796.48
BOY

Boykoff, Jules.

Activism an

Activism and the
Olympics

Critical Issues in Sport and Society

Michael Messner and Douglas Hartmann, Series Editors

Critical Issues in Sport and Society features scholarly books that help expand our understanding of the new and myriad ways in which sport is intertwined with social life in the contemporary world. Using the tools of various scholarly disciplines, including sociology, anthropology, history, media studies and others, books in this series investigate the growing impact of sport and sports-related activities on various aspects of social life as well as key developments and changes in the sporting world and emerging sporting practices. Series authors produce groundbreaking research that brings empirical and applied work together with cultural critique and historical perspectives written in an engaging, accessible format.

Activism and the Olympics

Dissent at the Games in Vancouver and London

JULES BOYKOFF

Rutgers University Press

New Brunswick, New Jersey, and London

Library of Congress Cataloging-in-Publication Data

Boykoff, Jules.
    Activism and the Olympics : dissent at the games in Vancouver and London / Jules Boykoff.
        pages cm.—(Critical issues in sport and society)
    Includes bibliographical references and index.
    ISBN 978–0-8135–6202–5 (hardback)—ISBN 978–0-8135–6201–8 (pbk.)—ISBN
978–0-8135–6203–2 (e-book)
    1. Olympics—Political aspects. 2. Olympics—Social aspects. 3. Dissenters. 4. Olympic
Winter Games (21st : 2010 Vancouver, B.C.) 5. Olympic Games (30th : 2012 : London, England) I. Title.

    GV721.5.B668 2014
    796.48—dc23

                                                                                    2013040634

A British Cataloging-in-Publication record for this book is available from the British Library.

Visit our website: http://rutgerspress.rutgers.edu

Manufactured in the United States of America

For Kaia and Jessi

Contents

Illustrations

Photographs

Figures

Tables

Acknowledgments

Thank you to the following people for their assistance, feedback, and encouragement during the writing of this book: Thomas F. Carter, Pete Fussey, Mike Geraci, Tina Gerhardt, Isaac Marrero-Guillamón, Ian McDonald, Tom Mertes, Alan Tomlinson, Paul Watt, Lissa Wolsak, and Dave Zirin. Thanks to Casey Nishimura and Matthew Yasuoka for fabulous research assistance. And big thanks also to all the political activists in Vancouver and London who took time to speak with me.

Thanks be to Douglas Hartmann, Michael Messner, and Peter Mickulas at Rutgers University Press. I feel fortunate to have worked with such a terrific trifecta of editorial sagacity and good cheer. I also appreciate the constructive feedback offered by this project's anonymous reviewers.

Some ideas in this book had a previous life in *Contemporary Social Science, CounterPunch, Dissent Magazine, Extra!,* the *Guardian, Human Geography,* the *Nation, New Left Review,* the *New York Times,* and *Red Pepper.* I also had the good fortune of presenting early stages of work from this book at the 2011 North American Society for the Sociology of Sport annual meeting and the 2012 International Symposium for Olympic Research at Western Ontario University. I would like to extend thanks to the University of Brighton for hosting me as a visiting scholar in spring 2012. This research was supported by a Graves Award in the Humanities, a Pacific University faculty development grant, and a Story-Dondero faculty development grant.

Finally, infinite gratitude to my two angels, Kaia Sand and Jessi Wahnetah, for their love and support, their creativity and zest. Together, all things are possible.

Activism and the Olympics

Introduction

The Olympics and Me

In his detective-fiction thriller *An Olympic Death,* Manuel Vásquez Montalbán captured what it was like to be in Barcelona as the city prepared to host the 1992 Summer Olympics. The acclaimed Spanish novelist and leftist columnist for *El País* presented one character in the book, a former Spanish revolutionary turned suit-sporting banker, to highlight the power of the Games to turn political beliefs into ideological jelly designed to sweeten capital accumulation. Underscoring the importance of international investment flows, the fictitious flip-flopper pivoted professionally to rivet his attention on profiteering from the Barcelona Games, audaciously declaiming, "Do you know how many foreigners we have in the city at this moment, all trying to get a piece of the Olympic action? An Olympics needs everything from a thimble to an elephant. Well, I have a complete collection of thimble salesmen, and another collection of elephant salesmen too." Another character in the novel, a formerly fledgling artist who sniffs Olympic-induced financial fortune, points toward the role of the culture industry in promoting the Games. He remarked, "Everything that moves in Barcelona these days is at the service of the Olympics. You have people coming to buy the place, people coming to see it all, and all the rest of us trying to sell it. There's not one artist in this city who's not looking out for what he can get out of the Olympics." Such connivance led Montalbán

1

to conclude, "In this city, you were either working for the Olympics, or you were dreading them—there was no middle ground."[1]

Such Manichaean framing—you're either for the Olympics or against them—becomes commonplace when the Games roll into a host city. Supporters of the Olympics sing full-throated music about the sporting brilliance that will soon grace the athletic terrain. Boosters also croon from the Olympic hymnal about benefits that will inexorably unfold for the city and its inhabitants. Elected officials, business leaders, and sports aficionados harmonize their messages, promising an influx of jobs, an uptick in urban development, and a spike in good cheer. Artists, entrepreneurs, and workers construct plans to profit from the two-and-a-half-week sports party. Urban planners and architects strategize, parlaying extant plans with Olympic needs, flinging ongoing projects into overdrive, and dreaming up fresh blueprints fit for the once-in-a-generation—if not once-in-a-lifetime—opportunity the Games present. As the Games approach, the media cover the building Olympic buzz.

Meanwhile, often in the margins of political discourse, the incorrigibly inquisitive raise skeptical, speculative questions about the bold promises and happy-faced assurances that Olympics boosters are piping into the social ether. Will the Games really create a booming economy replete with long-term jobs and investment? If so, for whom will it boom? Will hosting the Games discourage the tourism that would normally occur, creating an economic trade-off trending toward just breaking even? Why are police and security forces requesting extra weaponry? Will the Games intensify nationalism in an age of deterritorialized globalization? After pursuing answers to these questions, some decide the Games will only exacerbate inequality and drain taxpayer coffers in the name of a flag-waving festival of sport. And, of course, many people don't care about sports in the first place, viewing them as a nuisance, a distraction, a superfluous social sidecar, a new-wave opiate of the masses.

Although Montalbán asserts there is "no middle ground" when the Olympics come to town, there's actually more emotional and intellectual wiggle room than such a dichotomy proffers. When it comes to examining the Games, we need not obliterate shades of gray with the blunt instrument of the either-or. In fact, my own experience as an athlete and a scholar belies the idea that when it comes to the Olympics you have to either blithely champion them or impulsively spurn them.

Like many kids who grew up in the United States, I had unequivocally positive feelings about the Olympics. I did so, in part, because I was born and raised in Madison, Wisconsin, where local denizens followed winter sports with religious fervor. During the 1980 Winter Olympics in Lake Placid, New York, I cheered mightily for fellow Madisonian Eric Heiden as he won five gold medals in speed skating. His five-ring, five-medal performance had me continuously catapulting from my beanbag chair to cheer at the television screen as he swirled elegantly around the rink. Heiden's blend of grace and power even managed to extract the poet out of ABC's Keith Jackson who described him as "a spring breeze off the top of the Rockies."[2] To celebrate Heiden's triumphs, my parents gifted me with a stylish Eric Heiden-esque rainbow hat, which I wore with great delight. A few years later I proudly sported the cap at Madison West High School where Heiden had also gone to school as did his sister and fellow Lake Placid speed-skating Olympian Beth Heiden. That same Olympics the US hockey team won the gold medal, along the way vanquishing the Soviet hockey Goliath in the so-called "miracle on ice." I followed the team avidly, stacked as it was with University of Wisconsin players Mark Johnson—who scored two glorious goals against the USSR—and sure-sticked defenseman Bobby Suter. The moment the hockey team clinched the gold medal was etched in my mind. I can still recall my exhilaration.

My admiration for Olympics was rooted in an appreciation of athletic prowess, sangfroid under pressure, and the grit and determination to do one's best under the global media spotlight. At the time I knew nothing of the emergent commercialization of the Games, the behind-the-scenes political jockeying for sponsorship deals, the elitism that was bred into the International Olympic Committee (IOC).

In May 1990 I got my own personal taste of the Olympic movement when I represented the US Olympic Soccer Team—also known as the U-23 National Team—in an international tournament in France. After years of playing competitive soccer and taking the field for the Wisconsin state team and the Midwest regional team, I was selected by Olympic team coach Lothar Osiander to represent the United States on the international soccer stage. For me, this call-up to the national team was both a surprise and a thrill, and I was determined to make the most of it. I remember receiving a packet in the mail from the United States Soccer Federation (USSF) detailing Olympic team rules—from travel regulations to antidoping policies—and feeling overwhelmed by it all. And having never traveled outside the United States—truth be told, never even having considered the possibility of doing so—I needed to acquire a passport, and in expedited fashion. With the patient assistance of my parents, I managed to hop these logistical hurdles, and with the flexibility of my professors at the University of Wisconsin, I was able to take all my final exams early. Before I knew it, I was on an airplane heading to France.

In the tournament—the Festival International de Football 'Espoirs' de Toulon, it was called—we played against the Olympic teams from Brazil, Yugoslavia, Czechoslovakia, and the Soviet Union. My first full match was against the Brazilian Olympic Team. To say I was nervous is an egregious understatement. During the pregame inspection of the field, my chest was already buzzing with a mixture of tension and calm, as captured by a pregame photo snapped of me with teammate Mark Chung. We played the match in front of what seemed like some twenty-thousand fans, every last one of them rooting for Brazil to win, and we obliged them, losing by the respectable margin of 2–0. At the time I chalked up the pro-Brazil fervor to the assembled masses' wholly logical appreciation of the *seleção*'s imaginative, engaging style of play. After all, their line-up was brimming with skillful players like Cafu and Marcelinho, footballers who would go on to illustrious careers. One could hardly blame the fans for cheering for Brazilians playing "the beautiful game." But in a corner of my mind I entertained the idea that fans weren't just rooting *for* Brazil,

IMAGE 1 Jules Boykoff and Mark Chung, US Olympic Soccer Team, May 1990, Toulon, France. Courtesy of Jules Boykoff.

IMAGE 2 From left to right, Danny Barber, Jules Boykoff, and Manny Lagos, US Olympic Soccer Team, May 1990, Toulon, France. Courtesy of Jules Boykoff.

but also *against* us. And over the coming week or so, we received a similar cold French shoulder when we played Yugoslavia, Czechoslovakia, and the Soviet Union. Given that this was the tail end of the Cold War, and that France was a nominal US ally, I found our icy reception a bit baffling but also intriguing. There was something going on that I could sense but not fully understand.

In fact, there was a lot I didn't fully appreciate at the time. I was oblivious to the bigger-picture political and economic machinations that animated the Games. I never thought to consider whether taxpayers, private groups, or some combination thereof funded the activities of the U-23 national team let alone the actual Olympic Games. I was wholly unaware that in the 1980s and 1990s, while I was running up and down the pitch, then-IOC president Juan Antonio Samaranch was urgently commercializing the Olympics in an effort to create financial stability and even profit. By the late 1980s, the IOC had formalized cozy relations with the business world. This relationship was mutually beneficial. For the IOC it meant a steadier supply of cash.[3] For commercial partners, hooking onto the Olympic Games was golden goodness. As former IOC marketing guru Michael

Payne put it, "nothing has provided sponsors with a stronger or more powerful unified global platform to connect with their customers than the Olympics."[4] In short, the Olympics had been branded. And right in front of my very eyes, no less. But "the fetishism of commodities and the secret thereof," as Marx would have it, was far from my mind at the time. I wasn't contemplating the "metaphysical subtleties and theological niceties" of the political economy of sport.[5] I was just playing soccer and, I must say, quite enjoying it.

The years 1989 and 1990 will always stick out in my mind as the time I had the good fortune of playing for the United States Olympic Soccer Team. All in all, I ended up representing the United States in one international tournament and multiple exhibition games while also attending a number of Olympic team training camps. However, I was not chosen for the final roster for the 1992 Summer Games in Barcelona. In the summer of 1990, I broke my right foot in playing for my club team—the Madison 56ers—in Wisconsin. After an ambitious—in retrospect *over*-ambitious—rehabilitation effort, I returned to the field that fall for the University of Wisconsin. In a preseason match against the University of Wisconsin-Milwaukee, my friend and Olympic team teammate Manuel Lagos inadvertently rebroke my foot in total fluke encounter. Not realizing my foot was broken, I continued to play, only to dislocate my shoulder while doing a diving header. The double whammy landed me a long-term slot on the injured list.

Two surgeries and an über-zealous rehabilitation regimen later, I was back on the pitch, perhaps finding the best form of my career. I had earned a spot on the north regional team at the 1991 US Olympic Festival in Los Angeles. However, to my great elation, a few weeks before the tournament I received a call from the USSF informing me I had been called back up to the Olympic team for two Olympic qualifying matches against Panama, one in Panama and the other in Columbus, Ohio. A few days later, though, I received another call, letting me know there was a mix-up and that they originally thought they could bring twenty players for the qualifiers, but actually they could only bring eighteen. I was one of the two players on the chopping block. So, instead I went to Los Angeles for the Olympic Sports Festival where I captained the north team to a gold medal. I then returned home hoping I'd get the call from Coach Osiander. That call never came. I watched the 1992 Barcelona Olympics on television. My Olympic dream was never fully realized.

IMAGE 3 Author receiving gold medal at the 1991 US Olympic Festival in Los Angeles. Courtesy of Jules Boykoff.

Nevertheless, my Olympic experience ended up being pivotal in my life. After undergoing one surgery to place a steel pin in the fifth metatarsal of my right foot and another to reconstruct my right shoulder, I had some serious free time on my hands to ponder my future. I realized soccer was my ticket out of Madison, where I was born and had lived my entire life. I decided to transfer to the University of Portland in Oregon where I could play under the legendary coach Clive Charles and alongside my U-23 team teammates Yari Allnutt and Joey Leonetti. I also took more political science courses and studied Spanish, eventually graduating with a bachelor's degree in politics. The chilly reception we had received in France ghosted in my mind, impelling me to explore what might have given rise to it. All this led me to think more politically and critically about the world in general and in particular US foreign policy and the role that sports played in the geopolitical battle known as the Cold War.

Twenty years after narrowly missing a chance to play in the 1992 Barcelona Olympics, I finally went to Catalonia, not as an athlete, but as a scholar enjoying my first-ever sabbatical. It was January 2012, and my family lived for a month in Barcelona, in the Poble Sec neighborhood, just below majestic Montjuïc Park where the Olympics took place. Each morning I would go for a jog up the side of Montjuïc and to the Olympic Stadium, or the Estadi Olímpic Lluís Companys, named after the former president of Catalonia during the Spanish Civil War, who was executed by Francisco Franco's forces in 1940 at the nearby Montjuïc Castle. After circling the stadium a time or two, I would snake my way around the Olympic Ring (el Anillo Olímpico), where a bulk of the 1992 Games took place. Eventually I'd descend the terraces from the Olympic Stadium past the Olympic Tower—a sleek, steel structure designed by Valencian architect Santiago Calatrava and conspicuously branded by Telefónico—toward the National Institute of Physical Education of Catalonia where I would take advantage of the relatively soft dirt-graveled ground. There I would lope past a long stone monument on the open plaza, etched with famous names from Europe's past: Konrad Adenauer, John Maynard Keynes, Rosa Luxemburg, José Ortega y Gassett, Josep Tarradellas. Many of them were visionaries who were persecuted while they were alive, but who are being heralded as heroes today. As I jogged in circles, I thought about the complexities of dissident citizenship and historical memory. I also meditated on what the Olympics meant to me way back when and what it means to me now.

I am still a lover of sports. Every morning the first chunk of the newspaper I pick up is the sports section. I am a devoted supporter of my local soccer team, the Portland Timbers, as well as an avid admirer of FC Barcelona, whose former coach Josep "Pep" Guardiola had, as a player, helped Spain win gold in the 1992 Barcelona Games. For me, watching Pep guide Leo Messi, Andres Iniesta, Xavi Hernandez, Carles Puyol, and their comrades to "total football" victory was a pleasure, aesthetically, but also politically. FC Barcelona's unique, fan-oriented ownership structure and robust historical ties to politics make the club even more appealing to me. Under the Franco dictatorship, Camp Nou, where FC Barcelona plays its home matches, was a place—indeed, a rare place—where people could openly express their Catalonian dissent, as the fascist regime attempted to stamp out all traces of Catalan culture and ruthlessly enforce its version of Spanishness.[6] At Camp Nou, politics and sport cannot be completely disentangled without diminishing our understanding of both.

Such spaces of dissent interest me immensely. For more than a decade I have been researching and writing on the suppression of political dissent, focusing mostly on how that process has played out historically and contemporarily in the United States. I have written two books and numerous articles about how the state and mass media squelch activism and enforce the status quo, sometimes through obvious, visible means—the baton and the bullet—but more often through subtler, stealthier forms of suppression that take shape in the quiet corners of government planning and in media accounts of activists' efforts. Such research has opened my eyes to outside-the-frame political dynamics and has forced me to think critically about the way power exerts itself, especially when it feels like no one is looking. I bring this critical vantage to my thinking on the politics of sports.

In 2009 I made an intellectual pivot. I consciously decided to examine and analyze with more vim and depth the intersection of politics and sports. In advance of the 2010 Winter Olympics, I repeatedly headed north from where I live in Portland, Oregon, to Vancouver, Canada, to interview activists and civil libertarians about the repressive measures the Canadian state was instituting as the Games approached. I was covering these machinations of suppression for the political newsletter *CounterPunch* but quickly realized that what was happening in Vancouver was bigger than a straight-up repression story. It was about off-the-field political-economic forces that shaped what we eventually came to appreciate on the field, the slopes, and the rink. And it was also about creative activism and principled resistance in the face of the Olympics, the smiley-faced behemoth that enjoys wide public support.

Further personal experiences shaped my thinking about politics and sports. From 2008 through 2010 I was involved in a heated political battle in my hometown over whether to provide public funding for the Portland Timbers, as they made the transition to Major League Soccer. Despite my support for the team, I spoke out publicly against public funding for the franchise, arguing that taxpayer money was better spent on social programs, not subsidies for millionaires. The team was owned—and at the time of writing is still owned—by former treasury secretary Henry Paulson and his son Merritt. Such high-profile, high-roller owners brought the fracas into sharper focus and injected it with relevance beyond Portland. After meeting with city leaders behind the scenes, working alongside grassroots activist groups, and writing numerous articles—some of them with whip-smart sportswriter Dave Zirin—we succeeded in getting public funding for the project decreased from the Paulsons' original request of $85 million to about $11 million that would come out of a special spectator fund rather than the city's general fund. Through hard work and good luck we saw political fight-back with concrete results.

Despite my sincere appreciation for athleticism—and in particular Olympic athleticism—I could no longer experience sports without thinking about politics. So, when my family and I visited the Olympic Museum in Barcelona, I couldn't help but notice that curators had rinsed and wrung political controversy from the exhibitions. For instance, throughout the museum women Olympians were highlighted left and right, but there was no mention that for a long while, Olympic powerbrokers banned women from competing in most sports at the Games. Women were finally admitted to participate fully only with great hesitation. Writing in 1957, IOC president Avery Brundage opined in a circular letter to IOC members that there was "a well grounded protest against events which are not truly feminine, like putting a shot, or those too strenuous for most of the opposite sex, such as distance runs."[7] Rather than confronting these issues to highlight the evolution of the Games, the museum opted to bury them. When politics bubbled to the surface, as they did in the photo gallery where former IOC president Samaranch was shown with political leaders from George W. Bush to Fidel Castro to Vladimir Putin, it was if to say the IOC didn't take geopolitical sides. When it came to photo ops, the IOC was an equal opportunity crew.

Meanwhile the commercialism of the Games—so neon-clear today—was also airbrushed from the museum walls, as was the IOC's conflicted history with the amateur-professional divide. In fact, Brundage often counterposed amateurism, which he favored, and commercialism, which he fiercely denounced. He consistently critiqued "the materialistic world in which we live" and "a society which commercializes practically everything" and thus "fails to see the value of and the necessity for amateur regulations."[8] Sauntering through the memento-packed rooms, one would find it difficult to come to the conclusion that the IOC's position on commercialism has made a U-turn or that commercial interests have shaped the trajectory of the Games in extraordinary ways in our contemporary era. Nevertheless, in order to fully understand the Olympics, one must also examine commercialism. And, in fact, many political activists root their criticism in the corporate commercialization of the Games.

Such commercialism is a key cog in the machine of capitalism. The Olympics have thrived under capitalism and in particular during the era of neoliberal capitalism. With ideological roots extending back to Friedrich von Hayek and Milton Friedman, neoliberalism is marked by the concerted unfettering of market forces through privatization, deregulation, and the financialization of the economy. Such measures, which deliberately dismantle the social-welfare state while snuffing out Keynesian principles and programs, were embraced by President Ronald Reagan in the United States and Prime Minister Margaret Thatcher in Britain. "The basic prescription of neoliberalism," write sport scholars Michael Silk and David Andrews, is to "purge the system of obstacles to the functioning of free markets; celebrate the virtues of individualism . . . and competitiveness; foster economic self-sufficiency; [and] abolish or weaken social programs."[9] Neoliberal capitalism's guiding principle is letting the market decide. Joshua Newman and Michael Giardina add that neoliberalism and the claim that there is no viable alternative to it, "brought forth a new age of hyperconsumerism, media spectacularization, and market fetishism."[10] Today the Olympic Games marinate in this "new age," although the Olympics themselves are not necessarily neoliberal in character. After all, the public routinely pays for a large majority of Olympic costs, rather than privatizing them, and corporate sponsors hold a privileged position for future pacts—the free market does not "decide." Elsewhere I have argued this mode of economics is more "celebration capitalism" than neoliberalism.[11]

I am a child of neoliberalism, having come of age during the Reagan-Bush I era when the economic doctrine was forged on the ideological anvil of US Cold War politics. In 1991 I snapped a photograph of Ronald Reagan as he and Nancy glided past me with Secret Service officers in the wings at the 1991 Olympic Sports Festival in Los Angeles. As an athlete I had more access to the former president than I would ever have as a social scientist. Under the spell of Reagan's avuncular chumminess, and softened by his fragile appearance, I didn't even think to approach him to question his penchant for unregulated markets or his keenness to undercut the labor movement by unilaterally firing striking air traffic controllers in PATCO (Professional Air Traffic Controllers Organization). At the time I was only beginning to fully understand how Reagan had wielded the words and deeds of neoliberalism to fundamentally reshape economic and social relations. His policies and ideology carved a neoliberal path, marked by the mélange of deregulation, privatization, marketization, trade liberalization, financialization, and the state's evacuation from most economic planning and ownership. Many activists have rooted their anti-Olympics critiques in these very tenets.

Five-Ring Activism

More than a decade after the momentous protests against the World Trade Organization (WTO) known to many as the Battle in Seattle, social-movement activists and politically active artists are appraising the political topography of resistance, reassessing the socially produced spaces of dissent and the ways these spaces are shot through with conflict. Whenever supranational groups like the WTO, the International Monetary Fund, the World Bank, and the G8/G20 roll into a host city, activists and artists spring into action. Although the Olympic Games stoke the hopes of people around the world, they have also incited the ire of numerous activists. In recent years, the Olympic Games have generated a steadily increasing scale of dissent, despite the fact that a rule in the Olympic Charter explicitly outlaws Games-related political activism. This book examines the work of anti-Olympic activists in Vancouver and London who springboarded off the 2010 Winter Olympics and 2012 Summer Games to rescale politics to their advantage, using the Olympics as a stage for their own ideas and critiques.

And yet, when the Games come to town, there is tremendous social and cultural pressure to turn off your critical faculties and hop on the Olympic train. In an essay titled "I Do Not Hate the Olympics," Chuck Klosterman laments the disdain his friends pour upon him each time the Games roll around, and he fails to work up the requisite enthusiasm. Peer-pressured onto his back foot, he claims not to hate the Olympics—"I just don't like them at all (and there *is* a difference between those two sentiments)"—but maintains he's put off by the knee-jerk nationalism the Games tend do induce. He writes, "In order to enjoy the Olympics, you can't think critically about anything; you just have to root for America (or whatever country you're from) and assume that your feelings are inherently correct."[12]

Klosterman's observations jibe with George Orwell's famous quip that "international sporting contests lead to orgies of hatred." Orwell added, "There cannot be much doubt that the whole thing is bound up with the rise of nationalism—that is, with the lunatic modern habit of identifying oneself with large power units and seeing everything in terms of competitive prestige."[13] However, as activists, artists, and analysts have demonstrated in Orwell's wake, the situation is a great deal more complex. Indeed the Olympics can amplify nationalism, but modern-day five-ring devotees—including some human-rights advocates—also point out that the light cast by the Olympic flame can spotlight the negative, antidemocratic aspects of host countries, thereby moving them a step closer to concertedly ameliorating such conditions. The Olympics—replete with carefully choreographed opening and closing ceremonies and torch runs that snake across the land—can trigger fervent nationalism, but can also engender international camaraderie and good cheer.

And the Olympics are immensely popular. Although the Winter Games play second fiddle to the Summer Olympics, the Vancouver 2010 Games attracted more attention from US news consumers than any other story, including the flailing economy and the hot-button issue of health-care reform.[14] In a 2008 public-opinion poll, the Olympics won high approval ratings in the United States, with three in four opining the Olympics have been successful in fulfilling their stated mission of "building a peaceful and better world through sports."[15] Such widespread support does not leave a lot of wiggle room for Olympics critics or even those who wish simply to ask tough questions about the Games and their manifold promises. After all, Klosterman is a sports fan who could appreciate athletic prowess on the pitch, rink, and track, but his pals view his muted enthusiasm for the Olympics as words verging on treason. For many, supporting the Games is a civic obligation. As Finlo Rohrer noted for the *BBC News,* "If you believe in London's 2012 bid, you are a nice person who wants Britain to succeed. But express doubts and you are a Scrooge-like killjoy."[16]

And yet, short-term popularity in the public sphere is not always commensurate with the long view of history. Each time the Olympics approach, social euphoria builds to a crescendo rivaling a Beethoven symphony with its cresting boom of woodwinds, horns, and drums. But, it should be remembered that even the now-acclaimed Beethoven was not universally admired in his time. Many an audience member fled from his concerts in disgust. In France, for instance, his music was "first reviled as chaotic and incoherent" and out of tune with proper tradition before eventually being "worshipped as divine truth." When his first symphony made its 1807 Paris premier, it "was unanimously recognized as a ponderous flop" weighed down with "barbarous chords and incoherent progressions." Critics simply found his work meaningless.[17] In Vienna Beethoven was supported by a small sliver of the aristocratic elite but remained relatively unpopular in the middle-class concert halls until later in his career.[18] The esoteric nature of Beethoven's implicit critiques of dominant modes of music—and his thunderous response to the then-dominant, delicate, dulcet, styles that preceded him—were eventually celebrated of course. But, as sociologist of music Tia DeNora notes, at first Beethoven "fell outside conventional boundaries of musical worth."[19] His contemporaries simply lacked a musical vocabulary to help them appreciate his out-of-the-mainstream innovations. In some ways, political activists challenging the dominant logic of the Olympics face a similar situation. They can hold out the hope, though, that their beliefs, while largely marginalized, shunned, and distrusted in the present, prove to be as durable and deserved of serious consideration as Beethoven's ambitious, distinctive oeuvre.

The Accidental Ethnographer

Following my journalistic impulse while covering political activism in Vancouver put me on an inadvertent path toward what sports scholars John Sugden and Alan Tomlinson describe as "the investigative tradition for the sociology of sport." They assert this approach brings together ethnography, comparative methodologies, investigative sociological research, historiography, and a marked critical thrust.[20] My pursuit of satisfying explanations for the incipient militarism, repression, and special laws enacted to align with the demands of the IOC led to more questions than answers, which in turn demanded I speak with more people in the know. This led me to reach out to legal experts, grassroots activists, and social workers with on-the-ground experience and an openness to questioning the predominant logic that the Games were a win-win for the city.

Eventually I carried out seventy interviews with individuals who were challenging the machinations of the Olympic Games in Vancouver and London.[21] In Vancouver, a handful of politically active poets I know put me in touch with key activists in town, putting in a good word for this inquisitive outsider along the way. In London, I set up many of the interviews after I conducted ethnographic fieldwork at public meetings and demonstrations where I identified people who were speaking out publicly on these issues and the relationships they had with other actors.[22] After seeing them vocalize dissent at protests and meetings, I approached them to see if they would be willing to elaborate their thoughts in more detail. For activists in both Vancouver and London I conducted semistructured interviews that typically lasted between thirty minutes and an hour. Sometimes they entailed securing personal background information—what Robert

Sands calls in *Sport Ethnography* a "synoptic life history"—in order to better understand the individual's personal activist history and how this led the person to question the Olympics.[23] But a great bulk of each interview focused on activist strategies, tactics, and goals, as well as media coverage of their efforts.

I had the good fortune of engaging in snowball sampling whereby activists recommended other dissident citizens with whom they believed I should speak, thereby expanding the participant base.[24] I also benefited from what sociologist Richard Giulianotti calls "gatekeepers," trusted members of the group who were willing to introduce me to other actors, vouching for me along the way. As he notes, "Identifying and seeking out an influential 'gatekeeper' can circumvent much of the time-consuming and stress-inducing experiences of entrée."[25] All the while, I endeavored to create a diverse set of interviewees in regards to gender, race, class, and age. While a handful of the interviews were conducted via Skype and telephone, a great majority of them were face-to-face encounters. In every instance, I started off the exchange by explaining that I was writing general-audience articles for outlets like *CounterPunch*, the *Guardian*, and *Red Pepper* as well as a book-length scholarly project on activism and the Olympics. With the permission of each interviewee, I recorded the interviews to ensure faithful transcription of direct quotations.

These conversations raised connections to bigger-picture issues and wider concerns. This brought me full circle from journalism to my home turf: social science. The tools and methods of social science—in particular sociology, political science, and media studies—helped me deepen my inquiry, in some instances systemizing it so I could find more fulfilling answers. As such, this book is a concerted effort to carry out Sugden and Tomlinson's investigative, multimethod mode of critical sociological inquiry. And it is meant to be part of what Michael L., Silk, David L. Andrews, and Daniel S. Mason identify as an "increasingly interdisciplinary" zeitgeist within qualitative research in sports studies.[26]

A key element of such research involves deploying ethnographic methods. Numerous scholars working within the tradition of sport sociology have embraced ethnography, replete with cultural immersion and a nimble bundle of qualitative research methods. Silk, Andrews, and Mason assert that by situating sport as a key feature on the broader political and cultural landscape, qualitative inquiry into what they call "the sporting empirical" can help us "understand sport as a site through which various discourses are mobilized in regard to the organization and discipline of daily life in the service of particular political agendas."[27] In doing this, scholars of sport have made use of ethnography's two workhorses of data collection: participant observation and interviews. Some scholars—such as Daniel Burdsey, Ben Carrington, and Belinda Wheaton—have carried out ethnographic research on athletes.[28] Others—like Richard Giulanotti, Joshua Newman, and Paul Watt—have used ethnographic methods to make sense of subcultures and populations stemming from sports, often supporters and spectators but also everyday people.[29] Meanwhile, in social-movement studies, numerous scholars have used the techniques of ethnography, from Jacqueline Kennelly's research on youth cultures to Brian Wilson's examination of the relationship between online and offline activism to Luis Fernandez's work on the Global Justice Movement.[30] Notable among academics who have used ethnographic methods to bridge the gap between sports studies and research on activism is Helen Jefferson Lenskyj.[31] Although I came to ethnography through the back door of my journalism work, I believe it is a vital path for scholars working at the nexus of sports studies and social-movement studies. I am in full accord with Michael Silk's remark that "ethnography has an exciting place within the future of a democratic sports studies."[32]

I pressed forward with this work mindful of my own influence on the research setting and process, or my reflexivity. Kim England defines reflexivity as "self-critical sympathetic introspection and the self-conscious *analytical* scrutiny of the self as researcher."[33] Ben Carrington highlights the perpetual scale-shifting inherent to reflexivity and how it fits with the wider world beyond the scope of sociological inquiry, describing reflexivity as "a general positionality of heightened self-awareness . . . that problematize[s] the complex and mutually constituting relationship between the Self, Other, and society."[34] What he calls "*self-reflexive* modes of research" demand we flip the analytical gaze back toward ourselves as researchers in an effort to better understand how carrying out the research affects the outcomes.[35] Being reflexive also forced me to revisit my theoretical positions and predilections, which led to a book that embraces a wide range of social theory—from sociology to geography to communications—to make sense of what I came across in the field. Carrington argues—and I agree with him—that "a critical reflective engagement that contests the social and political worlds in which we live and research (and the tools and concepts of that research), holds out the promise . . . of a better, more humane, and committed sociology."[36] I aspire for this type of sociology in this book.

I carried out this research aware of my own "positionality" and how my own identity inflected the research process. My nationality gave me an outsider status that marked me as different from activists in Canada and England, freighting me with the baggage of geopolitical hegemony while simultaneously freeing me from local sectarian squabbles, allowing me to see the activist scene afresh and permitting me to ask basic questions. Meanwhile the privileged currency of my race (white) and gender (male) presented additional challenges, especially in activist cultures that were rightly skeptical of such historically drenched advantage. In this book I attempt to narrate myself into the text, not in a heavy-handed manner that foregrounds my role as researcher, but in a way that nevertheless acknowledges my presence in the processes of dissent under study. I do this in the spirit of Carrington's suggestion that we recognize "the importance of reflexive autobiographical approaches" to carrying out research with ethnographic dimensions, though I attempt to do this with a light touch.[37]

Social-movement scholars Kevin Gillan and Jenny Pickerill correctly point out that, as scholars, "we write with a subjectivity that is often formed by an embedded and sympathetic position" to the activists we study.[38] This is undoubtedly true. Nonetheless, I should note that while I share a political vantage with many anti-Olympics activists, I am determined to offer clear-eyed analysis rather than rote homage or knee-jerk apologia. Rather than sidestepping the shortcomings and contradictions of Olympic activism, I wade into their complexity, using "the metalanguage of social science" with the aim of better understanding the terrain of protest and social change.[39]

Situating the Book and Sketching Its Trajectory

Activism and the Olympics is an account of political protest in response to the 2010 Winter Games in Vancouver and the 2012 Summer Olympics in London. In addition to nestling within the tradition of qualitative research on sport, this book sits at the nexus of two main fields in sports studies: (1) work at the intersection of politics and sports and (2) critical research on the Olympic Games.

"The space of sports," noted Pierre Bourdieu, "is not a self-contained universe."[40] Despite repeated claims from IOC officials that the Games are apolitical, the Olympics—and sports more generally—are thrumming with politics. Scholars have long noted that sport both produces and reflects wider political dynamics; Carrington correctly states that sport is "a contested terrain wherein competing ideologies of domination and resistance can be traced."[41] The politics of sports affect local cultures, national policies, and geopolitical relations. In the last few decades sport's internationalization has surged, thanks in large part to the Olympic Games and the soccer World Cup. Andrei Markovits and Lars Rensmann note, "As sports have gone global they have become more embedded in politics, constituting an important display of political authority and even figuring into the most quotidian political matters."[42] Simultaneously, the commercialization of sport has intensified dramatically. Sport's symbolic, cultural, and economic capital has skyrocketed. Joseph Maguire has argued that the emergence and diffusion of competitive global sport has morphed into "the sports-industrial complex" that has come to dominate the world of sports and thwart the possibility of viable alternatives.[43] Meanwhile, women have enjoyed new opportunities on the global stage of sport. These trends ripple with political implications that journalists like Jemele Hill, Sally Jenkins, Andrew Jennings, Mike Marqusee, and Dave Zirin have addressed in the popular press. At the same time, academics across the disciplines have zeroed in on the politics of sports. Ben Carrington has carried out vital research on the politics of race, with a focus on the black athlete.[44] Richard Gruneau's seminal work on class formation and sports still carries relevance today.[45] Chris Gratton and others have analyzed the political economics of sport-driven regeneration schemes,[46] while scholars like Jennifer Hargreaves and Michael Messner have spotlighted the intersection of gender, politics, and sports.[47] Other researchers, such as Alan Bairner, study the geopolitical aspects of sports, how the globalization of sport has affected national identity.[48] Sports events can induce nationalism, but in the wake of World War II, they can, as David L. Andrews and Stephen Wagg write, also serve as a "hitherto unprecedented—and, arguably cathartic—vehicle for the expression of the new order of nation-based antagonisms."[49] In *Activism and the Olympics* I foreground the intersection of politics and sports, analyzing activist claims regarding race, class, gender, the environment, nationalism, and inequality. I investigate how and why activists dispute the political decisions of the IOC as well as the choices, policies, and priorities of local, regional, and national governments, sometimes acting at the behest of IOC demands.

This book also draws from—and is situated within—critical research on the Olympic Games. In the late 1980s Bourdieu remarked that sport sociologists were "doubly dominated" in that the serious study of sport was marginalized within the field of sociology and maligned by powerbrokers in the sports world. Nevertheless, despite "the special difficulties that the sociology of sport encounters," as Bourdieu would have it, the last twenty-five years have brought a remarkable outpouring of critical research on the Olympics, much of it emerging from the field of sociology.[50] Alan Tomlinson has consistently critiqued the Games for their commercialization, calculated construction of spectacle, and creation of a privileged "corporate class."[51] Garry Whannel has critically interrogated the role of the mass media—in particular, television—in the fashioning and fortification of the Olympic movement.[52] Investigative journalist Andrew Jennings has unearthed corruption within the IOC and been an outspoken, unswerving critic of the Games.[53] Similarly, but in a scholarly vein, Kevin Wamsley and colleagues have leveled intense criticism at Olympic "mythologies" and "the global sport monopoly," questioning the bigger picture of Olympism.[54] Meanwhile, scholars have zeroed in on particular aspects of the Games, with Janice Forsyth and Christine O'Bonsawin critiquing the co-optation of indigenous peoples[55] and John Karamichas questioning the IOC's claims of ecological sustainability.[56]

Helen Jefferson Lenskyj's research on what she calls "the Olympic industry"—and the activist response to it—is a vital precursor to this book. Yet, *Activism and the Olympics* differs from Lenskyj's commendable scholarship in numerous, significant ways. First, this book foregrounds theory and concepts from a variety of academic disciplines, leveraging them to deepen our understanding of on-the-ground activism. While her scholarship is largely descriptive, in this book I gain analytical leverage through the application—and development—of concepts and theories.[57] I make use of my background working in the fields of social-movement studies, political science, and media studies to bring together a unique, interdisciplinary set of concepts and theories in order to analyze anti-Olympics activism in Vancouver and London. I believe an interdisciplinary approach is not only useful but *necessary* for understanding the complexities of anti-Olympics fight-back. In addition, I also carry out systematic media analysis that relies on methodologically rigorous standards. While Lenskyj does some revealing exploratory media analysis, it is largely anecdotal and reliant on Noam Chomsky and Ed Herman's "propaganda model" from the

1980s.[58] I employ a wider range of modern-day conceptual tools, including frame analysis, indexing, and journalistic-norm analysis. Finally, my book draws primary evidence from numerous personal interviews with activists, journalists, civil libertarians, and Olympics organizers, angling in on the Games from numerous viewpoints. It is more analytic and less polemic.

This book directly addresses the critiques that emanate from critical scholarly research on the Olympic Games. At the same time, the book takes its vantage from the ground up, offering an empirical examination of activist denunciations of the Olympic machine. In fact, one of the central aims of this book is to bring the criticism of activists and the analysis of scholars into productive conversation.

In the following chapter, I lay out the theoretical and conceptual tools I will use to make sense of anti-Olympics activism in Vancouver and London. I also present a typology for Olympics-related political activism containing two axes: the character of the activist (whether athlete or non-athlete) and the target of the activism (the Olympics or wider social issues). Along the way, I ante up prominent examples of activist action from the past that provide us with essential context for the two case studies. In chapter 2, I examine the robust, concerted political activism that occurred in Vancouver, Canada, before, during, and after the 2010 Winter Olympics. In doing so I highlight the importance of geographical theory—in particular, the production of space and scale—for achieving greater understanding of this activism. Chapter 3 considers the 2012 Summer Olympics in London and the activist response, from dissident citizens who opposed the Games to organizers who attempted to convert the situation into a social-justice boost for their groups. I also zero in on the role that both humor and preemptive policing played in the anti-Olympics campaign. In chapter 4, I offer a systematic, comparative media analysis of the two Olympic Games, highlighting the patterns in coverage and the possibilities for activists. In chapter 5, I situate Olympics activism in the wider pattern of increased protest across the world at the outset of the twenty-first century, from the Occupy Movement in the United States to the Arab Spring in the Middle East. What does this spike in dissident citizenship mean for Olympics activists? What lessons can we learn from Vancouver and London? What might activists have in store for Sochi, for the 2014 Winter Games, and Rio de Janeiro, where the 2016 Summer Olympics will take place?

1

Understanding the Olympic Games

————————————●

The Olympic Games are shrouded in an apoliticism that is in fact eminently political. The notion that the Olympics can sidestep politics is one of the guiding fictions of our times, and one propped up by major players in the Olympic movement. Avery Brundage, who headed the International Olympic Committee from 1952 to 1972, chanted the mantra that politics and Olympics shouldn't mix. For instance, in a 1969 letter he wrote, "we actively combat the introduction of politics into the Olympic movement and are adamant against the use of the Olympic Games as a tool or as a weapon by any organization."[1] More recently, IOC leaders have adopted a subtler approach. While not expressly stating the Olympics are a political juggernaut in and of themselves, IOC president Jacques Rogge remarked at the 113th IOC session in 2002, "sport is closely linked to the political and economic framework within which it develops."[2]

In reality, the Olympics are a cauldron of ever-bubbling politics on low boil. At the same time, the Olympics are an important and wildly popular cultural event. As Sir Alan Collins, managing director for Olympic legacy at UK Trade and Investment, remarked as London prepared to host the 2012 Summer Games, the Olympics "is obviously the greatest show on

Earth." He also acknowledged the economic importance of the Games, describing them as "the biggest possible networking opportunity" before concluding "we would be remiss if we didn't take maximum advantage of that while we have the eyes of the world on us."[3] Over time the Olympics have transmogrified into a gargantuan economic force nestled in a political thicket.

Sport is a site of political struggle. The political complexion of sport crystallized in the case of 1976 Winter Olympics, which were originally slated for Denver, Colorado, until an upsurge of dissent derailed the IOC's plans. In May 1970, the IOC selected Denver to host the 1976 Winter Games. Upon winning the bid contest, Colorado governor John Love vowed, "It's going to be a great thing for Colorado" while the president of Denver's Chamber of Commerce promised the Games would make a "great economic impact," adding, "It makes us look like we're alive and we're recognized worldwide as a major city."[4]

Not everyone shared their enthusiasm. After the IOC awarded the Olympics to Denver, activists rallied against hosting the Games for fear of the ecological degradation it could trigger. Groups like Protect Our Mountain Environment and the Rocky Mountain Center on Environment deluged IOC officials with letters laying out the case to move the Games from Denver.[5] A range of organizations kicked into action under the umbrella group Citizens for Colorado's Future, jumpstarting a petition drive and pressing for a state referendum on a $5 million bond issue to fund the Games. They won the public vote in November 1972 with 60 percent of the final tally, thereby shutting off the potential money spigot.[6] In undercutting the funding mechanism, Colorado activists rebuffed the 1976 Winter Games. This made Denver the first city to reject the Games after having been granted them by the IOC.

Nonathlete actors in Colorado cobbled together a multifaceted antiGames rationale that serves as a vital antecedent for Olympics activists today. Citing escalating costs, a tax hike, potential ecological scarring, and a population explosion that could raise the cost of living, these groups banded together to run a hardscrabble grassroots campaign to convince voters that the Olympics would be ruinous for Denver and the surrounding areas. One popular bumper sticker at the time read, "Don't Californicate Colorado!"[7] Although Denver organizers originally asserted the cost of the Olympics would be contained at $14 million and the Games would be geographically limited to the Denver area, projected costs eventually climbed to $35 million and planned venues began to stretch as far as four hours away into the Rocky Mountains.[8]

Campaigners showered IOC officials with letters demanding reconsideration—the Avery Brundage archive alone contains four full folders with letters from concerned Colorado citizens and elected officials. Richard Lamm, the assistant minority leader in the Colorado House of Representatives, penned a letter to Brundage highlighting fiscal concerns as well as the opportunity costs of hosting the Games. "Colorado, painfully, cannot afford to host the 1976 Olympics," he wrote. "We are a small state, already on the verge of taxpayer revolt. We cannot afford to do justice to our schools, to our institutions, to our many other pressing needs now; and as we become aware of the vast financial commitment to host the 1976 Olympics we see increasingly that we do not have the will or the tax base to afford the 1976 Olympics."[9] In a subsequent letter to Canadian IOC member James Worrall, Lamm added, "The debate over the ability of our small state to properly host the Games is tearing us apart and dividing our people. Candidates of both parties are lining up to run on the anti-Olympics platform." He concluded, "I urge you to remove the Games from Colorado. It would be to the benefit of both Colorado and the Olympics."[10]

Other letter writers also highlighted the opportunity costs of the Games. Al Nielson wrote Brundage to suggest that instead of spending money on Olympic construction, funds could be spent on "the purchasing of food, medicine, and education for those unfortunate people throughout the world." He concluded, "It is my opinion that dollars spent in this manner will certainly benefit mankind far greater than a new ski jump in Evergreen, Colorado." Another private citizen wrote to Brundage suggesting the Games be held in the same facilities every four years: "The millions of dollars that would be saved by such a program might well be channeled into activities which more directly might meet the need for improved health, education, and job training throughout the world." Activists also criticized the Denver Organizing Committee (DOC) for its lack of transparency and unwillingness to register citizen input. The communications director from Citizens for Colorado's Future said the local organizing committee "has to date shown itself to be insensitive to citizen opinion, undemocratic and secretive in its operations, and careless to the point of negligence in its management."[11] The messages were getting through. In May 1972, Brundage wrote a memo cataloging activist critiques and logging the number of telephone calls he had received over the matter.[12] While in general activists engaged in lawful contention, the *New York Times* reported that resistance occasionally verged into sabotage: "Somebody even burned down the steep-slope ski jump that towers above town" in Steamboat Springs, "scribbling anti-Olympic obscenities on the charred remains."[13] This persistent mix of legal and transgressive activism proved to be powerful enough to fight back the Olympic machine.

When it came to the November 1972 referendum, pro-Olympics forces held key advantages. They poured more than $175,000 into a slick marketing campaign, relied on big-name Olympians for public endorsement, and enjoyed a generous assist from the press. As *Sports Illustrated* put it at the time, Olympic supporters "trotted out that old pro-Olympian Jesse Owens and flooded the state with entreaties to 'light the torch now,' meanwhile receiving sustenance from the *Denver Post,* which in the campaign's final days devoted up to five times more news space to Olympic boosters than to critics."[14] Activists ran a ramshackle campaign—Citizens for Colorado's Future spent less than $24,000 during its entire existence, with most of those funds secured in $5 to $10 donations. The group's media budget barely topped $2,000. Yet the activists emerged triumphant, winning the referendum handily: 537,440 to 358,906. Afterwards, the chairman of the DOC conceded defeat, flatly stating, "The voters made their position clear. . . . They don't want the Olympics."[15] The IOC eventually opted to relocate the 1976 Winter Olympics to Innsbruck, handing the Austrian city a victory by attrition. *Sports Illustrated* concluded that the activist campaign and referendum in Colorado "was not a vote against the Olympics per se, nor a vote against sport. But it was a vote against sporting facilities that cost taxpayers millions of dollars and work against essential conservation attitudes in the area concerned."[16] This distinction remains important for understanding anti-Olympics activism in the twenty-first century.

To be sure, a great deal has changed since the activist battle in Colorado. The Olympics have evolved from a relatively modest festival of amateur athleticism into a shimmering, capitalist dynamo. By the end of the 1980s the IOC had made great strides in transforming itself into the powerful behemoth we know today. Nonetheless, the case of Denver highlights the possibilities of political dissent that challenges the Games. The activist efforts in Denver spotlight the complex relationship between sport and politics and the strategic interplay between everyday people and those in positions of power. It also helps illuminate aspects of social theory that will be useful as we consider dissident citizenship on the Olympic terrain in the twenty-first century.

A Moment of Movements

Writing in 1992, social-movement scholar Mario Diani synthesized existing conceptualizations of the term *social movement* before offering his own: "a network of informal interactions between a plurality of individuals, groups, and/or organizations, engaged in a political or cultural conflict, on the basis of a shared collective identity."[17] While Diani's useful fusion captured many key dimensions of collective action, it deemphasized two elements that are significant to social movements: formalized politics and sustained interaction. Social movements often engage in regularized, formal political activity inside the institutionalized pathways of political power, translating their efforts into crisp demands of elected officials and other authorities. Also, to be a social movement, such activity and organizing cannot be a one-off—it must be *sustained* through time. Diani's conceptual work fashioned a pathway for Sidney Tarrow to offer what is now a widely accepted definition of social movements—"collective challenges, based on common purposes and social solidarities, in sustained interactions with elites, opponents, and authorities."[18] While this is a valuable definition, it doesn't quite fit the sorts of organizing that often emerge to challenge the Olympics since this activism is only barely maintained through time and from site to site.

Writing about the modern-day Global Justice Movement, Tom Mertes has asserted that it's "useful to conceptualize the relation between the various groups as an ongoing series of alliances and coalitions, whose convergences remain contingent. Genuine solidarity can only be built up through a process of testing and questioning, through a real overlap of affinities and interests."[19] Anti-Olympics activism aligns more with this conception of organizing—which highlights contingency and convergence—than the idea of an old-school social movement, despite the fact that at least one scholar has described anti-Olympics activism as "a quite significant social movement."[20] It would be more correct to call anti-Olympic resistance an "event coalition" than a social movement proper, since the activism is only scarcely sustained through time; protesters hobble on a shoestring budget from Olympic host city to host city. Sidney Tarrow distinguishes movements from event coalitions, or groups coming together for a single event where there is relatively shallow, temporary cooperation between organizations that decreases after the event transpires, when demonstrators return to the "normal activism" surrounding their central issues. As we will see, while the transnational site-to-site activist ties between anti-Olympics activists are becoming stronger, the idea of an event coalition captures the formal aspects of anti-Olympics activism in the early twenty-first century.[21] Protesting the Olympics is akin to an activist version of Whac-A-Mole. The Games pop up in one city, generating dissent, and then quickly plunge beneath the discursive surface, rearing their head in another city two years later. Protesters meanwhile fall back into their pre-Games patterns of protest, returning to their main targets and objectives.

Anti-Olympics activism is not so much a "movement of movements" as it is a *moment* of movements. During the Olympics moment, extant activist groups come together using the Olympics as their fight-back focal point. As we shall see, their efforts are often filtered through tactical and strategic hubs, the coming-together points of loose networks that share a five-ring bête noire. Viewing anti-Olympics activism in this way is not merely an academic exercise in definition construction; it's a clear reflection of twenty-first-century activist groups finding ways to organize with greater flexibility, spontaneity, and lateral solidarity. Anti-Olympics activism in Vancouver and London provide prime examples of these dynamics.

Social-movement scholars distinguish between *contained contention* and *transgressive contention,* with the former meaning activists who are "previously established actors employing well established means of claim making" and the latter indicating contenders who are "newly self-identified political actors" who engage in "innovative political action" that is either unprecedented or outlawed.[22] In the conceptually murkier world of boots-to-pavement activism, such dichotomies often don't hold up, which led Tarrow to delineate *multiform* activist coalitions that employ traditional and imaginative tactics and strategies both inside and outside the institutional pathways of political power.[23] As Jack Goldstone puts it, "the organizations that channel protest and 'conventional' political actions, are increasingly intertwined."[24] Anti-Olympics event coalitions are multiform, often adopting traditional forms of dissent, such as testifying at local meetings and lobbying elected leaders, while also making use of novel repertoires of contention with targets outside traditional politics.

While Olympics activists are not strictly speaking part of social movements, social-movement theory nevertheless offers a rich theoretical seam from which we can draw to make sense of anti-Olympics campaigners. One useful conceptual apparatus that can help us organize our thinking in a bigger-picture way is *political opportunity structure* (POS). POS encompasses both longer-term, relatively fixed institutional structures (for example, the constitutional role of the military in a given country) as well as medium-term, more dynamic structures that can more readily shift (for example, political alignments among elite policymakers).[25] POS affects the social receptivity of groups that are challenging dominant power relations. In an effort to enhance the analytical precision of POS, Doug McAdam delineates what he views as its four central dimensions: "the relative openness or closure of the institutionalized political system, the stability or instability of that broad set of elite alignments that typically undergird a polity, the presence or absence of elite allies, the state's capacity and propensity for repression."[26] To this I add the presence of international pressures[27] and the openness and receptivity of the mass media. Moreover, Goldstone makes the important point that bursts of activism "are likely to be triggered by major society-wide crises, such as military or economic challenges that weaken support for a government."[28] In other words, structure matters, but so do the less-predictable quirks, flurries, and upsurges that can roil the political world. These state-of-exception moments can loosen the political ties that bind elites, thereby creating space in which activists can work with more freedom and efficacy.

POS has been robustly critiqued by social-movement scholars on a variety of grounds.[29] Nevertheless, for the purposes of this book, POS serves as a useful heuristic that can sensitize us to some of the unique issues, dilemmas, and factors in the political environment that anti-Olympics activists face. This book examines how anti-Olympics activists foment creative, complex repertoires of contention in the face of structural impediments and atmospheric challenges. It does not attempt to forge a one-size-fits-all, causal, universal, or predictive theory for understanding the emergence or success-failure of anti-Olympics event coalitions.

Thinking through the elements of political opportunity structure help us better understand Colorado's unique rebuff of the Olympic Games in the 1970s. Activists operated within a relatively open, democratic political system and benefited from the option of concocting a statewide referendum on Olympic funding. Additionally, protesters were able to link up with elite allies who shared their environmental and economic concerns. Richard Lamm, the outspoken member of Colorado House of Representatives, echoed the sentiments of activists when he said, "The people behind the Olympics are the same ones who stand to profit—the airlines, hotels, banks and ski resorts." Like protesters, he believed that playing host to the Olympics meant vulnerability to "economic land mines."[30] While Olympics boosters benefited from the support of the *Denver Post,* major national news outlets like the *New York Times* and *Sports Illustrated* transmitted activist grievances at face value for the world—and perhaps more importantly, Colorado voters—to consider. Such media could leverage international consideration in ways the local press could not. Overall, the political opportunity structure confronted by Colorado activists was relatively propitious. The Olympic movement was comparatively weak; whereas today it is a powerful force with high approval ratings worldwide. Under such conditions, activists were able to blend contained and transgressive contention to their advantage.

Anti-Olympics activists in the twenty-first century face a formidable political opportunity structure. Depending on the host city, the openness of the institutionalized political system can vary widely, from Sydney (2000) to Sochi (2014), from Salt Lake City (2002) to Beijing (2008). But regardless of the political system, elites of all stripes tend to unite under the glow of the five rings when a city from their homeland is hosting the Games. These strengthened alignments minimize the possibility of securing elite allies with whom activists can work to amplify their claims in the public sphere. Since mass media often use elite decision makers as a barometer for agenda setting, this united elite front also tends to manifest itself in the press, marginalizing the critiques of activists. Although in specific instances involving less democratic host regimes (for example Seoul 1988, Beijing 2008), international pressures can carve out space for activists to act. However, the general trend is for international forces to reinforce the values of the Olympic Movement. Breaking down political opportunity structure into its component parts helps us make sense of Finlo Rohrer's aforementioned remark on the BBC that if you were a supporter of the London 2012 Games "you are a nice person who wants Britain to succeed" but if you raised concerns "you are a Scrooge-like killjoy."[31]

Media Matters

The mass media collectively constitute a crucial social circuit, a key conveyor of information that shapes our understanding of the issues, ideas, and ideologies of our day. Mass media—especially television— have played a pivotal role in the ascension of the Olympic Games. But the media are not simply a bullhorn that proliferates Olympism to the general public. The media also serve as an informational judge and jury, tacitly constructing discursive brackets that—ever-shifting as they may be—hem in what is socially acceptable political opinion and what is outside the boundaries of tolerability. This brings us to another vital theoretical concern from the field of social-movement studies, the two-pronged concept of *framing:* (1) activist attempts to frame their grievances in the most appealing, sympathetic ways, and (2) the mass media's framing of issues and ideas, condensing the whirl and swirl of the world into consumable strips of information.

When social-movement scholars discuss framing they usually mean "conscious strategic efforts by groups of people to fashion shared understandings of the world and of themselves that legitimate and motivate collective action."[32] These efforts often come into direct conflict with the "shared understandings" of state agents, economic elites, and other pockets of socio-political and economic power. This leads to what William Gamson describes as "framing contests" whereby activists and their adversaries discursively jockey for political advantage by expressing their grievances to the media, political elites, other activists, and the general public as persuasively as possible.[33] Robert Benford and David Snow assert that social movements attempt to fulfill three "core framing tasks" as they pursue social change: diagnostic, prognostic, and motivational framing. With diagnostic framing, activists pinpoint socio-political problems and attribute blame for extant injustices. Through prognostic framing, dissident citizens ante up solutions and pathways for realizing them. Motivational framing aims to catalyze social-movement action.[34]

When communications scholars use the term *framing* they mean something different: consistent, coherent bundles of information that journalists provide to instill real-world events with structure and meaning. Media frames organize issues and offer interpretive cues, pointing both backward at what happened and forward to what it all means.[35] So, when it comes to Gamson's "framing contests," mass media are the arbiters. As such, the media are of vital importance when it comes to constructing discourse. Media coverage of dissent matters—it can help activists circulate their ideas or it can undercut their efforts. Through framing, journalists tacitly fashion discursive brackets that classify certain ideas and political actors as rational and thus to be taken seriously, while other ideas and actors are framed as extremist and therefore unacceptable. Are campaigners framed as thoughtful citizens exercising their rights and freedoms? Or are activists' critiques framed as offering "the reflexive complaints of Negative Nigels who would rain on any parade"?[36] In this book I argue that the machinations of mass media are crucial in understanding activism vis-à-vis the Olympics. The quality and quantity of media coverage of dissent is critical. Mass-media coverage can help activists legitimize and disseminate their ideas to potential supporters. Or it can alienate campaigners from potential allies in the public sphere. As Robert Entman notes, "the frame in the news text is really the imprint of power—it registers the identity of actors or interests that competed to dominate the text."[37] Thanks to their access and clout, political elites have more influence over the mediated "imprint of power," but savvy activists can nevertheless pry open propitious possibilities through dexterous strategies and tactics.

The fact that mass media reflect, reproduce, and sometimes help activists challenge power relations links laterally to what Ruud Koopmans and Paul Statham call the "discursive opportunity structure," or the set of variables "determining which ideas are considered 'sensible,' which constructions of reality are seen as 'realistic,' and which claims are held as 'legitimate' within a certain polity at a specific time."[38] In a way, they're pointing to the crux of activist resonance: the space where dissident framing meet media frames. To maximize the impact of their ideas and critiques, activists need to pay heed to—while simultaneously questioning—hegemonic discourses. Holly McCammon and her colleagues note, "if activists frame their grievances without regard to dynamics in the broader cultural context, their messages are far less likely to be politically effective."[39] The reverse is also true. Activists can try to shape their frames to resonate with the wider discursive field, adopting tropes and lingo that ride the political zeitgeist. At the same time they can try to wedge open the discursive fractures that exist, occasionally even rupturing the dominant modes of social dialogue when they verge on being outdated.

Online and Social Media Matter, Too

The ever-building maelstrom of Internet and social-media activism complicates the media field in ways that both reinforce and undermine corporate media power. According to Brett Hutchins and Janine Mikosza, new media create possibilities for undermining the International Olympic Committee: "From the perspective of the IOC," decentralized media "possess a Janus-faced character, simultaneously offering additional avenues to promote the Olympic brand and experience across the globe *and* challenging their capacity to maintain control over Olympic related media in unpredictable online environments."[40] The IOC is more than aware of these possibilities and has moved to circumscribe the use of social media. In 2009, at the IOC's 13th Olympic Congress in Copenhagen, one of the central themes was the "digital revolution." A final recommendation emerging from the meeting was that "the Olympic Movement should undertake a fundamental review of their communication strategies, taking into account the fast-moving developments in information technology and, more recently, the digital revolution" in order to spread the Olympic spirit far and wide.[41] The IOC has subsequently issued "Social Media, Blogging and Internet Guidelines" for Olympic participants and other accredited individuals that restrict how they can act online. In the guidelines for the 2014 Winter Games in Sochi, the IOC encouraged Games participants to blog and tweet. However, "postings, blogs or tweets must be in a first-person, diary-type format" and the social-media user "must not assume the role of a journalist, reporter or any other media capacity." Moreover, participants must "at all times conform to the Olympic spirit and fundamental principles of Olympism as contained in the Olympic Charter." Failure to comply means one's accreditation "may be withdrawn without notice, at the discretion of the IOC" while the committee also reserves the right to take legal action and impose other sanctions.[42]

Political activists operating outside the orbit of the IOC are not inhibited by such strictures; dissident citizens have crafted digital repertoires of contention designed to reach wide audiences while simultaneously chewing up less resources on outreach and coordination. Social-movement scholars have placed increasing focus on what W. Lance Bennett and Alexandra Segerberg call "digitally networked action."[43] In one typology, scholars delineate four general classifications of Internet activism: (1) "brochure-ware" web sites that house relatively static information related to various campaigns and causes; (2) online activity that catalyzes offline activism; (3) participation in online protest activity like petition signing, and (4) completely virtual organization of online protest campaigns.[44] This led Jennifer Earl and Katrina Kimport to construct a "continuum of online activism" that ranges from, on one pole, "E-mobilizations" that use the Internet to aid in information sharing that contributes to offline protest to "E-movements" on the other pole, whereby both organization and participation in activist activity occurs online. In the middle of the continuum sits collective action that blends—in diverging degrees—online and offline elements. This is where keyboard activism sparks boots-to-pavement mobilization. These activist interventions can be affiliated with social movements in variegated ways.[45]

Social-movement scholar Victoria Carty examined an array of campaigns and movements on the continuum—from Students Against Sweatshops' anti-Nike Campaign to the post–September 11 peace movement to the online group MoveOn.org—and concluded, "E-activism and e-mobilizations have allowed for new forms of grassroots participatory democracy" that can productively bypass the mainstream media and create a "symbiotic relationship between e-activism and local organizing." In short, she found "online and offline activism tends to reinforce each with groups straddling cyberspace and local mobilizations."[46] Sociologists Glenn Stalker and Lesley Wood found in regards to the 2010 G20 protests in Toronto that more than half of those who participated found out about the demonstrations through an Internet communication technology, with more than one in four learning through social-networking sites. Online communication tended to reinforce and reproduce extant political circuits and social networks, but also served as a promising outreach tool for new recruits and participants.[47]

While many scholars are intrigued—and even heartened—by the possibilities of online activism, not everyone is so sanguine. Media scholar Robert McChesney asserts, "The tremendous power of the digital revolution has been compromised by capitalist appropriation and development of the Internet" whose internal logic is "inimical to much of the democratic potential of digital communication."[48] Skepticism of this sort emerges not only from the tendency for corporate behemoths to predominate on the Internet,[49] but also in part from the propensity of Internet connections to forge "weak ties" rather than deep, meaningful relationships rooted in commitment and trust. Yet as sociologist Mark Granovetter famously pointed out, "Weak ties are more likely to link members of *different* small groups than are strong ones, which tend to be concentrated within particular groups."[50] Such lateral connection can be vital in the mobilization process, as it can aid in the diffusion of ideas and information. However, as social-movement scholar Doug McAdam pointed out, "strong ties" are more important for understanding why activists engage in high-risk protest. In analyzing the Student Nonviolent Coordinating Committee's Freedom Summer program, he learned that those who had more "strong ties" tended to stick with the program, while those who lacked such ties were more inclined to withdraw. McAdam noted, "it is the sum of a person's ties to other applicants or known activists . . . that bears the strongest relationship to participation."[51] When the stakes were high, strong ties mattered.

The difference between strong and weak ties brings us to the relationship between social media and political activism. In regards to social media like Facebook and Twitter, social commentators and scholars have debated the power and influence of such social-networking media for the purposes of political organizing. As Bennett and Segerberg have noted, unlocking the logic of collective action—replete with free riders—has been complicated further by "the logic of connective action," which "applies increasingly to life in late-modern societies in which formal organizations are losing their grip on individuals, and group ties are being replaced by large-scale, fluid social networks." They argue that social media are vital to such networks "and their logic does not require strong organizational control or the symbolic construction of a united 'we.'"[52] "Connective action" is reliant on highly personalized forms of socially mediated communication whereby digital media are the "organizing agents."[53]

In the academy, activist circles, and the public sphere, participants in the debate over the efficacy and effectiveness of social media in political organizing fall into two predominant camps: techno-optimists and techno-pessimists.[54] The question is whether keyboard clicktivism can translate into the clacking of shoes to pavement. On one hand, techno-optimists like Clay Shirky argue that thanks to the rise of social-media technologies, collective action is easier than ever: "most of the barriers to group action have collapsed, and without those barriers, we are free to explore new ways of gathering together and getting things done."[55] The power—and limits—of traditional media have diminished considerably, he asserts, and social media have made the task of organizing people around a common cause "ridiculously easy."[56] Social media allow for lightning-quick communication and mobilization, swift conglomerations of ideas and bodies, collecting from the ground up. For Shirky, "The story of rapidly coordinated protest by ordinary citizens is one of the most durable stories we have about social media."[57] Political activism, this line of thinking goes, has experienced a preternatural techno-reinvention. Academics studying topics as diverse as a Guatemalan justice movement to protests in Egypt's Tahrir Square to #Occupy Everywhere have assembled evidence that social media can mobilize people from the cybersphere to the streets.[58]

On the other hand, techno-pessimists like Malcolm Gladwell of the *New Yorker* argue that because social media engender weak ties and rely on horizontal structures, they are ill-suited for challenging power. He asserts that hierarchy makes for effective protest and that social-media organizing, "shifts our energies from organizations that promote strategic and disciplined activity and toward those which promote resilience and adaptability. It makes it easier for activists to express themselves, and harder for that expression to have any impact." Furthermore, he writes, "The instruments of social media are well suited to making the existing social order more efficient. They are not a natural enemy of the status quo." If it's minor reform you want, social media might help, but if you desire structural change, Twitter is not the solution.[59] This approach is bolstered by social critics like Evgeny Morozov who claims online efforts are more likely to devolve into "slacktivism" than meaningful activism: it "makes online activists feel useful and important while having preciously little political impact." He surmises that social-media activism "may be eroding, rather than augmenting older, more effective forms of activism and organizing."[60] In a sense, clicktivism can become an alibi for offline inaction. Social media can also be an effective surveillance tool for those who wish to undercut political change. Scholars share many of these concerns, with Ingrid Hoofd arguing that activists in the "era of acceleration" have become so obsessed with the technological tools of dissent that they have "increasingly *no choice* but to *accelerate* neo-liberal production" as they pursue their goals. Activists incessantly churn out more information, and this plays into the interests of "the speed elite," who would prefer to see activists on a cyber-treadmill of their own choosing than taking to the streets. Media technologies, she states, leads to "increasing social retrenchment and division rather than connection and liberation."[61]

Scholar-activist Paolo Gerbaudo slices an analytical path between techno-optimism and techno-pessimism, arguing that social media can facilitate "a choreography of assembly" whereby social-media users shepherd people toward activist events. Facebook and Twitter can also play a role in "providing participants with suggestions and instructions about how to act" and aid in "the construction of an emotional narration to sustain their coming together in public space."[62] In his comparative analysis of social-media use in the Egyptian revolution, the *indignados* protests in Spain, and Occupy Wall Street, he finds that such choreography entails "the mediated 'scene-setting' and 'scripting' of people's physical assembling in public space." Vital to this process is the way social media can foment "emotional condensation" for activists around a common cause or identity.[63] But for Gerbaudo the linchpin is that such "condensation" must lead to "material precipitation in public space"—on-the-ground activism.[64] Gerbaudo's emphasis on social media becoming "emotional conduits for restructuring a sense of togetherness among a spatially dispersed constituency" gels with Bennett and Segerberg's concept of the "personal action frames," which activists deploy in hopes of galvanizing action.[65] This brings us back to Benford and Snow's "core framing tasks"—diagnosis, prognosis, and motivation—albeit with a techno-twist.[66]

The perils and possibilities of digital-media technologies have a lot to do with the political opportunity structure that anti-Olympics activists face. As we shall see, activists at the 2010 Winter Games in Vancouver and the 2012 Summer Olympics in London took advantage of digital media in differing degrees in an effort to organize, educate, and inspire. In general, activists in Vancouver were more skeptical of social media, while in London the technologies were more widely embraced.

Dissent and Its Suppression

In many ways, anti-Olympics activists face an uphill battle, but there are circumstances that, if they're able to create them, make achieving their activist goals more possible. Social-movement scholars have identified key preconditions for collective action, factors that structurally and strategically make dissent more viable. These preconditions include the ability to (1) maintain solidarity; (2) attract new recruits; (3) create, nurture, and support movement leaders; (4) generate preferably favorable media coverage;

(5) mobilize support from potentially sympathetic bystander publics; and (6) carve out the tactical freedom to pursue social-change goals, rather than put resources toward defensive maintenance needs.[67] Olympics activists have met these preconditions with varying levels of success.

The state and media can make achieving these conditions more difficult, whether through intentional maneuverings designed to stifle dissent or through less deliberate actions that render dissent less visible and thus less viable.[68] As criminologist Luis Fernandez notes, the suppression of dissent is complex, spanning the legal, physical, and psychological spheres.[69] Sociologist Jennifer Earl makes the important point that sometimes repressive forces can engage in coercion (for example, use of force), while at other times they undertake channeling (for example, negotiating over the timing and form of protest activities). She also notes the mounting importance of private agents (for example, vigilantes, private police) in suppressing activism, what we might call the outsourcing of repression.[70]

Policing protest has undergone discernible shifts through time, as "repertoires of protest control" have evolved.[71] Prior to the 1970s, the principal method for responding to activist demonstrations was "escalated force," a blend of aggressive actions, including arrests and physical coercion. Use of lethal weapons as well as tear gas and other technologies of crowd control were commonplace. From the perspective of police, protesting was not considered a legitimate form of political activity. This changed in the 1970s and 1980s when a "negotiated management" approach emerged that viewed protest as a viable mode of political expression, but one that needed to be heavily supervised and surveilled. Under this policing regime, security officials aimed to protect speech rights while fortifying social order. Softer policing techniques emerged, such as the joint negotiation over the timing and location of protest events. The requirement that activists secure protest permits became routine. This permitting process subtly doubled as a way the state could gather data on protesters and their strategies. Meanwhile, the negotiation process made each side—protesters and the police—more legible to each other.[72] In the late 1990s, policing practices shifted toward a "strategic incapacitation" model which Patrick Gillham and John Noakes describe as "a range of tactical innovations aimed at temporarily incapacitating transgressive protesters, including the establishment of extensive no-protest zones, the increased use of less-lethal weapons, the strategic use of arrests, and a reinvigoration of surveillance and infiltration of movement organizations."[73] The approach—backboned by the good-protester–bad-protester dynamic—relies on the prevention of protest and the targeting of specific social-movement activists for neutralization. It also entails an upsurge in the militarization of policing—the line between police and military institutions has become increasingly fuzzy.[74]

In the twenty-first century, highly militarized security forces have become a familiar part of the five-ring terrain. To understand why, one must go back four decades to the 1972 Munich Summer Games where on 5 September members of a Palestinian group called Black September sneaked into the Olympic Village and kidnapped Israeli athletes. This eventually led to a gun battle where all the Israeli athletes and five Palestinians were killed on the airport tarmac as they prepared to board a plane. In the wake of this violent debacle, Avery Brundage was faced with the difficult decision of what to do. Brundage opted to press ahead with the Games. He said in swiftly prepared remarks:

> Every civilized person recoils in horror at the barberous [sic] criminal intrusion of terrorists into peaceful Olympic precincts. We mourn our Isreal [sic] friends victims of this brutal assault. The Olympic flag and all the flags of the world fly at half mast. Sadly, in this imperfect world, the greater and more important the Olympic Games become, the more they are open to commercial, political, and now criminal pressure. . . . I am sure that the public will agree that we cannot allow a handful of terrorists to destroy this nucleus of international cooperation and good will we have in the Olympic Movement. The Games must go on and we must continue our efforts to keep them clean, pure and honest and try to extend the sportsmanship of the athletic field into other areas. We declare today a day of mourning and will continue all the events one day later than originally scheduled.[75]

The terrorist attack in Munich became a pivot point in Olympic history. Since then, terrorism has justifiably become a major concern, and host cities have ramped up their security forces to prevent attacks. This has proved controversial, however, as those same security forces can also be used to squelch—or at least intimidate—political activism, even if that's not their primary or stated function. The distinctions that policing bodies make between terrorist security threats and "social disorder" can be elided by those with the institutional power and incentives to do so. In fact, terrorism and political protest are often conflated in official rhetoric by blurring the two into the catch-all categories of "threats" or "risks" to the Games.

Activists in Vancouver and London repeatedly pointed to the fact that heavily armed police forces affected their dissident practices. And many argued that enhanced security measures—carried out in the name of combating terrorism—unduly militarized public space, all in the name of a two-and-a-half week sports extravaganza.

The Dialectic of Resistance and Restriction

Activists are involved in an ever-present dance with their detractors. This dialectic of resistance and restriction, whereby dissident citizens adapt their strategies and tactics in response to efforts to squelch their effectiveness, is a perpetual battle of adaptation. By a dissident citizen I do not mean "citizen" in the relatively static, state-sanctioned, legalistic mode. Rather, I mean people who engage in the active process of citizenship through voicing their opinions and grievances and participating in political life, oftentimes in the public sphere. Dissident citizenship moves beyond mere disagreement—as with, say, a dissenting judge—to embracing active efforts to make social change.[76]

The smooth veneer of frictionless spatial relations is vital to the Olympic spectacle. The Olympic brand as pushed forward by the IOC demands what Sze Tsung Leong calls "control space," which he describes as "a cartography in continuous flux" that bestows passageway for the machinations of capital, instilling the "vicissitudes of the market" into everyday life.[77] The IOC demands that host countries scour social spaces so they are free from political dissidence that might stain the high-stakes sports gala. To do this, policing entities amass caches of weaponry, insulating the IOC and local boosters from unwanted criticism. The IOC has also written extraordinary rules and laws that mandate dissent-free, highly controlled zones teeming with sports and commerce. The Olympic Charter tees up an enlightening requirement mandating "control space" while exerting an iron-fisted grip on its commercial interests. In a section of its charter titled "Advertising, Demonstrations, Propaganda," the IOC states, "No form of advertising or other publicity shall be allowed in and above the stadia, venues and other competition areas which are considered as part of the Olympic sites. Commercial installations and advertising signs shall not be allowed in the stadia, venues or other sports grounds." It also strictly prohibits political activism at the Games: "No kind of demonstration or political, religious or racial propaganda is permitted in any Olympic sites, venues or other areas."[78] What constitutes "other areas" is open to broad interpretation. Thus, despite the rhetoric of human rights and freedom that abound in IOC official discourse, the Olympic Charter dictates—if indirectly—that local authorities suppress not just ambush marketing, but also political activism during the Games. The IOC's daunting demands have led to the fortressification of host cities before, during, and after the Olympic Games.

The Olympics ante up a genuinely unique moment for political activists. On one hand, the Games are a multifaceted, far-reaching behemoth that touches many issues that often galvanize protest, from public-spending concerns to civil-liberties issues to environmental matters. On the other hand, as I argue in this book, there's no established, transnational enduring anti-Olympics movement—campaigns in particular host cities have an expiration date, the end of the Games. When it comes to the dialectic of resistance and restriction, on one hand the Olympics give rise to a burgeoning security apparatus designed to quash terrorism but that can also double to suppress dissent. On the other hand, the police don't want to appear thuggish under the hot glare of the media spotlight. Olympics organizers wish to create a festive sphere of celebration, not a repressive urbanism that will make Olympics-goers feel queasy. Activists often chant "the whole world is watching" and with the Olympics, it actually is.

Olympic Activism

The modern Olympics have generated a wide range of response, from blissful sports boosterism to staunch political dissent. While some see the Games as a sanguine sportstopia, others argue it exacerbates the already uneven topography of political economics. Despite the fact that, for some people, protesting the Games borders on the sacrilegious, numerous political activists around the world have challenged various aspects of the Olympics. In the 1920s and 1930s, the worker sports movement organized alternative games to the Olympics, and women created the Women's Olympics.[79] In the 1960s and 1970s, poet Dennis Brutus led an effort to boycott apartheid South Africa's participation in the Games.[80] John Carlos and Tommie Smith raised their black-glove-clad fists in the air during the medal ceremonies in 1968 to protest racism and poverty in the United States and around the world, while Australian sprinter Peter Norman joined them in medal-stand solidarity. More recently, before the 2004 Summer Games in Athens, activists challenged organizers set on intensifying development in an environmentally sensitive part of the metropolis that was already overpopulated. Dissidents in China rallied against human-rights abuses on the platform of the 2008 Summer Games in Beijing. Activists in Vancouver used the 2010 Winter Olympics to challenge historically unsettled indigenous land claims, while campaigners in London questioned public-spending priorities with the 2012 Summer Games.[81] The Olympics ritually rivets our collective attention, not only zeroing in on awe-inspiring athletic prowess, but also enhancing the possibility of high-profile dissident citizenship on the global media terrain. The frequency of Olympic protests has skyrocketed in the last thirty years, in part because of the rise and evolution of transnational activist networks that are more effectively engaging four types of politics: informational, symbolic, leverage-oriented, and accountability-centered.[82]

Pierre de Coubertin, the founder of the modern Olympics, had high hopes for the socio-political power of sport, despite the fact he largely sidestepped taking stands on the big political issues of his day. In a January 1919 letter to the members of the International Olympic Committee, he linked sport and democracy, writing, "Athleticism has a major role to play in the bringing about of social reforms. . . . [T]he athletic group is, in a way, the basic cell of democracy." Coubertin went on to assert there was almost nothing sport couldn't do in society: "Mutual assistance and competition, the two essential elements of any democratic society, necessary [sic] rub shoulders in this group, because sports—the leveler of class distinctions—, is also a powerful alternative to bad instincts, an antidote for alcoholism, a pursuer of tuberculosis, an unequaled agent for physical and moral health in our time. Finally, these groups sow the seeds of observation, critical thinking, self-control, calculated effort, expenditure of energy, and a practical philosophy in the face of failure. These are qualities this generation needs desperately."[83] Coubertin believed in the transformative power of sport, especially on the level of the individual. And he wasn't naïve when it came to mixing politics and sport. In 1936, as the Berlin Games—also known as the Nazi Olympics[84]—approached, Coubertin observed, "Today, politics is making its way into the heart of every issue. How can we expect athletics, the culture of the muscles, and Olympism itself to be immune?" He went on to argue "the ravages that this phenomenon can cause" did not affect real-deal Olympism, the "soul" of the movement, which "remains as steadfast as the principles on which the institution is based" and there-fore immune from the fractious perils of politics.[85] Thirty years later, Avery Brundage followed his predecessor's lead, contending, "The Olympic Movement appears as a ray of sunshine through clouds of racial animosity, religious bigotry, and political chicanery."[86] Brundage often championed, as he put it, "the necessity of preventing the Olympic Movement from being used as a tool or weapon for other causes." Yet, like Coubertin, he thought the Games could offer up a positive demonstration effect for foun-dering politicos: "The IOC cannot very well reform the world; it can only set, in the Olympic Games, a good example for the politicians to follow," he wrote.[87]

Contemporary critics may view Coubertin's absolution and Brundage's exuberance as the justificatory contortions of true believers, who, faithful to their status as five-ring elites, wished to insulate Olympism from brass-tacks politics, brute economics, and all their complications. Dave Zirin, for example, argues the muscular religiosity promoted by the Baron and his ilk, "provided the perfect place for the rulers of imperialist nations to assert their rights to symbolic domination."[88] Sports academic Alan Tomlinson maintains the Games have "become what successive political or economic ideologues and entrepreneurs have wanted them to become."[89] Meanwhile, Lenskyj asserts there is "a fundamental problem that permeates all aspects of the Olympic industry: a failure to conduct business in a socially respon-sible and ethical manner."[90] Critics like Zirin, Tomlinson, and Lenskyj contend that neo-aristocratic privilege, concealed behind the veil of grand Olympic ideals, boosts and buoys the Games while reinforcing inequality, with the rich snagging the proverbial gold and the poor being shunted fur-ther to the political and economic margins.

Despite the staggering disadvantage political activists have in terms of resources, they have consistently waged an asymmetrical discourse battle against the Olympic Movement. The fact that the Olympics occur under the hot glare of the global media spotlight abets political activism, as dis-sidents have a prime opportunity to engage in "piggyjacking."[91] Savvy activ-ists have the potential to deflect attention from the sports spectacle and swerve the narrative toward political issues that matter to them, in a sense, "seizing the Olympic platform." The essence of this discursive seizure is, as Monroe E. Price puts it, "to find a platform that has proven highly suc-cessful in establishing a major constituency for one purpose and then con-vert that constituency to a different, unintended objective."[92] This helps political activists jump scale with their dissent, reaching bystander publics who might otherwise be inaccessible or disinterested.

Contemporary activism is marked by creativity and appropriation, which lend themselves well to the possibility of piggyjacking. Given the fact many of the official Olympic events—including the opening and closing ceremonies as well as the pre-Games torch run—are designed for both maximum emotional impact and a certain amount of public participation, they are often seen as political spectacle. Situationist Guy Debord theorizes, "The spectacle is not a collection of images; rather, it is a social relationship between people that is mediated by images."[93] This image-induced "social relationship" is key to understanding both the Olympics and the activist response.

Some contemporary theorists argue that the energy and intrigue of the spectacle can be harnessed and redirected for positive political purposes. For instance, Douglas Kellner advances "progressive spectacle politics" in order to snap people from their spectator-politics trance and offer them concrete channels for becoming active in political struggle and for making substantive political headway. Such a spectacle is designed to "further the goals of democracy, justice, human rights, environmental protection, and a progressive agenda" while eschewing passive acquiescence to the political status quo.[94] This chimes with scholar-activist Stephen Duncombe's notion of the "progressive ethical spectacle," which is participatory, horizontal, and willing to embrace humor, fun, and productive estrangement. The ethical spectacle veers toward direct democracy as it "breaks down hierarchies, fosters community, allows for diversity, and engages with reality while asking what new realities might be possible."[95] Political actors are thus co-creators of a spectacle of their choosing. This is carnivalesque spectacle with a purposeful political pulse.

Yet a guiding principle of such activism is often the idea that being more politically effective can often derive from being less overtly political. With contemporary activism, humor can often smooth the path toward alternative interpretations and possibilities. As anthropologist Angelique Haugerud puts it, satire-oriented activism "can disrupt politicians' branding messages . . . and destabilize dominant corporate and discursive frames by exposing contradictory meanings."[96] Through the one-two punch of irony and parody—satire's go-to moves—activists can activate "spectacular dissent" that "does not necessarily yield predictable meanings for participants or wider publics," which many protesters point to as a strength.[97] In other words, "parody is serious business"[98] as it can both loosen up and open up the political field, something anti-Olympics activists in Vancouver—and especially London—recognized.

Attempting to recapture the term *spectacle* and drag it into the service of progressive activism is a tall order, demanding an enormously valiant effort. And even if dissidents can pull it off, important questions loom. Could they merely be replacing one form of alienation with hyperactive participation that values process but that doesn't transform material reality? Can such an emphasis on horizontal participation overshadow—and perhaps even trump—outcome? There's also the possible danger of simply replacing "the manufacture of consent" with the manufacture of enthusiasm, whereby politically engaged activists tread water and feel self-satisfied, while the powerful continue to pull the marionette strings like an invisible—and untroubled—puppeteer.

Forging a progressive spectacle is made all the more complicated in the context of challenging the Olympics. After all, the Games are extraordinarily popular. As mentioned earlier, the 2010 Vancouver Winter Games garnered more attention from USAmerican news consumers than any other story.[99] This resembled public interest in the 2008 Summer Games in Beijing, which drew the biggest television audience in US history.[100] This record was shattered four years later in London where 219.4 million people tuned in to NBC for the Games, surpassing Beijing's 215 million viewers.[101] The *New York Times* reported that London 2012 was the most watched event in the history of US television.[102] Meanwhile, in the United Kingdom, almost 52 million tuned in to the BBC to watch the Games, a full 90 percent of the population.[103] And the London Olympics enjoyed widespread public approval: 92 percent of those polled after the London Olympics viewed the Games as "very successful" or "somewhat successful."[104]

Nevertheless, even if the Olympics are tantamount to a hegemonic "subject-making apparatus," as anthropologist Thomas F. Carter suggests, political activists have not stood passive in the face of the shiny behemoth.[105] While some have argued this apparatus "squeezes out any possibility of counterhegemonic challenge and resistance, instead being absorbed in popular consciousness as an unquestioned social good," over the last thirty years activists have consistently challenged the hegemonic view of the Games.[106] The flame of resistance has not been—and never can be—entirely engulfed by the Olympic flame. This activism takes the form of both contained politics largely carried out by NGOs running Olympic watchdog campaigns and transgressive politics mostly performed by anti-Olympics direct-action activists. In this book I emphasize the latter as well as the interchange that occurs between groups embedded in these "multi-form" event coalitions.

The Olympics and Activism—A Typology

The political history of Olympics-induced activism is rich and complex. In an attempt to organize the fray, I offer a typology of Olympics dissent, laying out the categories of activism that will be fleshed out in the chapters that follow. One axis of this typology encompasses the political actor: who is engaging in politics vis-à-vis the Games? The two main political participants are athletes and nonathletes. The second axis involves the target of the activism: Is it the Olympics that are being protested? Or are activists piggyjacking the Games to highlight extant socio-political issues that are related to the Olympics? This renders four categories: (1) athletes protesting the machinations of the Games themselves; (2) athletes protesting wider socio-political issues; (3) nonathletes challenging the Olympics; (4) nonathletes using the Games to widen the audience for non-sports-related issues. These four analytical boxes are not airtight: some groups and individuals, for example, push for the reform of the Olympic structure while advancing wider socio-political goals. Figure 1.1 summarizes the four analytical categories.[107] In *Activism and the Olympics,* I focus on nonathlete activists who challenge the Games, transforming the mega-event into a prism that refracts political light onto ongoing, contentious social issues.

A number of Olympic athletes have taken public positions on political issues. This often means they forfeit their status as what sociologist John Horne calls the "polysemic athlete."[108] The term *polysemic* comes from linguistics and denotes having multiple meanings or interpretations. With polysemic athletes, spectators can map onto the athlete a wide range of understandings, thereby making that athlete appealing to a diverse range of people. Horne invokes the example of soccer superstar David Beckham: "fans can read into Beckham whatever they want."[109] When an athlete becomes "a polysemic signifier," as Kellner puts it, that person "mobilizes many fantasies (i.e. athletic greatness, wealth, success,

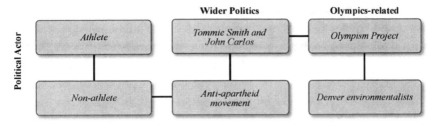

FIGURE 1.1 Typology of Olympics Political Activism. Source: Jules Boykoff.

and upward mobility) for the national and global imaginary, providing a spectacle who embodies many desirable national and global features and aspirations."[110] Polysemic athletes exude a fuzzy legibility that can be conveniently converted into a workhorse for capital accumulation, whether symbolic or material. However, when athletes take a specific political stand—especially one that is controversial—they narrow the interpretive field, thereby sacrificing the possibility that the masses will be attracted to their nebulous persona. Corporate sponsors hesitate, and the possibility of product spokespersonhood dwindles. The same principle applies to candidates running for political office; taking specific stances might alienate potential voters. Instead, when possible, they speak in generalities—and often platitudes—so voters can see in them whatever they wish.[111]

Despite the risks involved, Olympic athletes have used the Games as both a platform for fomenting social change and for attempting to reform the Games in order to bring them into tighter alignment with principles of equity and fairness. A high-profile example of this is the aforementioned instance when John Carlos and Tommie Smith famously—or infamously, depending on one's political vantage—thrust their clenched, black-gloved fists skyward during medal ceremonies at the 1968 Summer Games, creating what has become an iconic snapshot of resistance. Carlos and Smith were protesting widespread political problems like poverty and racism that plagued the United States and the world. Their choreographed symbology pointed to the macrosocial issues they wished to address. Their shoeless feet and black socks represented poverty. The black scarf and gloves signified black pride. Carlos's open jacket symbolized the working class that included his parents. Around their necks they wore beads that represented their African heritage as well as thick strings signifying the ropes of lynching in the US South. They sported human-rights pins on their coats and were joined by silver-medal-winning Australian Peter Norman who wore a political button in solidarity. Carlos and Smith were part of the Olympic Project for Human Rights (OPHR), a group that had specific goals such as the restoration of the heavyweight title to Muhammad Ali and the termination of apartheid in South Africa. In April 1968, as the Mexico City Games approached, sixty-five US athletes signed on to a list support-ing the boycott of the Games if South Africa were allowed to participate. Signatories included Arthur Ashe, Wilt Chamberlain, Jim Bouton, Len Wilkins, Oscar Robertson, Jackie Robinson, and Ruben Amaro, as well as US tracksters John Carlos and Lee Evans.[112] But the OPHR also wanted to reform the Olympics themselves. For example, OPHR demanded the "[d]esegregation of the United States Olympic Games Committee and assignment of more Negro coaches to the US Olympic teams."[113]

The sports media establishment attacked Carlos and Smith's action, turning their black-glove-clad hands into lightning rods for media heat. Arthur Daley of the *New York Times* wrote, "Smith and Carlos brought their world smack into the Olympic Games, where it did not belong, and created a shattering situation that shook this international sports carnival to its very core. They were also divisive."[114] Calling them "unimaginative blokes" and "a couple of black-skinned storm troopers," Brent Musburger, railed in the *Chicago American,* "One gets a little tired of having the United States run down by athletes who are enjoying themselves at the expense of their country." He continued, "Protesting and working constructively against racism in the United States is one thing, but airing one's dirty clothing before the entire world during a fun and games tournament was no more than a juvenile gesture by a couple of athletes who should have known better."[115] The entire episode highlights, as Douglas Hartmann puts it, "the thrill of victory and the agony of activism," and gives us insight as to why more Olympic athletes don't use their high-profile athletic stage to make political statements, and if they do, they often stick to safe trails.[116]

In another quadrant on the typology, other athletes, such as those asso-ciated with the Olympism Project, restrict their efforts to reforming the Olympics. Co-founded by Nathaniel Mills and Eli Wolff, the Olympism Project engages in educational programming to promote humanitarian and peace pursuits. Mills, a speed skater who participated in three Olym-pics (1992, 1994, and 1998), and Wolff, a Paralympic soccer player (1996 and 2004), adopted the motto "making ideals real." The group stresses internationalism and goodwill while downplaying nationalism and zeal-ousness.[117] Eli Wolff said the organization consciously foregrounds peace education, social justice, and human rights in order to create "a safe place to have conversations about the Olympic ideals" and figure out ways these conversations can translate "ideals into action." They do workshops in various cities in the United States and abroad (for example, Chicago, Boston, London). He said they are trying to jumpstart dialogue and debate in order "to get issues that are not talked about talked about." On the road to awareness raising, the group tries "to create a platform for athletes to learn about Olympism and what it means." Sometimes working with indi-viduals in the IOC and United States Olympic Committee (USOC), these activists provide a process-oriented educational platform that allows people interested in the Games "to work together, even though it can be challenging and even frustrating." They concertedly embrace tactics that Wolff says "are maybe more comfortable and a little more inviting" and less in-your-face. They've harnessed the power of social media—like Facebook and Twitter—to get the word out about their philosophy and efforts.[118]

Historically, nonathletes have also challenged various the tenets of the Olympics as well as the socio-political effects of hosting the Games (the final two quadrants of figure 1). The actions, strategies, and tactics of these activists—who operate outside the locus of Olympic athletics—constitute the analytical focus of this book. Former IOC marketing head Michael Payne once approvingly referred to the Games as "the world's longest commercial."[119] Many political activists would not dispute Payne's characterization but view it as a crass dynamic in need of reform. Politi-cal activists have critiqued the lopsided public funding of the Games, the private profiteering that can emerge, and the intense commercialism inher-ent to the modern Olympics. Other concerns raised by nonathlete activists include civil-liberties issues, environmental destruction to make way for the Olympics, and the ritualized nationalism that can at times transmog-rify into jingoism.

Activist Precedent in South Africa

Since this type of nonathlete activism is my focus in this book, it is impor-tant to elucidate two instructive episodes of contention that serve as vital political-historical context: (1) the South African anti-apartheid move-ment's use of the Games as a platform to both reform the Olympics and to draw attention to wider, ongoing political struggles in the 1960s and 1970s; (2) dissidents in Sydney who protested how the 2000 Summer Games would have grave environmental and social impacts. Activists in South Africa were tremendously successful in meeting their stated goals, while those in Sydney were less effective in their fight against the Olympic machine.

Behind the scenes at the IOC, South Africa had long been a vexing topic. IOC president Brundage, who had for years argued tenaciously against the country's exclusion from the Olympic family, couldn't stop the IOC from saying enough's enough.[120] Thanks to its overtly racist social policies, South Africa had its invitation to the 1964 Tokyo Games withdrawn by the IOC.[121] But to understand how the IOC came to exclude the South African National Olympic Committee, one needs to bring dissident citizenship into the picture. The pressure of nation-states played an important role—numerous countries supported a boycott of South Africa based on its apartheid system—but beneath the surface a band of savvy activists employing a wide-ranging, innovative repertoire of contention was the difference maker. In 1962, these activists started a strategically named group: the South African Non-Racial Olympic Committee (SANROC). On the surface, the acronym sounded like an official national Olympic committee, which Brundage objected to vigorously. In 1967, Brundage asserted the IOC would not deal with SANROC unless it changed its name, removing the word "Olympic." SANROC technically obliged, inserting "Open" for "Olympic," but its stationery still read "South Africa Non-Racial Olympic Committee" through the 1970s.[122]

SANROC emerged out of the South African Sports Association, a group founded by poet-activist Dennis Brutus in 1958. As president of SANROC, Brutus endeavored to use sport to leverage antiracist social change in South Africa. To achieve this, SANROC carried out an innovative, multifaceted campaign. SANROC frequently framed its claims as efforts simply to work in compliance with IOC policies and requirements, thereby rhetorically sanding away the sharp-edged radicality of their social-movement goals. They implored the IOC and the international federations to live up to the antiracist principles enshrined in their own charters. SANROC is a classic example of activists using sport to jump scale regarding their previously held grievances, what Harvey, Horne, and Safai refer to as "nonsport organizations that use sport to achieve broader social change or try to change sport and its institutions."[123]

SANROC's road of resistance was by no means easy. They operated in apartheid South Africa after all. Afrikaners were hardly willing to give up their racist policies without a fight. Amid SANROC's political pressure Jan De Klerk delineated four essential tenets for the National Party's approach to sports: (1) "Each racial group would form a separate controlling association in each sport," (2) "white associations would control the code, send representatives to the world federation, and assist the development of black associations," (3) "racially mixed teams would not represent South Africa," and (4) "sports officials would not invite racially mixed teams from abroad to play in the Republic."[124] This explicitly racist framework provided activists with a concrete set of policies to challenge. But the South African government had placed banning orders on Brutus, which prohibited him from writing (in 1961) and from belonging to any organization or meeting with more than two people (in 1963).[125] When he met with a former Swiss sports administrator in South Africa, police clamped down on him. Later, when attempting to travel to Baden-Baden, Germany, to meet IOC officials, Portuguese authorities in Mozambique intervened, taking Brutus into custody and handing him over to South African officials. When Brutus attempted to escape—he feared for his life—he was shot on a Johannesburg street and left to bleed for an hour before a "Coloured ambulance" picked him up to transport him to a hospital. Meanwhile South African officials and members of the IOC chastised SANROC for blending politics and sports. Red-baiting was rampant, with SANROC labeled communist by their detractors. Under such intense repression, SANROC went underground in 1965, emerging in 1966 outside South Africa.[126]

After establishing themselves in exile in London, Brutus and his fellow dissident citizens—like Sam Ramsamy, Reg Hlongwane, Chris de Broglio—continued their efforts. They pressed national governments to sign on to an Olympic boycott, despite the fact that Brundage asserted, "The word 'boycott' is a political word not used in Olympic circles."[127] They linked with sympathetic anti-apartheid groups as far away as New Zealand and worked with the United Nations International Committee against Apartheid Sport.[128] SANROC also bombarded IOC officials with letters reinforcing its anti-apartheid position and requesting to be treated like a national Olympic committee. For instance, in a letter to the Montreal Organizing Committee, Sam Ramsamy informed organizers that SANROC would be sending delegates to Montreal and called for "the usual courtesies which will facilitate our entry into the Olympic Village and other venues where the meetings will be held."[129] SANROC also pressured regional games officials to refuse hosting apartheid teams from South Africa. In a letter to the lead organizer of the Commonwealth Games, Dennis Brutus wrote, "It is my duty to advise you that SAN-ROC is prepared to campaign vigorously for Commonwealth countries to decline to participate in the Games this year, if a team from South Africa is touring Britain at the same time." He urged organizers "to use whatever pressures are available" to avoid taking the "wrongheaded and unwise" course.[130] Such persistence eventually led IOC president Lord Killanin to distribute a SANROC circular to IOC officials that clearly elucidated the anti-apartheid group's central grievances and implored the IOC to stamp out racism from the Games.[131]

SANROC also enlisted sympathetic allies from countries around the world to support their cause. Former Canadian Olympian Bruce Kidd, then an assistant professor in the School of Physical and Health Education at the University of Toronto, wrote to Harry Kerrison, the head of the Canadian Track and Field Association, to protest sending athletes to participate in a track meet in South Africa. He argued, "Very few of our members would like to see our national champions lend their support to the repressive system" of apartheid. "And yet that's exactly what happens when they compete under the contrived conditions of the South African Games." He vowed, "I am not prepared to leave it at writing one letter" and followed through on that promise, engaging in wide-ranging pressure on Canadian officials to line up their rhetoric and their actions on the South African racial question.[132]

The persistence of political activists paid off. South Africa's invitation to the Mexico City Games was withdrawn. Brundage wrote in a cable to IOC members, "In view of all the information on the international climate received by the executive board. . . . [i]t is unanimously of the opinion that it would be most unwise for a South African team to participate" in Mexico City.[133] SANROC had played a vital role in creating the "international climate" that severely limited Brundage's range of choices, as did the promise of twenty-five countries boycotting the Games if South African was allowed to compete. South Africa did not send athletes to Mexico City. African countries organized another boycott for the 1976 Games. After South Africa's expulsion from Olympic movement, it languished in the sports wilderness. SANROC's campaign to dismantle South Africa's racist sport structure and replace it with a merit-based system more in alignment with the rest of the world and with the stated principles of groups like the IOC finally succeeded, and the country was readmitted in the post-apartheid era to participate in the 1992 Barcelona Games."⁴ Such success reforming the Olympic movement is an important precursor for contemporary activists who wish to reform the Games.'³⁵ Yet the Olympics could also be an effective lever for wider social change.

Dissident Citizenship in Sydney

Like the activists in Denver described at the outset of this chapter, anti-Olympics protesters at the Sydney Summer Games in 2000 zeroed in on the environmental and social impacts of hosting the Games. But campaigners in Sydney faced a markedly different political opportunity structure. Not only had the IOC solidified its income streams and stabilized its status as a top-shelf mega-event, but higher-ups in the IOC were ready—and even eager—to talk about green objectives. By the time Sydney rolled around, the IOC had raised its environmental game, declaring ecological concerns "an essential component of Olympism" during its 1994 Olympic Congress in Paris. '³⁶ Soon after it added ecological considerations to the 1995 Olympic Charter. In this version of the charter, Rule 2 declared that the IOC, "sees to it that the Olympic Games are held in conditions which demonstrate a responsible concern for environmental issues."'³⁷ In Sydney this translated into remediating the highly polluted Homebush Bay, making it home to the Olympic Village and a number of other Olympic venues.

The IOC's green proclamations were put to the test in the lead-up to the Games when the Sydney Organizing Committee announced it would hold the beach volleyball competition at Bondi Beach, a venerated, scenic location along the Pacific Ocean. Holding the event there meant constructing a ten-thousand-seat temporary stadium that would restrict access for regular beachgoers for a sizable chunk of the summer. This, argued Bondi residents and their supporters, could cause ecological harm while simultaneously cutting into local commerce. The beach was already a tourist hotspot, and critics didn't believe it needed an Olympic boost. Yet NBC, which had doled out $600 million for television rights for the Sydney Games, insisted that beach volleyball happen at Bondi Beach because of the spot's international reputation and the picturesque Pacific bay background that would make for appealing TV programming.'³⁸

In May 2000, as construction on the temporary stadium began, direct-actionistas from Bondi Olympic Watch hit the sand, staging a raucous protest where activists buried themselves in sand to the neck to prevent bulldozers from getting to work.[139] Their efforts gained significant attention from the local press, not all of it positive. One opinion piece in Sydney's *Daily Telegraph*, titled "Sun, Sand and Angry Hippies," derided the group as "a bunch of septuagenarians, leftover hippies and the odd goatied [*sic*] youth," some of whom were "squawking about police brutality."[140] Other articles highlighted the low number of protesters and the fact that there were more curious onlookers and pro-Olympics hecklers than activists.[141] And as Lenskyj notes, the assembled security forces were overwhelming and intimidating; on hand were "three Blackhawk helicopters, two police launches, fifteen mounted police officers, and one hundred and fifty SWAT team police on foot," all ready for action.[142] In the end, the activists were thwarted and Olympic volleyball took place on Bondi Beach.

But environmentalism was not the only concern of campaigners in Sydney. Dissident citizens sounded the alarm on Games-induced gentrification in the Olympic corridor as well as the disproportionate effects development could have on Aboriginal peoples. They also raised concerns about special laws for the Games that would have the effect of criminalizing poverty.[143] Others questioned the hefty five-ring price tag, and in the end, activists had a point: the Sydney Games accumulated a $1.7 billion debt, an unwanted legacy for the New South Wales taxpaying public.[144] Lenskyj argues that by relying on the caveat that "'I'm not against the Olympics/I don't hate sport/I like the Olympics, but . . .' many Olympic-related groups diluted their message significantly." On the other hand, they left themselves less susceptible to attacks that claimed they were lacking patriotism or the Australian spirit.[145] As we shall see, appreciating sports but questioning the Olympics is a bind many activists find themselves in, and how they reconcile this quandary often informs their dissident practice in terms of both on-the-ground tactics and rhetorical strategy.

The IOC's Relationship to Politics and Dissent

Throughout the IOC's history, politics have been verboten. The aforementioned "Advertising, Demonstrations, Propaganda" rules have a long and vertiginous, if somewhat consistent history. Tracing this history helps us better understand how the IOC's position on politics and activism has evolved and how it has come to dovetail with commercial concerns.

An important predecessor to the rule was the IOC's demand in the 1933 Olympic Charter that National Olympic Committees (NOCs) avoid the temptation of favoritism and completely sidestep all politics. In order "to fulfill their duty," NOCs "must avoid any political or other influence and when called upon to take a decision be actuated only by general interest without taking into consideration local questions or the desire to favour national competitors."[146] In other words, politics had the power to induce bias that could take the form of favoritism, and more particularly nationalism. The following decade, the 1946 Olympic Rules contained a resolution on the "[e]xamination of the question of the nationalisation of sports for political aims." After praising governments for developing physical-education and sports programs in support of the Olympic movement, it stated, "Nevertheless it regards as a danger to the Olympic ideal that by the side of the legitimate development of sports in conformity with the principles of amateurism there can be propagated certain tendencies which envisage above all a national exultation of success achieved rather than the realization of the common and harmonious objective which is the essential Olympic law."[147] Nationalistic politics were perforating the IOC's desire for universalism and fair competition, and the organization wasn't going to sit around passively while it happened.

The 1950 Olympic Charter continued to press for this apolitical mandate, sharpening up the verbiage in an effort to quell political impulse and linking this to the greater good of Olympism: "National Olympic Committees must be independent and autonomous. They must avoid any political, commercial or religious interference, and, consider when decisions have to be taken only the general interest of the Olympic movement and without being swayed by local questions or by the desire to favour their athletes."[148] This sentiment was reinforced in the 1952 IOC "Rules for Regional Games," where, again, politics were explicitly mentioned: "There must be no extraneous events connected with the Games, particularly those of a political nature." IOC honchos weren't taking any chances, micromanaging minutiae, down to the way the public-announcement system would be employed: "The loud speaker must be used for sport purposes."[149]

In 1955 the IOC introduced language similar to what eventually ended up as the "Advertising, Demonstrations, Propaganda" provision. In a section called "Information for Cities which desire to stage the Olympic Games," the IOC announced: "Invitations must state that no political demonstrations will be held in the stadium or other sport grounds, or in the Olympic Village, during the Games, and that it is not the intention to use the Games for any other purpose than for the advancement of the Olympic Movement." This repeated language above from the 1952 "Rules for Regional Games" and expanded it a bit: "The loud speaker must be used for sport purposes only and no political speeches are to be permitted. In fact there must be no commercial or political intervention whatsoever."[150] The IOC's preoccupation with politics was taking a turn toward political activism.

The IOC continued to ramp up its prohibitive precision, as it ever more tightly circumscribed activities that could be construed as political. For instance, the 1974 Olympic Charter, stated: "No political meetings or demonstrations will be held in the stadium or other sports grounds, nor in the Olympic Villages, during the Games, nor in the preceding or the following week. The candidate city will officially confirm that it is not its intention to use the Games for any purpose other than the interest of the Olympic movement."[151] Later in that same charter, in a section called "Questionnaire for Candidate Cities Staging the Games," the IOC posed this subtext-laden question: "Can you guarantee that no political meeting or demonstration will take place in the stadium, or any other sports ground or in the Olympic Village during the Games?"[152]

In 1975, the prohibitions in "Advertising, Demonstrations, Propaganda" took fully recognizable shape. Originally appearing in Rule 55 under a section called "Advertising and Propaganda," the following strikingly detailed section appeared, the bones of which eventually became enshrined in Rule 50 in the 2013 version of the Olympic Charter:

> Every kind of demonstration or propaganda, whether political, religious or racial, in the Olympic areas is forbidden. Commercial installations and advertising signs shall not be permitted inside the stadium or other sports arenas. No commercial advertising is permitted on equipment used in the Games nor on the uniforms or numbers worn by contestants or officials, in fact nothing may be worn on the uniforms of contestants or officials except

the flag or emblem of the National Olympic Committee, which must meet with the approval of the International Olympic Committee. The display of any clothing or equipment such as shoes, skis, handbags, hats, etc. marked conspicuously for advertising purposes in any Olympic venue (training grounds, Olympic Village, or fields of competition), by participants either competitors, coaches, trainers or anyone else associated with an Olympic team in official capacity, will normally result in immediate disqualification or withdrawal of credentials.[153]

This tacit acknowledgement of the official, sanctioned commercialization of the Games and its importance is a clear marker of the post-Brundage era. Brundage vociferously abhorred the encroaching commercialization and professionalization of the Olympic Games. But while the IOC eventually eased its position on commercialization—making its revamped stance a vital aspect of the Olympics juggernaut—its antipolitics stance did not budge.

In the 1978 Olympic Charter, this rule was moved to Rule 57, again titled "Advertising and Propaganda." Once more, the specificity gets ramped up, as if written by lawyers keen on preventing copyright infringement. Again, we see evidence of the IOC's conflation of advertising and political speech. The slightly revamped rule added the phrase "No publicity whatsoever shall be allowed in the sky above the stadia and other Olympic areas, since this is part of the Olympic sites." It also noted in precise terms, "The trade marks even on timing equipment and scoreboards may on no account be larger than 1/10th of the height of the equipment itself, and shall never be greater than 10 cm. high. All contracts that contain any element whatsoever of advertising or are related to publicity must, before they are entered into, be submitted to the IOC for its necessary consent."[154]

This formation of the advertising and propaganda prohibition stabilized until the June 1991 Charter, where it became Rule 61 and was condensed to read: "1—No kind of demonstration or political, religious or racial propaganda is permitted in the Olympic areas. No form of publicity shall be allowed in and above the stadia and other competition areas which are considered as part of the Olympic sites. Commercial installations and advertising signs shall not be allowed in the stadia, nor in the other sports grounds. 2—The IOC Executive Board alone has the competence to determine the principles and conditions under which any form of publicity may be authorized."[155] In the June 2004 Olympic Charter the provision changed to more completely resemble its current form. Rule 53, titled "Advertising, Demonstrations, Propaganda," stated:

1 The IOC Executive Board determines the principles and conditions under which any form of advertising or other publicity may be authorised.

2 No form of advertising or other publicity shall be allowed in and above the stadia, venues and other competition areas which are considered as part of the Olympic sites. Commercial installations and advertising signs shall not be allowed in the stadia, venues or other sports grounds.

3 No kind of demonstration or political, religious or racial propaganda is permitted in any Olympic sites, venues or other areas.[156]

This remains the same in the current Olympic Charter (2013) where it is Rule 50.[157]

When new members are sworn into the IOC's inner circle, they are required to take the following oath during the induction ceremony, which they recite in front of the full assembly: "Recognizing the responsibilities that go with the great honour of serving as (one of) the representative(s) of the International Olympic Committee in my country, (name of his country), I bind myself to promote the Olympic Movement to the best of my ability and to guard and preserve its fundamental principles as conceived by the Baron Pierre de Coubertin, keeping myself as a member free from all political, sectarian or commercial influence."[158] This oath is striking for its requirement to sidestep politics and for its plea to avoid the corrupting sway of commercialism.

Yet in his autobiography, Lord Killanin, an Irishman who served as president of the IOC from 1972 to 1980, complicated the well-cultivated myth of Olympic apoliticism. He wrote, "Ninety-five percent of my problems as president of the IOC involved national and international politics." He went on to offer nuanced commentary on the politicization of the Games, "Clearly politics are 'in' sports and have always been. Everything in our lives is governed by political decisions. We have varying degrees of freedom, but that freedom is obtained by political decision. Yet what we need in sport is the interest and support of politicians, not their interference."[159] It was as if Killanin were channeling a slightly watered-down version of George Orwell who once wrote, "All issues are political issues, and politics itself is a mass of lies, evasions, folly, [and] hatred."[160] This book shares the sentiment that politics infuse our everyday microinteractions and decisions as well as the bigger-picture macrotrends that bracket our social horizons. By excavating the politics sunk beneath the smooth surface of sports history, we can more effectively leverage a textured, nuanced understanding of the Olympic Games and the social relations that both animate and emerge from them. The modern Olympics afford us an opportunity to rethink the relation between sports and politics, and between security and freedom. All this on the terrain of power under the shimmering din of the spectacle.

2

Space Matters

————————————————————●

The Vancouver 2010
Winter Olympics

Walking along West Hastings Street in the Downtown Eastside of Vancouver, British Columbia, one crisp January morning in 2010, I came across a perplexing set of white panels on the outer flank of the refurbished Woodward's building. The panels featured a verbal explosion of repudiation: simple black-lettered phrases like "Hell no," "I said no," "No bloody way," and "No way José." Four placards simply read "No." It was only later I learned this was a site-specific installation by Vancouver artist Ken Lum for Simon Fraser University's Audain Gallery that was challenging a "2010 Winter Games By-law" passed by the City of Vancouver in the run-up to the Olympics. This "Sign By-Law" outlawed placards, posters, and banners that were not "celebratory," though people were allowed to display "a sign that celebrates the 2010 Winter Games, and creates or enhances a festive environment and atmosphere." The ordinance criminalized anti-Olympics signs and gave Canadian authorities the right to remove them, even if it meant entering private property to seize them. The city seemed to be telling its citizens that the Canadian Charter of Rights and Freedoms was being granted a temporary vacation while the Olympic juggernaut rolled into town. Audain Gallery curator Sabine Bitter noted, "This project understood art itself as a public discourse at a time when public space was being dramatically altered and contested from different directions. One of the questions was what role art can play within this context in which public space does not simply exist, but is struggled over and actively produced."[1] Vancouverites fully understood the intensely politicized context that spurred Lum's visible dissent. The Canadian state's questionable lawmaking and Lum's creative response highlight the ever-present dialectic of restriction and resistance, sharpening our focus on the emergent socio-spatialities of dissent and its suppression.

The following month I returned to Vancouver to see how anti-Olympic organizing was taking shape. Strolling near the Olympic Village in the days before the Games began, I encountered a contradiction-laden mélange of genial sports enthusiasm and the militarized feel of a surveillance state. The place was teeming with sprightly tourists, athletes, Olympics officials, and journalists—cameras and press badges swinging from their necks—who waded through a sea of teal, one of the perky, focus-group-tested official colors of the 2010 Winter Games. At the same time, I felt like I was entering some sort of immaculate repression zone—what Vancouver-based activist Harsha Walia described as "the overall militarization of Van-couver, an encroaching police and surveillance state."[2] Officers from the newly formed Vancouver Integrated Security Unit (VISU)—headed by the Royal Canadian Mounted Police and composed of more than twenty policing agencies—clumped together on every street corner and patrolled the bustling footpaths around the False Creek inlet. Surveillance cameras loomed above, pegged to poles in regular intervals around the perimeter of the area. Helicopters whirred overhead. CF-18 Hornet fighter jets occasionally zinged by. Ersatz Christo and Jeanne-Claude–style banners in the ubiquitous Olympic teal enveloped chain link fences that channeled people into permissible zones while concealing significant chunks of so-called public space.

Numerous social commentators have examined resistance to the workings and meetings of supranational groups like the World Trade Organization, the International Monetary Fund, the World Bank, and the Group of 8,[3] but the Olympic Games are another international mega-event that has generated steadily increasing dissent. As noted in the previous chapter, the International Olympic Committee's official charter forbids the expression of anti-Olympics activism, stating, "No kind of demonstration or political, religious or racial propaganda is permitted in any Olympic sites, venues or other areas."[4] Nevertheless, when the Olympics touch down in a host city, dissent soon follows, and political activists in Vancouver springboarded off the event in an attempt to rescale politics to their advantage.

Anti-Olympics activists in Vancouver appraised the political topography of resistance in their city, reassessing the socially produced spaces of dissent and the ways these spaces are shot through with conflict. They sliced against the zeitgeist of deterritorialization whereby a fuzzily defined "multitude" harnesses its "deterritorializing desire" as it struggles against empire's domination. Instead, dissidents snubbed the notion that "the strategy of local resistance misidentifies and thus masks the enemy" and concertedly re-territorialized the struggle, foregrounding the production of space.[5] In short, activists in Vancouver got their space on. At the same time, anti-Olympics resistance in Vancouver jump-started intense, fruitful discussions around two questions that have fractured social movements since what feels like time immemorial: What strategies and tactics to adopt when challenging the inequities of power? What does "diversity of tactics" mean and should it be the preferred path forward? All too often these questions have been posed in dichotomous, either-or terms ensconced in the tired reform-versus-revolution narrative. Activists in Vancouver aimed to paint a more complex picture. Before and during the 2010 Winter Olympics, activists did a whole lot that was innovative and effective, and scholars and activists alike would do well to pause and reconsider their accomplishments, strategies, tactics, and shortcomings.

Who Are the "Grumble-Bunnies"?

> that insurrection of a personal nature
> that illumination
> which produces an idea-force inside us
> in opposition to the chatter of opinion
> —Reg Johanson[6]

To some sports fans in Canada, protesting the Olympics is not only unseemly, but borderline sacrilegious, too. Yet activists insisted that the Games' three-legged stool of ethics, politics, and economics has become increasingly wobbly in the modern era. Activists in Vancouver were early adopters of anti-Olympics dissent. Campaigners emerged in 2002—even before the city was granted the bid by the International Olympic Committee the following year—and built momentum right through the Olympics. And while the *Vancouver Sun* pegged protesters as a collection of "whiner and grumble-bunnies" who couldn't "hold their tongues even on a special occasion" so Canadians could "relax and cheer on the home team,"[7] anti-Olympics activists put forth spirited, wide-ranging criticism: The Olympics were taking place on unceded Aboriginal (Coast Salish) land; taxpayer money was being squandered on a two-and-a-half week sports party rather than indispensable social services for those who truly needed them; and civil liberties were being threatened by a massively militarized police force.

This confluence of concerns roused a groundswell of dissent. Groups like the No Games 2010 Coalition pinpointed the potential perils of the Olympics and began a long-term public education project to demystify the ostensibly win-win nature of the Games. Watchdog groups like the Impact on Community Coalition adopted a neutral stance at first, hosting numerous panels and seminars, though the group shed its nonaligned status after a change in leadership and once the contradictions of hosting the Olympics simply became too saw-toothed to downplay. Extant groups like No One Is Illegal and the Anti-Poverty Committee lent a radical analysis of the Olympic juggernaut, with religious, environmental, and Aboriginal groups also getting involved. Other prime movers included Streams of Justice, the Power of Women Group, No 2010 Olympics on Stolen Native Land, Native Youth Movement, and Van.Act! (an outgrowth of the University of British Columbia's Students for a Democratic Society). Many people in these groups also worked with the Olympic Resistance Network, formed in spring 2008, a highly effective, decentralized, nonhierarchical, anti-authoritarian alliance rooted in consensus-style democracy and mutual aid. The resistance benefited from the fact that local universities opted to cancel classes for the duration of the Games, which meant a fresh infusion of young people with more free time for activism.

In Vancouver we very clearly saw a *moment* of movements, not a movement of movements. Anti-Olympics activism aimed at the 2010 Winter Games was a highly contingent process, built astride an intricate mosaic of affinities and goals. This was not a traditional social movement replete with *sustained* challenges to authority *through time,* but rather a short-term "event coalition" galvanized by the Games.[8] Many activists in Vancouver were aware of the distinction between "movement" and "event coalition," concertedly calling their actions a "convergence of movements" around "the Olympic moment" rather than a "social movement," a term they viewed as tending to flatten out multiplicity and heterogeneity while over-stating temporal continuity. The anti-Olympics convergence in Vancouver coheres with W. Lance Bennett's definition of an organizational hybrid he dubs "embedded networks" whereby direct-action activists nestle within "established NGO-centered networks in sprawling, loosely intercon-nected network webs populated by organizations and individuals who are more resistant to conventional social movement practices."[9]

In February 2003, Vancouver voters were presented with a plebiscite to gauge public support for hosting the Games. The pro-Olympics "Yes" side won out with 64 percent of the vote, though only 40 percent of eli-gible voters opted to weigh in and boosters spent $700,000 to persuade the public, 140 times more than the "No" side.[10] This relatively weak yet media-trumpeted endorsement of the Games did not stunt dissent. An uncommon blend of activists joined forces—from indigenous dissidents to antipoverty boosters to environmentalists to anarchists to civil libertar-ians and numerous combinations thereof—resulting in remarkable, cross-cutting solidarity in opposition to the Games. As David Eby, the executive director of the British Columbia Civil Liberties Association (BCCLA), told me on the eve of the Games, "There is a real unanimity of purpose around NGOs in Vancouver as a result of the Olympics," with the activist atmosphere "cooperative and reinforcing."[11] Resistance went well beyond the NGO circuit, taking the form of a unique, effective two-track fight-back, with one wing working inside the institutional corridors of power and another applying pressure from the outside through direct action.

Dissident citizens carried out an array of direct-action protests leading up to and during the Olympics. In what became known as the Eagleridge Bluffs Blockade, environmental and First Nations activists teamed up to oppose the expansion of the Sea-to-Sky Highway connecting Vancouver to Whistler. In late May 2006 First Nations elder and activist Harriet Nah-anee was arrested along with environmentalist Betty Krawczyk. Despite their age they were both unceremoniously tossed in jail. In February 2007, while Krawczyk and Nahanee languished behind bars, the Vancouver Organizing Committee (VANOC) held an "Olympic Countdown Cer-emony" to drum up excitement. Activists attended the event, and two of them—Anti-Poverty Committee activist David Cunningham and indigenous dissident Gord Hill—spontaneously hopped onto the stage, seized the microphone, and disrupted the event with the chants "Homes not Games" and "Fuck 2010." Tragically, Nahanee contracted pneumonia in jail, which ultimately led to her death in 2007. Her memory lived on, however, as activists consistently invoked her name, drawing motivation from her lifetime of dissent. Her passing was both a powerful reminder of the stakes involved and a key part of the symbolic architecture that animated the resistance. The following month, activists caused a stir when they made off with the gargantuan Olympic flag that had been hoisted at city hall. Shortly thereafter, a photograph of three masked activists posing in front of the flag and carrying a photograph of Nahanee was released by a group calling itself the Native Warrior Society. Hill later commented that the pair of direct actions "set the tone for the resistance with a very strong anti-colonial, anti-capitalist analysis."[12] Such media-savvy maneuvers helped place the issue in front of the general public.

The Olympics and Indigenous Peoples

First Nations peoples had good reason to be skeptical they'd be treated respectfully and honorably. After all, as Native scholar Christine O'Bonsawin notes, "Indigenous Peoples have forever served the spectacle and performance needs of Olympic organizers."[13] To fully understand what O'Bonsawin means, we need to take a brief foray into Olympic history.

The Olympics have come a long way. The 1900 Olympics in Paris and the 1904 Games in St. Louis were appended to the massive international exhibitions—or World Fairs—of the time. These Games were sideshows to the World Fairs rather than the main attraction on the world stage they have come to be today. Yet, to understand indigenous resistance during subsequent Olympiads, it's imperative to consider the 1904 Games, which were marked by the inclusion of the Anthropology Days, a series of athletic events that transmogrified the Games into a testing ground for the racial theories of the day.

Part research and part athletic competition, the basic idea of Anthropology Days was to pit ethnic groups and races against each other in Western sports like track and field to see which race was the most athletic. Organizers also wanted to compare indigenous peoples to top athletes from the United States and Europe. While not strictly an Olympic event, Anthropology Days did occur as part of the Louisiana Purchase Exposition (LPE), as did many other athletic competitions, including the Games. Anthropology Days organizers—who called the event the "Special Olympics"—wished to both capitalize on interest in the Olympics while attracting spectators to the Olympic Games that followed two weeks later.

The Anthropology Days should be understood in the context of the burgeoning field of anthropology. At the time, academic disciplines—like political science and anthropology—were aiming to put the "science" in "social science" with as much technical gravitas as possible. In anthropology, anthropometry was the science du jour in the early 1900s: making biometric measurements in order to identify racial trends in body shape and size that ostensibly correlated with labels like "natural athlete" and "born criminal." Anthropologists assumed race existed as a category that was commensurate with various physical, psychological, and cultural traits. Such ostensibly objective measures were freighted with politics.

William J. McGee and James E. Sullivan were largely responsible for Anthropology Days. McGee was an anthropologist and an anthropometry true believer. Sullivan was the head of the Department of Physical Culture for the exposition and was also a former athlete and a prolific writer. McGee was biased toward his anthropological theories, which argued Native men and Caucasians were subject to scientific laws governing their physical prowess. McGee wanted the "savage Olympics," as he was apt to call them, to demonstrate the use value of anthropology as a discipline while simultaneously drumming up exchange value for his stash of anthropological artifacts, which he intended to vend to raise funds for future research. He also hoped to garner support for his evolutionary theory that environmental factors affected physical skills, which in turn would provide political grist for the assimilation of Native Americans and others. Meanwhile, Sullivan was biased toward US athletes and their training methods, which he championed as the best in the world, and sought a testing ground to prove their preeminence. Although for different reasons, both men were in search of ways to improve athletic performance. And both came supplied with precooked conclusions in search of data that would support their theories.[14]

Sullivan initially proposed the "Special Olympics" to prove that that nonwhite athletes were inferior. His efforts were foiled in part by Native Americans like the Osage and Ojibwe who refused to go along with the anthropometric measuring scheme. Others, like the Cocopas, rebuffed attempts to snap their photograph. Many refused to participate because no monetary rewards were being offered to the winners, whereas other competitions at the exhibition came with cash prizes. Others declined to play along because, lacking any experience in the sports they were being asked to demonstrate, they did not understand the rules. This led organizers to shepherd the potential participants to a few Olympic trials to see if they would pick up some pointers. But no one actually elucidated the rules and regulations for the athletic competitions, and no one was allowed to even practice. Some Native Americans—like the Arapahos—vamoosed rather than succumbing to the emerging farce. Surely even more would have vacated had they known they were taking part in a large-scale racial experiment.[15] Others—including seven Kwakwaka'waka and Nuu-chah-nulth people—used the event as a pedestal for dissent. At one LPE event, in an effort to challenge the so-called civilizing policies of Canadian assimilation, a handful of indigenous people from Vancouver Island choreographed an over-the-top, sleight-of-hand performance that led audience-goers to believe they had witnessed an act of cannibalism. Thus, they "engaged in an ingenious process of political resistance," notes O'Bonsawin, "thereby negotiating and challenging the oppressive conditions of colonial Canada" on the global stage.[16]

McGee and Sullivan pressed ahead. After their colleague Martin Delaney explained the rules to Native participants—in English and without interpreters—heats for running events were organized, one for each ostensible race. As Sullivan reported, there were heats for "Africans, Moros (Philippines), Patagonians, and the Ainu (Japanese), Cocopa (Mexican), and Sioux Indian tribes."[17] The idea was to ascertain the fastest person from each group and then have them compete in a final race. Those times would be compared with those of top-flight athletes from the United States and northern Europe. However, the heats did not go according to plan due to different cultural mores vis-à-vis individualism, collectivism, and competition. Rather than running through the finish-line ribbon, runners would wait for other runners or duck under it instead. As Nancy Parezo notes, "Cooperation was more important than 'victory' . . . waiting for friends was a sign of graciousness and a symbol of respect in many cultures."[18] Stephen C. Simms, who had been brought in from the Field Columbian Museum of Natural History in Chicago to manage the competition, was aghast, demonstrating it was possible to not get sucked into the vortex of racism masquerading as science.[19]

While McGee initially downplayed the results of Anthropology Days, Sullivan formed wide-reaching generalizations about the "utter lack of athletic ability on the part of the savages" that supported his political pet project: assimilation.[20] Comparing the Anthropology Days athletes with elite competitors from the United States helped him prove his pre-ordained point. He wrote that multiple-gold-medal-winning Olympian "Ray Ewry jumped further in the standing jump than any of them could go in a running broad jump. The broad jump, like other sports the savages took part in, proves conclusively that the savage is not the natural athlete we have been led to believe."[21] He chalked up the inability of sport new-comers to equal the best efforts of highly trained Olympians as evidence of Native deficiencies. On this, McGee seemed to agree, writing in his final Anthropology Days report that "the lesson" of their "Special Olympics" was that "[d]espite fair proficiency in the few lines specialized by each group, primitive men are far inferior to modern Caucasians in both physical and mental development."[22]

IOC president Pierre de Coubertin did not agree with the founders of this "Special Olympics" believing it was a negative mark against his beloved Olympic Games. He called Anthropology Days "a mistake," "inhuman," "embarrassing," and something that made the Olympics "flawed."[23] In 1913, he reflected on the Anthropology Days as "the beginnings of exotic athleticism" that were "hardly flattering."[24]

The Anthropology Days were not the only example of Native appropriation for Olympic purposes in North America. During the closing ceremonies of the 1976 Summer Olympics in Montreal, nine First Nations agreed to participate in a "commemoration ceremony" in which two hundred representatives of these nine Nations were joined by 250 non-indigenous dancers sporting costumes and paint in an effort to pass themselves off as First Nations people. According to the Games' "Official Report," the "sumptuous procession" was "made even more exciting by the play of lights and the theatrical music based on André Mathieu's *Danse sauvage*."[25] Janice Forsyth, director of the International Centre for Olympic Studies, concluded, "In the end, non-Aboriginal performers dressed and painted to look like 'Indians' led the Aboriginal participants through their own commemoration."[26] One can hardly blame indigenous peoples for skepticism they may hold for the spirit of Olympics. These episodes poured a firm foundation for contemporary indigenous resistance to the Games, but many Native people found the Games to be alluring.

Four Host First Nations and Their Discontents

As in 1976, many indigenous groups were willing to play ball with the International Olympic Committee, participating in opening and closing ceremonies. In 2010 Aboriginal people played a more prominent role

IMAGE 4 Anti-Olympics banner designed by Gord Hill, who also goes by the pen name Zig Zag. Courtesy of Gord Hill.

than in any previous Olympics. In advance of the Winter Olympics, four First Nations from British Columbia joined forces to create the Four Host First Nations. In November 2004 leaders from the Lil'wat, Musqueam, Squamish, and Tsleil-Waututh agreed to work together to host and assist with the Games. For the first time ever, the IOC recognized Aboriginal people as official host partners. The three official mascots were also First Nations–inspired: Miga, a mythical sea bear; Quatchi, a sasquatch; and Sumi, an animal spirit. *Indian Country Today,* a weekly national newspaper that focuses on indigenous issues across the Americas, retrospectively assessed the event favorably as "a showcase for Native culture," where "the vibrant and integral involvement of Native people in the Games" was evident.[27]

But not everyone held such a sanguine view. While it was true that Aboriginal peoples were not being outrageously typecast and imitated—as with Montreal in 1976—and that First Nations peoples were getting a seat at the table for 2010 Olympic programming, anti-Olympics activists were quick to point out that even though the Olympic Charter endorses "promoting a peaceful society concerned with the preservation of human dignity" the IOC chose to hold the games on unceded Coast Salish territory.[28] Thus, the specter of dispossession haunted the Olympics and "No Olympics on Stolen Native Land" became one of the predominant anti-Olympic slogans. While the Four Host First Nations took center stage at the Olympics— and benefited economically from their willingness to partake—80 of the 203 indigenous bands in British Columbia refused to participate, which is remarkable in light of ubiquitous pro-Olympic propaganda and the possibility of economic gain.[29]

In British Columbia, First Nations have a unique relationship with the Canadian state. In other areas in Canada the British Crown signed treaties with Aboriginal groups in alignment with the Royal Proclamation of 1763, which declared that only the Crown could obtain indigenous lands. In 1867, when British colonies became confederated as Canadian provinces, Aboriginal-settler treaties had already been established. However, in British Columbia, which joined the Confederation in 1871, only fifteen treaties had been agreed to (the Vancouver Island Treaties, also known as the Douglas Treaties), while Aboriginal title to the remainder of the region was left unresolved. With the exception of Treaty 8, negotiated in 1899, and the Nisga'a Treaty, which was completed in 2000, treaty making was stultified, though a 1973 Supreme Court decision—*Calder v. British*

Columbia—jumpstarted the possibility of negotiations, with the court ruling that Aboriginal title had actually not been extinguished in British Columbia.[30] According to indigenous intellectual Taiaiake Alfred, lacking treaty relations, British Columbia "remains in a perpetual colonialism-resistance dynamic."[31] Fast-forwarding to 2010, this dynamic was evident in full force in anti-Olympics activism, with perpetual acknowledgement that athletes were skiing the slopes and hitting the halfpipes on Aboriginal land.[32] As scholar and Olympics critic O'Bonsawin noted, "The inclusion of colonial narratives has tacitly been enshrined in the Olympic formula. . . . Such storylines position the subjugation and containment of indigenous peoples within national histories, thereby removing them in time and space from present-day realities."[33]

It's the Economy, Mayor

In some ways, Vancouver has become the poster city for neoliberal-era gentrification, with the gap between rich and poor widening into an abyss. The perils of neoliberal "success" are captured in a tandem of facts in tension: Vancouver is reputedly the most livable yet the least affordable global city. On the eve of the Olympic Games, the Economist Intelligence Unit named Vancouver the most livable city in the world.[34] In 2010 the Frontier Centre for Public Policy issued the sixth annual Demographia International Housing Affordability Survey, which found Vancouver to be the least affordable of the nearly three hundred cities it considered: the median house price in Vancouver was a whopping $540,900 while the median household income was $58,200.[35] Nowhere is the difference between nouveau riche and old-school poor more glaring than in Vancouver's Downtown Eastside (DTES) neighborhood, an eight-by-fifteen-block strip of gritty urban intensity that—outside Aboriginal reserves—is Canada's poorest postal code. Yet the sharp juxtaposition between extreme "livability" and dire poverty does not undermine Vancouver's exchange value on the silver-frosted terrain of global capitalism. Andy Merrifield's description of the modern-day cosmopolitan city fits Vancouver like a spandex speedskating suit: "cities *themselves* have become exchange values, lucre *in situ,* jostling with other exchange values (cities) nearby, competing with their neighbors to hustle some action."[36] Per the machinations of capitalism, hosting mega-events like the Olympics tends to enhance urban exchange value as it kickstarts gentrification, even if the project loses money for the host governments.

Days before the Games began, activist Am Johal told me, "The Olympics are a corporate franchise that you buy with public money."[37] Only one modern-era Olympics has ever achieved economic success: the 1984 Summer Olympics in Los Angeles, which ended with a surplus of more than $220 million.[38] This singular—and singularly privatized—monetary success helped proliferate the conception that the Olympics were a money-making enterprise and that dumping public money into the Games was a sound investment. Vancouver—and British Columbia more generally— was persuaded by this possibility, and followed the predominant logic of the pre-economic meltdown, fashioning public-private partnerships as a funding structure. However, with Olympic funding, the established trend is that the public pays and private entities profit, thereby socializing the costs of economic development while privatizing the benefits.[39] Vancouver mayor Gregor Robertson—a New Democratic Party–style liberal— was no exception; when it came to the Olympics, the cofounder of the Happy Planet organic juice company was guzzling the public-private partnership Kool-Aid.

Boosters routinely overestimate the economic benefits of hosting the Olympics while understating the costs.[40] Whether British Columbians liked it or not, the IOC introduced them to Games-induced capitalism, and from early on the Olympics were a full-on budget buster. The five-ring price tag was originally estimated to be $1 billion. The month before the Games, costs had ballooned to $6 billion, and post-Olympics estimates soared into the $8 to 10 billion range, with the City of Vancouver alone kicking in nearly $1,000 for every single person in town.[41] And these numbers don't reflect the fact that the city used its precious loan guarantees to rescue dithering developers who went belly up while the athletes' Olympic Village was only half built. To be sure, the economic collapse of 2008 couldn't have come at a worse time for Olympic organizers, but they had already made a habit of incessantly lowballing costs.

After the Olympics, Canadian officials announced severe budget cuts that many activists connected to the Games. Funding for the arts was slashed drastically, leading to the BC Arts Council chairwoman's abrupt resignation in August 2010. The Vancouver School Board announced an $18 million funding shortfall for the 2010–2011 school year, which translated to reduced music programs and hundreds of Vancouver teachers receiving pink slips. To add propaganda to injury, the province made receiving money from its 2010 Sports and Arts Legacy Fund contingent on participating in "Spirit Festivals" designed to fabricate a positive Olympic legacy.[42] To be sure, Vancouverites got the Canada Line, a much-needed train connecting downtown Vancouver to Richmond and the airport, but it also acquired significant debt. And those who have tried to follow the Olympic money have been stymied. The complex patchwork of public-private partnerships demands a fastidious audit, but neither the auditor general of British Columbia nor the Canadian auditor general was granted access to VANOC's books. Summing it up, Micheal Vonn, the policy director at the BCCLA remarked, "the Olympics were an anti-transparency device."[43]

Policing Dissent

The military-grade fortressification of host cites during sports mega-events has become par for the neoliberal course, and the Winter Olympics in Vancouver was no exception. The security budget was originally estimated at $175 million, but eventually skyrocketed to more than $1 billion, a process Gord Hill characterized as "police extortion from the ruling class."[44] Canadian authorities used the Olympics as an opportunity to jack up the Kevlar-per-capita quotient, and in the process accelerated the militarization of everyday life. Even Olympics supporters were alarmed by the ever-ascending price tag for policing, with a *Globe and Mail* op-ed asserting, "You don't have to be a disciple of dissent to be dismayed at the amount of money being spent on security for the Vancouver Olympics."[45] Canadian officials used that money to establish a surveillance-drenched urban terrain, employing seventeen thousand security agents, including people from the RCMP, the Canadian Security Intelligence Service, city police forces, and private security officers. The Canadian Border Services Agency inserted their officers—essentially the immigration police—into the DTES, demanding residents provide proof of citizenship. Police with semiautomatic weapons attended demonstrations, thus normalizing authoritarianism while proliferating fear.

This heavy police presence produced not only jittery citizens, but floated an array of repressive measures. Ahead of the opening ceremonies the Office of the Privacy Commissioner of Canada reported the installation

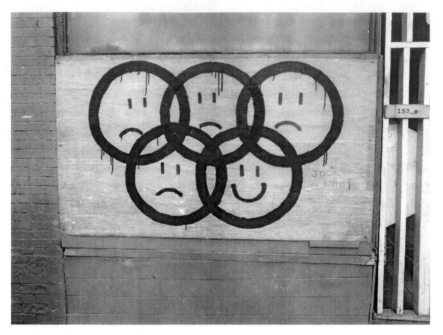

IMAGE 5 Jesse Corcoran's controversial mural at the Crying Room Gallery in Vancouver
Courtesy of Jules Boykoff.

of nearly one thousand surveillance cameras in greater Vancouver.[46] VISU
promised to take down the cameras after the Olympics, and many cameras
were disconnected but "take down" does not mean "go away," and trying to track the cameras' whereabouts has been virtually impossible. The
BCCLA submitted freedom-of-information requests to the Vancouver
Police Department regarding the cameras, but the police were evasive as
to whether they intend to exercise their option to purchase them. Activists argued that by standardizing tactics of obfuscation—or as Vonn put
it, "wielding the mighty sword of vagueness"—the Canadian state turned
the democratic ideal of transparency into overdetermined political theater.
"It's the kind of shell game we've come to expect around CCTV," she said.[47]
More importantly, the high-tech policing equipment for today's state of
exception becomes the quotidian instruments of tomorrow's new normal:
military-style weaponry that can be employed in day-to-day policing.

But surveillance went beyond the ever-winking cameras that dot-
ted the urban microgeographies of social control. Ahead of the Games
the Canadian Security Intelligence Service (CSIS) and other VISU officials refused to rule out the possibility that their infiltrating agents would

break the law or try to assume leadership positions within anti-Olympics groups. Victoria police chief Jamie Graham even bragged to the audience at the Vancouver International Security Conference that a police infiltrator had wormed his way into the movement, becoming a bus driver who carted around activists attending a protest of the Olympic torch relay.[48] Outspoken Olympics critic Christopher Shaw, the author of *Five Ring Circus: Myths and Realities of the Olympic Games,* experienced intense harassment from VISU. Beginning in June 2009, he started getting VISU visits at home, at work, and on the street. Sometimes officials would be holding a copy of his book, saying they found "disturbing information" they wanted to discuss and that VISU investigator Jeff Francis "says hi." By the time

IMAGE 6 Anti-Olympics artwork and photo by Gord Hill (Zig Zag). Courtesy of Gord Hill.

2010 rolled around these visits were almost daily occurrences, with VISU also questioning his friends, girlfriend, and ex-wife. VISU paid yet another visit to Shaw just before the G8/G20 summit in Toronto, attempting to flip him into becoming an informant, an offer he flatly declined.[49] Activists reported to me that nearly everyone involved in the Olympic Resistance Network was visited by VISU for questioning.

All this was supplemented by a slew of extraordinary rules and laws, including the aforementioned Sign By-Law prohibiting signage that didn't celebrate the Olympics. A legal challenge from the BCCLA and plaintiffs Chris Shaw and Alissa Westergard-Thorpe, helped defang the bylaw. However, in line with the IOC's "Clean Venue Guidelines," the revamped bylaw still forbade signs that undermined the logos of Olympic corporate sponsors.[50] The spirit of political censorship was evident in December 2009, when City of Vancouver staff insisted Jesse Corcoran remove his anti-Olympics mural from the front of the Crying Room Gallery at 157 E. Cordova Street in Vancouver. The mural depicted the Olympics rings as four frowning faces and one smiling face. After an outcry from artists, activists, and civil-liberties groups, the city backpedaled, arguing that the mural was actually removed because of an antigraffiti bylaw, before ultimately relenting and allowing the piece to be reinstalled.

Meanwhile, at the provincial level, British Columbia passed the Assistance to Shelter Act, which activists argued criminalized homelessness while sacrificing human rights on the altar of property rights. The law allowed police to forcibly place the homeless into shelters; the timing of the law made it clear it was designed for social cleansing in the name of Olympics spectacle production. Michael Barnholden, author of *Reading the Riot Act: A Brief History of Rioting in Vancouver,* put it this way: "During the Olympics it was like you could have all the human rights you could afford."[51] All together these repressive measures produced a scenario whereby the state created, nurtured, and amplified the conditions for its own continued growth.

Yet the incident at the art gallery also exemplifies the successful push-back on the part of civil libertarians and activists in advance of the Games, demonstrating the importance of organizing early and often around questionable measures. The BCCLA was an important part of this process of push-back, but so were direct-actionistas. As Eby noted, the goal was "to be out front of the rights violations, to identify as many of the potential violations in advance as you can and to put pressure on government officials to commit to not using those tactics and, even if they refuse to, to raise public awareness of it so the public can recognize the problems when they see them."[52] In the lead-up to the Games, VISU purchased a medium-range acoustic device (MRAD)—the notorious military-grade weapon used in Pittsburgh during the G-20 protests in 2009—though because of negative press and intense pressure from activists, the MRAD was kept in the box during the Games. Canadian officials promised "safe assembly areas"— tantamount to the "protest pens" at US political-party conventions and the Beijing Olympics—but were forced to abandon this measure after wide-spread public outcry. Nevertheless, the Canadian state's efforts to acquire high-tech weaponry exemplified what Neil Smith and Deborah Cowen have called "the intensified *weaponization* of social control."[53]

Space Matters

With the recent "spatial turn" in critical geography, a baseline assumption is that space is not an empty apolitical parcel of turf waiting to be trod-den upon by people and ideas. Nor is it a passive receptacle, wooden-stiff in its physicality. Rather, space is dynamic, ever-unfolding, and socially produced through material and discursive practices playing out on the uneven geography of power relations. This production of space highlights multiplicity, heterogeneity, and conflict—three concepts that are key to understanding anti-Olympics resistance as adjunct to the Global Justice Movement. Space conceived in this way points toward what Edward Soja calls a "socio-spatial dialectic" whereby the social and the spatial are indis-solubly linked, mutually constituting each other.[54] As such, space pro-duces and reinforces social relations but also sometimes challenges them. This chimes with Henri Lefebvre's critical insight: "Socio-political contra-dictions are realized spatially. The contradictions of space thus make the contradictions of social relations operative. In other words, spatial contra-dictions 'express' conflicts between socio-political interests and forces; it is only *in* space that such conflicts come effectively into play, and in so doing they become contradictions of space."[55]

"Contradictions of space" were brought into sharp focus at the outset of the Olympics by the fact that there was a lack of access to the Olym-pic cauldron, which Games organizers placed within the perimeter of a tall fence. This intense sensitivity to security raised the highly symbolic spatialized contradiction whereby Olympics-goers were unable to secure satisfying snapshots of the cauldron, a contradiction that was widely reported in the mainstream press.[56] In this context, the Canadian state and dissident citizens engaged in spatial struggle, with the state attempting to construct, constrict, and regulate public space, while activists engaged in spatially conscious politics, flexing their right to protest and a wider right to the city as they engaged in the process of "seeking spatial justice." Activists foregrounded the fact that space is an active aspect of social-movement organizing and demonstrated that the production of space is vital to counterhegemonic practices. Mustafa Dikeç points us to a valuable socio-spatial heuristic for thinking about anti-Olympics resistance: the dialectical relationship between the "the *spatiality of injustice*—from physical or locational aspects to more abstract spaces of social and economic relationships that sustain the production of injustice—and the *injustice of spatiality*—the elimination of the possibilities for the formation of political responses."[57] Activists in Vancouver dealt directly with spatial injustice as they captured corporeal space and produced it in line with the values that motivated them.

Anti-Olympics activists made the Downtown Eastside neighborhood of Vancouver an anchor of resistance. As activist and local professor Reg Johanson put it, "The Downtown Eastside crystallizes issues around space in Vancouver."[58] Dissident citizens joined forces in solidarity with the annual Women's Memorial March, bolstering its ranks for one of its biggest-ever turnouts. Downtown Eastside residents were the targets of extraordinary laws such as the aforementioned Assistance to Shelter Act, a provincial law passed in 2009 that allowed police to force the homeless into shelters. Before that, Vancouver mayor Sam Sullivan pushed Project Civil City, a measure designed to curtail panhandling, homelessness, drug use, and public-nuisance complaints in the lead-up to the Games. This allowed Vancouver police to engage in what activists viewed as a selectively enforced ticketing blitz for minor infractions, effectively criminalizing homelessness. Demonstrators took to public space in the Downtown Eastside to challenge the Assistance to Shelter Act, reframing it as the "Olympic Kidnapping Act," taking the battle straight to the spaces where the law would be enforced. Activists linked this laterally to a persistent critique of the "increasing organization of sport as spectacle, sport as industry."[59] Cecily Nicholson, activist and coordinator of the Downtown Eastside Women's Center, said, "Our physical presence of a diverse collection of people in a public space, does create a kind of solidarity with those who are always there [on the streets] long before the Olympics and will be there long after. . . . A greater interconnectedness has been established."[60] Numerous activists emphasized the strategic and ethical importance of centering resistance in the Downtown Eastside where spatial injustice is unmistakably etched into the socio-political landscape.

For the anti-Olympics resistance, participatory democracy was a contact sport. Against the frictionless notion of "the deterritorializing power of the multitude" constructing "a powerful non-place" concretely realized on the global terrain, activists in Vancouver resolutely reterritorialized their struggle, rejecting the repudiation of "the *localization of struggles.*"[61] They forged a place-based spatial analysis, and according to activist Aaron Vidaver, within that analysis "the seizure of space was crucial, central."[62] Nathan Crompton of Van.Act!—a group of younger activists that emerged in the lead-up to the Games and that has remained active in its wake—added, "when you take a space and make it concrete, people can get empowered."[63] An important instructive example of the significance of spatial strategies within repertoires of resistance emerged on 15 February 2010, a few days after the Games' opening ceremonies. Following a rally at Pigeon Park, challenging the twin processes of gentrification and homelessness criminalization, campaigners descended on 58 W. Hastings Street where they took control of the space owned by bête-noire developer Concord Pacific and leased to VANOC for use as a parking lot during the Olympics. The site was strategic: the lot was a highly visible location where spatial injustice is indelibly inscribed in the social landscape. Concord Pacific had a permit in hand to develop a nest of high-priced condominiums on the plot, but it was also capacious enough to fit the more than one hundred tents that were eventually pitched there.

In what became known as the Olympic Tent Village, activists didn't just seize space, they produced it. Upon entering the tent village, one saw a sacred fire tended to by indigenous elders. Another community fire burned in the back of the lot, with music, workshops, and skill-share sessions filling the area. Food Not Bombs provided victuals. Activists from Streams of Justice (a Christian social-justice group) and Van.Act! helped with logistics. A security crew prevented unwanted outsiders—like the camera-wielding media—from entering camp and helped assuage tensions that arose inside the village, at one point ejecting two suspected police infiltrators from the encampment. Leadership emerged organically from the vital organizing efforts of the Power of Women Group, a collection of DTES residents—many of them Aboriginal elders—with deep roots in the neighborhood and widespread respect within activist circles. Individuals from this group, along with Dave Diewert of Streams of Justice and Harsha Walia of No One Is Illegal, served as media spokespeople. Every day or so community meetings helped set and enforce camp protocols and create work schedules.[64] Tom Mertes dubs such necessary activity the "nano-level processes of forging solidarity," which he describes as unpredictable, open-ended, and desirably untidy, "the life-blood of any movement."[65] Such open-endedness and spontaneity can blast open the barn doors of creativity, too. Activists used the direct action to reframe gentrification as new-wave recolonization. Walia, who was at the center of organizing the tent city, noted the action demonstrated "there's an increasing willingness to engage in more creative tactics . . . that break the ritual of protest."[66]

Creating safe spaces for dissent is important in that they provide non-competitive contact points where a diversity of individuals and organizations can work together. The Olympic Tent Village led to unique social interactions, where university students could intermingle with street people, the professoriat with the subproletariat, rich exchanges that would not have happened with more traditional forms of protest.[67] The action helped crystallize relationships between groups that hadn't worked together before, bridging what Lefebvre dubbed the "double morphology" of the city—"practico-sensible or material on the one hand, social on the other."[68] Vidaver, who worked the graveyard security shift, touched on this "double morphology," noting the importance of "these autonomous or semi-autonomous reclamations and then the kind of interactions that one has with people within those spaces once they're set up and can be defended and made safe."[69] All these horizontal, space-producing processes sliced backward against what Dikeç describes as "the spatialization of the Other" by which he means "depriving the inhabitants of certain areas of their rights to the city in the political sense of the term."[70] Those who moved into and volunteered at the Olympic Tent Village lived politics through the quotidian interactions of self-management and in the age of breakneck globalization found ways to slow down and relate to others. Originally, the plan was to run the tent village for five days, but because of the energy and political considerations, the space seizure was extended beyond the end of the Olympics. Numerous activists I spoke with stressed that the Olympic Tent Village was not merely a symbolic act, but a material victory, too. Because of the action, approximately eighty-five people secured housing through the City of Vancouver and the state agency B.C. Housing.[71]

In tune with to the activists' two-track strategy, the Olympic Tent Village wasn't the only shelter-related protest in town; the Pivot Legal Society spearheaded a Red Tent Campaign whereby bright red tents were plunked down around town to raise awareness of homelessness and to press for a national housing policy. For one hundred dollars, one could sponsor a tent emblazoned with the slogan "Housing Is a Right," which would be given to a homeless person for temporary shelter. Influenced by the French antipoverty organization Children of Don Quixote, which used a similar strategy in late 2006 to raise consciousness about homelessness in Paris, Red Tent campaigners in Vancouver erected tents in high-traffic areas outside Olympic venues where they also leafleted to sportsgoers and wrapped the Canadian Pavilion in red tarps, in the process going for a Guinness Book World Record for longest banner wrap. Though the group embraced a legalist approach—aiming to publically pressure the federal government to create a national housing strategy—it also donated red tents to the Olympic Tent Village, the illegal seizure of space where confronting the state was a goal, not conversing with it.[72]

Both the Olympic Tent Village and the Red Tent Campaign forged what Lefebvre called "counter-space," or "counter-plans and counter-projects designed to thwart strategies, plans, and programmes imposed from above." Relevant to the anti-Olympics activism in Vancouver, Lefebvre wrote, "The quest for 'counter-space' overwhelms the supposedly ironclad distinction between 'reform' and 'revolution.'"[73] Another vital "counter-space" that circumvented overdetermined dichotomous thinking was forged at the VIVO Media Arts Centre, an artist-run space whose "Safe Assembly Project" featured programming like "Afternoon School" workshops, screenings, and art productions; a pirate radio poetry project; and "Evening News" events organized by Am Johal, Cecily Nicholson, and Nicholas Perrin that occurred every other night for the duration of the Games. The Evening News forum brought together video activists and their raw protest footage, practicing artists who wished to respond the Olympics industry and its effects, and panels of activists and academics organized around particular themes. According to Nicholson, whose day job was coordinator of the Downtown Eastside Women's Center, the two aims of the Evening News events were to construct semiautonomous cultural space conducive to dialogue and to create an archive of community response and critique, goals that "coalesced in the construction of the space."[74] The Evening News forums constructed space in an inclusive way that fostered participation and lateral learning, performing the intermediary function of political-cultural brokerage: connecting previously isolated actors and social sites and putting them in conversation through the explosion of socio-spatial barriers that preclude such relations.

The events at VIVO demanded that art play a pivotal role in reformatting anti-Olympics resistance, rather than be relegated to acting as colorful window dressing. Organizers effectively brought together Vancouver art and activist communities in a neutral space devoid of political-historical baggage. VIVO scheduled formally innovative poets and artists who leveled more questions than answers, more open-endedness than tidy poetic closure. Rather than anteing up a didactic brand of art, organizers facilitated antiauthoritarian political work that demanded a thoughtful active audience and trusted such an audience was possible. This tactical decision on the part of organizers aimed to achieve a dialogical depth not possible with more traditional protest forms, thereby widening the discussion—by harnessing the poetic power of lateral association—and expanding the audience to those who identified more as culture workers than straight-up political activists. The poetry scheduled into the Evening News events was supplemented with a pirate radio program called *Short Range Poetic Device* hosted by poet-activists and local professors Stephen Collis and Roger Farr. The program sat at the nexus of poetry, politics, and anti-Olympics resistance, featuring readings and discussions with local poet-activists such as Donato Mancini, Rita Wong, Jeff Derksen, Kim Duff, and Naava Smolash. These shows played periodically throughout the Olympics and were cached online.[75] Although the pirate radio station was shut down in the early days of the Olympics by Industry Canada—the governmental body that oversees radio spectrum and telecommunications standards across the country—whose intervening officials were sporting Olympic apparel, the poet-activists pressed ahead, streaming their show online. This not only allowed locals to continue to tune in, but it also fomented what Jennifer Earl and Katrina Kimport call "copresence"—a sense of "collectiveness" that even without "physical togetherness" can produce the emotional buy-in that bolsters collective action.[76]

The Evening News events jumpstarted fine-grained analysis in real time that crowbarred open the all-too-often black-boxified dialectic of resistance and restriction. Without succumbing to process fetishism, Perrin remarked: "The dialogue we created didn't come to a resolution based on Habermasian rationality . . . but even when there were deep divides, people stayed in the room and continued the conversation."[77] An instructive example of this occurred on 17 February when the BCCLA's David Eby, who was slated to participate on a civil-liberties panel, was pied by a disgruntled activist who felt Eby had spoken negatively about the actions of window-smashing protesters, thereby violating the spirit of solidarity that undergirds the diversity-of-tactics approach. Numerous activists reported to me how the aggressive action against Eby was an intense, bracing event.

To fully comprehend the pie incident and the conversation it created, one first needs to understand the Heart Attack March, which occurred on 13 February, and how it fit into discussions around diversity of tactics. The diversity-of-tactics approach allows protesters with diverging styles and preferred methods to make a pact to support each other—or at least not publically denigrate each other—during an episode of contention. Particular tactics are not ruled out from the get-go, and criticism is to remain internal to the movement rather than blathered onto the media terrain. The approach can form a solidaristic bridge between ardent supporters of Gandhi-style nonviolence and those who may accept property destruction as a legitimate tactic—and this is where cracks in the approach usually emerge. Sometimes activists agree to allow for certain tactics to occur on particular days or in specific geographical zones in order to lessen the possibilities of intragroup friction. Diversity of tactics makes room for spontaneity, uncertainty, and illegibility; the approach relates to what social-movement scholars have identified as "the radical flank effect" whereby movements can benefit from having a radical wing that makes progressive goals, tactics, and strategies seem relatively moderate—and thus more palatable to the power structure.[78] Given that tactical and strategic differences can be a real solidarity squelcher, anti-Olympics activists tried to ride a fine diversity-of-tactics line that, while theoretically crystalline, is inevitably messy—not unlike democracy itself—once activist boots hit the pavement. In advance of the Games, the Olympic Resistance Network put forth a statement of unity featuring the diversity-of-tactics approach that was signed by numerous anti-Olympics entities.

The Heart Attack March—to "clog the arteries of capitalism"—was Vancouver's Seattle moment: activists smashed corporate windows, setting off intense discussions around tactics and strategies both inside and outside the Global Justice Movement. In Vancouver, militants broke off from a planned march and used newspaper boxes and metal chairs to break plate-glass windows at corporations like the Hudson's Bay Company. Critics maintained such tactics would only alienate the general public and invite the wrath of the cops, while supporters argued that the company's historical ties to British colonialism justified property damage; after all, the Hudson's Bay Company was an integral actor in the Canadian state's effort to extinguish Aboriginal title in British Columbia during the nineteenth century.[79] Eby was quoted in the media as saying he was "sickened" by the action, dubbing it "thuggery."[80] This diversity-of-tactics no-no led to him being aggressively pied at VIVO and condemned by militants as a traitor. It also sparked a lively debate at VIVO where the conversational temperature was high, but calming yet forceful interventions by Nicholson kept the event moving forward constructively. Months after the pie incident Eby dryly noted, "It began a conversation with groups that are concerned about how we make a better world. It began a conversation about tactics . . . and about the black-bloc tactic in particular and whether or not it's actually helping move towards, from a civil-liberties perspective, a more democratic, equal, and participatory kind of culture in Canada, or otherwise." Demonstrating reflexivity, he said he learned a lesson: not to act as a legal observer and be perceived as movement lawyer during the same episode of contention.[81]

The Evening News helped surface—in a productive way—the ever-present tension between direct-action activists who want immediate change and extant, formalized NGOs that trend toward incremental change. Activists in Vancouver made it clear this tension is not reducible to dichotomous camps, with "the traditional parties and centralized campaigns" on one side and "the new movements organized in horizontal networks" on the other.[82] VIVO's Evening News events created safe space, which in turn wedged open tactical space where decisive questions could be raised, questions with significance that extended forward to London 2012 and beyond: Does a diversity-of-tactics approach socialize an alibi for property destruction? Does it dull the knife-edge of direct action's effectiveness? Does it alienate bystander publics? Does it pave a path for symbolic solidarity? Does it allow the media to slide into the well-worn grooves of dissident denunciation? Has it ossified into hollow catchphrase that distracts activists? Does a focus on diversity of tactics mean we're not talking about strategies anymore? Do debates over tactics need to happen *during* the episode of contention or should they happen afterwards? Do hypermasculinist shout-downs—replete with belligerent pie smashing—create a fracture point that the state can take advantage of by having macho, braggadocio-bandying infiltrators enter movements as agent provocateurs since what some in Vancouver were calling "the angry manarchist white boys" are relatively easy to emulate? The answers to these questions are to be found on the ground in particular contexts, not in the universalized ether of one-size-fits-all finality.

Solidarity and Scale

If Vancouver was a "relational incubator" for dissent and social movements as geographer Walter Nicholls has suggested the city can be,[83] then the Olympic Tent Village and VIVO were praxis inducers within the "relational incubator." This praxis has fed a spate of protest events that have emerged from the solidarity achieved during the Olympics moment. Numerous activists I spoke with rattled off lists of subsequent activist interventions emanating from the anti-Olympics struggle, and almost all of them mentioned the False Promises on False Creek event on 15 May 2010. This protest capitalized on widespread disgruntlement with the government's reneging on promises—ostensibly because of fiscal exigency—to convert a sizable swathe of the Olympic Village along the False Creek inlet into social housing. The athletes' Olympic Village was supposed to be the crown jewel of the social-sustainability promise, but the city government has prioritized market rental units while ignoring social-housing units.[84] Critics like the BCCLA's Eby told me, "Frankly it's a total fuck-up."[85] The building of the Olympic Village—thanks only to a last-minute infusion of taxpayer funds—transmuted the Vancouver waterfront into an intensely politicized space. As Vancouver-based social critic Jeff Derksen noted,

> The Olympic Village in Vancouver, hunched on the post-industrial waterfront, is an aluminum-clad symbol of neoliberal governmentality and of a specific production of spatial injustice . . . this new building also marks the long reter-ritorialization of the waterfront as an elite space, burying its working-class history deeper into the mud to have the waterfront transformation emerge as a real-estate gamble that hopes to shape the city's future yet again. The class-anxiety around the complex, particularly who deserves to live in the subsidized housing, also marks the shift in the constitution of the public.

> And the nervousness around the "non-owners" who could live in the building (subsidized or renting at market) catches the antagonism that the sociospatial program of neoliberalism has built.[86]

While city planners channeled their inner Milton Friedman, activists ramped up their dissent, descending on the condo site during the grand opening and disrupting sales for the day. Dissident citizens from groups like Van.Act!, who had been radicalized by the anti-Olympics round of contention, were joined by activists from Streams of Justice, the Power of Women Group, the Citywide Housing Coalition, and the Impact on Community Coalition. Again, we don't see the emergence of a single movement but, as Dave Diewert put it, we see "a sense of solidarity or camaraderie so when a group calls for an action, then others come along and participate." Emerging from actions like the Olympic Tent Village, he pointed to a "deepened the sense of trust" among activists and marginalized populations in Vancouver, which "has led to a strengthening of communities of resistance" and "a deeper appreciation of the collective wisdom of people." Media activist Franklin López said, "The city hasn't felt this good in many, many years, activism-wise."[87] Whether this momentum carries and builds into the future remains to be seen, but the Olympics undoubtedly gave long-time Vancouver activists a positive boost while refreshing the ranks with energetic, mostly younger protesters who were given a once-in-a-lifetime opportunity to soar over the hurdles that might have otherwise been present during "normal" political times.

As with the concept of space, scale should not be viewed monochromatically as fixed, if nested, levels of analysis (for example, local, national, global). Scale is not an inexorable, hierarchical stairway to spatial heaven, but a temporary, ever-emergent outgrowth of human agents struggling within and stretching social structures and assumptions. As such, scale both demarcates the boundaries where socio-political contestation occurs as it plays an important role in how these contests play out. In the run-up to the Olympics, activists engaged in what Neil Smith dubbed "scale bending," the production of geographical scale in ways that the "entrenched assumptions about what kinds of social activities fit properly at which scales are being systematically challenged and upset."[88] The 2010 Winter Olympics was an international mega-event that doubled as a fulcrum for scale bending, a ready-made platform for restructuring scale through social struggle. Harsha Walia articulated this fact: "The Olympics provided a foundation for a much longer-term analysis and debate and vision of our terrain of struggle. It was pivotal for bringing the local terrain of struggle to a national and international scale."[89] Her remarks highlight the possibility of dissident struggle at multiple scales simultaneously.

An example of this is the multiscalar work Am Johal and his group Impact on Community Coalition did with representatives of the United Nations. In late 2009, Johal teamed up with Miloon Kothari, the former UN special *rapporteur* on the Right to Adequate Housing to raise global awareness of the social stakes. Kothari visited Vancouver in the lead-up to the Olympics to take stock of the effects the Games were having on low-income housing. The UN official was alarmed by the rampant loss of low-income housing units and did the favor of stating the obvious that "the real estate speculation generated by the Olympics" was likely "a contributing cause." After taking the baton from Kothari, UN special rapporteur Raquel Rolnik issued another report critical of Olympic spending and the lack of an adequate housing strategy, critiquing Olympics-induced real estate speculation and the use of private security guards to remove homeless people from commercial hotspots.[90]

The spread of contention beyond the local occurred through the work of globe-trotting, political-cultural entrepreneurs who bridged grievances and identities, which helped bend the scale of dissent. Such transnational scaffolding between people opposing the Olympics on their home turf has become an enduring facet of Olympics resistance. Activists from Salt Lake City, which hosted the 2002 Winter Olympics, traveled north to Vancouver to give talks and tips in the run-up to the Games. Anti-Olympics activists from London and Sochi—hosts of the Olympics in 2012 and 2014 respectively—were in Vancouver to register their dissent and to coordinate efforts with local demonstrators. Transnational activists help us think through the politics of scale.

Discursive Space

One way activists can bend scale to their advantage is, as geographer Paul Routledge puts it, by "going globile." He notes, "Through their use of media vectors social movements can escape the social confines of territorial space," combating the mass media's tendency to deprecate activists.[91] In Vancouver, the prospect of using mainstream media to carve out strategic freedom was not especially promising. Both Canwest—which owns the *Vancouver Sun* and the *Vancouver Province* newspapers—and the *Globe and Mail* were official sponsors, or "print media suppliers," of the Games.[92] On top of this, the International Media Centre for the Olympics engaged in scale squelching when it refused to distribute the BCCLA's press releases during the Games.[93] The group applied to have its work sent out through the center months in advance but were informed they would not be allowed to participate a mere three days before the Games began, thus precluding the possibility of appeal.[94]

As we will see in more detail in chapter 4, the US mainstream media's coverage was relatively parochial, with major newspapers virtually ignoring anti-Olympics dissent. The coverage that did emerge was superficial and monolithic, embracing a sports-only frame of the Games that reflected the all-too-common Olympics-related apoliticism that is in fact deeply political. When the US media did cover politics, they parachuted journalists into Vancouver to peddle what some activists described to me as "poverty porn": capturing images of the intense poverty in the Downtown Eastside without sufficiently exploring its socio-political roots. If demonstrators were mentioned, they were often disparaged as "small" groups bent on disrupting the lives of everyday Vancouverites and sports lovers or as "emotional" troublemakers who seemed hardwired to whine about police. Canadian press coverage was more complex, breaking down into three sequential phases: pre-Games articles that made space for dissent; articles appearing once the Olympics commenced where media tended to deprecate activists' efforts and; articles appearing near the conclusion of the Olympics that extolled the police and hailed the mega-event as a "unifying force" for Canada.

Since the days of Samaranch, TV broadcasting revenues have provided the ocean of money that floats the IOC's fiscal boat. An exemplary case of the low-budget alternative media strategies that emerged from the anti-Olympics moment was the Vancouver Media Co-op (VMC). Led by Franklin López and Dawn Paley, and composed of numerous citizen journalists, the VMC, which was born from the Olympic Resistance Network's Media and Communications Committee, had the radical-media machine firing on all cylinders, providing the public with up-to-date information, politically driven art, and all the news that's unfit to print in the corporate media. The VMC consistently mobilized alternative versions of the Olympics and shifted the scale of anti-Olympics dissent by producing two segments for *Democracy Now!*, the leading community media outfit in the United States. López, who once worked for *Democracy Now!* as a television producer, helped put anti-Olympics resistance on the program's radar. After *Democracy Now!* host Amy Goodman and two of her colleagues were detained and questioned at the US-Canada border in November 2009 on their way to Vancouver where Goodman was scheduled to speak at the public library, the show's producers were definitely aware something unique was going on. Suspicious that she intended to speak out against the Olympics, border guards rifled through her personal effects and questioned her about the topics she intended to cover in her talk and whether one of them was the Winter Olympics.

The VMC's roots go back a half-decade to a publication called the *Dominion*. Once the magazine incorporated as a federal cooperative, Paley set up a co-op local in Halifax in January 2009 and then in Vancouver the following summer. The VMC is reader owned, advancing a revenue model based on sustainers who chip in between five and twenty dollars per month. The co-op put out a broadsheet called *Balaclava* during the Games, which has continued through today. The VMC infrastructure, which activists across the anti-Olympics spectrum pointed to as a chief legacy of the Winter Olympics, forms an online node for system-change sociability where independent journalists can post their blow-by-blow documentary work and critical analysis for a wider audience. According to Gord Hill, "the VMC reenergized and raised the standard of the radical alternative media structures that we have in this country."[95] It fulfilled many of the preconditions of collective action that social-movement scholars have enumerated in that it facilitated the organization of protests, productively and efficiently shared information, bolstered solidarity, fortified collective identity, and allowed dissidents to test-drive arguments that challenged the pro-Olympic zeitgeist.[96]

While the received wisdom on social media like Twitter and Facebook is that they allow for everyday people to create content and document experience in lateral fashion, VMC journalists were skeptical of its potential, dubbing it the "social media mafia." As López remarked, it "pushes the model of corporate social media as an alternative media, which it really isn't. A lot of it is ad-driven and event-driven." VMC journalists were aware of what Mark Andrejevic calls the "digital enclosure," whereby we create an interactive, online field in which all of our actions—and transactions—generate a slew of information about ourselves. The tradeoff for activist interventions in the digital realm is a quiet, yet vital shift in social relations: submission to surveillance, or "the monitoring embrace of an interactive (virtual) space."[97] In other words, dealing with the social media mafia meant risking the increased possibility of the suppression of political dissent. Vancouver activists were also tuned in to Andrejevic's additional meaning for digital enclosure, and one that echoes Marx's concern with the privatization of communal space for the dual purpose of capital accumulation and the refashioning of labor relations; using the online realm for activism was simultaneously an enticement into a monitored space with rippling significance not only for the relations of consumption and production, but also for the social relations of anti-Olympics activism. Nevertheless, even López and his VMC colleagues used social media like YouTube during the Olympics, though he found that a number of his videos were swiftly removed: "During the Olympics it was almost as if they had it automated to take down anything the IOC didn't like."[98] The VMC had neither the resources nor the time to fight these questionable take-down notices.

VMC journalists' critique of social media chimes with Jodi Dean's conception of "communicative capitalism," which reframes the proliferation of social media as ersatz political participation: "Communicative capitalism captures our political interventions, formatting them as contributions to its circuits of affect and entertainment—*we feel political, involved, like contributors who really matter.*" She adds, "the intense circulation of content in communicative capitalism occludes the antagonism necessary for politics, multiplying antagonism into myriad minor issues and events."[99] Although many anti-Olympics activists employed social media to get the word out about events (for example, using Facebook's events function), it was striking how many activists told me they were offline and in the streets for most of the Olympics. They argued that keyboard activism may supplement boots-to-pavement protest, but it cannot—and should not—supplant it.

Some contend the Global Justice Movement may well be the first that doesn't need the mainstream media as a communication conduit.[100] We're certainly at a unique moment in history when the mainstream media are becoming increasingly immaterial, yet they still matter in terms of reaching a general audience. Dawn Paley, who dubbed the mainstream media "SQUM," or "status-quo media," rightly pointed out that even if we don't admire the mass media, they're not obsolete information dinosaurs: "Mainstream media are very relevant because they set the agenda."[101] Social media may help generate numbers at protest events and get information out to external audiences, as evidenced by the recent Arab Spring. And independent media activists who are taking and tweaking the journalistic norms of the mainstream media—for instance sourcing and subverting the mainstream media with content should be supported at every turn. But when it comes to proliferating messages and images to bystander publics, the mainstream media still matter. Activists in Vancouver knew this, placing op-eds in newspapers like the *Vancouver Sun* and appearing as sources in numerous outlets, offering quotes that helped educate the public about why they were protesting. This opens up a key question for activists: how can they infiltrate and build relationships with mainstream media while continuing to grow alternative and radical media? As with many dichotomies that were exploded in Vancouver, the mainstream media vs. alternative media quandary was not an either-or but a both-both.

The Right to the City?

Baron Pierre de Coubertin, the founder of the modern Olympics, once said, "The important thing in life is not the victory but the contest; the essential thing is not to have won but to have fought well." Anti-Olympics activists "fought well" in Vancouver and many of them carried this momentum east in June 2010 to the G8/G-20 meetings in Huntsville and Toronto where they faced a very different scenario.[102] After debuting in Vancouver for the Olympics, the Integrated Security Unit reemerged in Toronto as the new normal for policing international mega-events in Canada. Its own website divulged, "The approach to the Summit would be best described as an expanded version of our approach to previous events based on best practices and the lessons learned."[103] With a $1 billion security budget, one of the "lessons learned" seemed to be to use state funds to build their arsenal whenever the opportunity presents itself.

Unlike the Olympics convergence where the Vancouver Police Department—which had years of experience policing protests—took the lead, often looking the other way at key junctures, the Ontario Provincial Police came out with batons flying, arresting more than ten times as many protesters as were cuffed and stuffed in Vancouver. The authorities in Toronto deployed preemptive arrests, snatch squads, and kettling tactics and created dire detention conditions. Harsha Walia, who traveled to Toronto, noted a key contextual difference between policing strategies in

Vancouver and Toronto: "The Olympics is a brand protecting the tourist industry where the police are actively trying to avoid a police confrontation" whereas Toronto could go into temporary lock-down mode—dispensing with legal niceties like the presumption of innocence—to protect the G-20 plenipotentiaries flooding their city for the weekend.[104] Also, Toronto learned only months before the summit that they'd be hosting, as Huntsville was deemed inadequate for the G-20 event, so both activists and the state had a tighter timeline in which to prepare.

One palpable legacy of the Vancouver Olympics is a revivification of the coercive capacity of the Canadian state. But from the activist perspective, a more hopeful legacy is an emergent Right to the City Coalition that slices against what David Harvey calls "the spreading malaise of a neoliberal ethic."[105] This coalition goes beyond the legalistic framework of rights- and freedoms-based discourse to grapple with ways we can collectively reshape the urbanscape by vamping the processes of urbanization in a more participatory, equitable direction. The movement draws energy from both the theoretical writings of Henri Lefebvre—who saw the right to the city as "a transformed and renewed right to urban life"—and the Right to the City Movement in the United States.[106] Soja points to the strategic savvy of building such a movement: "Grounding the global justice movement in the right to the city creates more tangible and achievable targets than simply organizing against neoliberal capitalism, globalization, or global warming, especially as all three are primarily generated from and made concrete in the major city regions of the contemporary world."[107] The Olympics rejuvenated activist circles, imbuing them with renewed excitement and energy. As Franklin López put it in the wake of the Games, "It's a really special time to be in Vancouver."[108] Reg Johanson chimed in, "If the goal of the anti-Olympics convergence was to get people more involved in their activism, then that happened," with poet-activist Mercedes Eng adding, "It was really, really, really fun, too."[109] In 2012 the fun shifted to London where campaigners aimed to challenge the hegemony of the IOC and its corporate allies.

3

London Calling

————————————————●

Activism and the 2012
Summer Olympics

In late February 2012, the antisecrecy group WikiLeaks began releasing
"The Global Intelligence Files," a trove of more than five million internal
e-mails from Stratfor Global Intelligence, a private intelligence firm head-
quartered in Texas.[1] Stratfor gathers and analyzes information under con-
tract with private corporations like Goldman Sachs and Lockheed Martin,
as well as numerous government agencies, such as the Department of
Homeland Security. The documents contained some politically explosive
information, including speculation that WikiLeaks founder Julian Assange
would soon be indicted by the US Justice Department. The e-mails also
revealed that Stratfor client and "Worldwide Olympic Partner" Coca-Cola
was concerned that the animal-rights group People for the Ethical Treatment of Animals (PETA) might interfere with the smooth runnings of
the 2010 Winter Games in Vancouver. In a June 2009 e-mail, one Stratfor employee anted up "a long list of questions regarding PETA/Animal
Activism and the upcoming Olympics in Vancouver." Among Coke's que-
ries were "How many PETA supporters are there in Canada?"; "How many

of these are inclined toward activism?"; and "To what extent could non-PETA hangers-on (such as anarchists or ALF [Animal Liberation Front] supporters) get involved in any protest activity?"[2]

As the London Games approached, another Stratfor client, Dow Chemical, tasked the firm with tracking activism related to the 1984 Union Carbide gas disaster in Bhopal, India. Dow acquired Union Carbide in 1999 and insisted it was not responsible for the debacle that had killed thousands and sickened many more. As another Worldwide Olympics Partner, Dow provided $100 million (£63 million) to the IOC. In addition, it supplied an $11 million (£7 million) decorative wrap for the Olympic Stadium. Stratfor kept a Bhopal activism file for Dow, which included entries on activist Colin Toogood of the Bhopal Medical Appeal (BMA). Stratfor noted that Toogood had used Facebook and Twitter to disseminate information critical of Dow in the context of the upcoming Olympics.[3] Julian Cheyne of the online anti-Olympics group Games Monitor was also ensnared in Stratfor's surveillance net after receiving a tweet from the BMA.[4] Neither activist appeared overly concerned. Toogood nonchalantly noted, "None of it was that much of a surprise. We had suspected such surveillance for years." He went on to say, "It showed that clearly they were worried. They saw the Bhopal campaign as a threat. If they didn't have a case to answer, they wouldn't bother surveilling us."[5] Cheyne echoed this sentiment. Pointing to Dow's corporate strategy of oppositional research, he told me, "I take it as a considerable compliment because if they think it's worth investigating somebody, if they're spending money on something, then that is the indication of value for them."[6] He even remarked, "I think we should be quite pleased to be mentioned."[7]

Cheyne also found Statfor's fine-grained surveillance to be "in a sense rather extraordinary" in that it pointed toward a remarkable asymmetry in resources.[8] WikiLeaks helped highlight the asset chasm that allowed Dow and its Olympic-sponsor associates to remain one step ahead in the ongoing discursive battle between corporations and campaigners. In London, the clash with the Olympic juggernaut seemed Sisyphean in scope, and as many activists admitted, all too often the opposition was a step ahead. As Meredith Alexander of the Greenwash Gold campaign put it, "The Olympics is a big money and power machine. There is definitely a massive David and Goliath scenario here."[9] In London, the underdogs did not achieve the political traction they envisioned. However, a year before the Games began, it appeared there might not be any significant fight-back. Only nine months before the Olympics commenced, Cheyne said, "There isn't really a concerted campaign like there was in Vancouver," adding, "This is not a coalition of powerful groups. This is just a coalition of people who are easily marginalized and written off as insignificant and out there to make a nuisance of themselves."[10]

Fomenting activism was complicated by the fact that the London Games was a tri-partisan affair, with the Labour Party, Liberal Democrats, and the Tories all championing the Olympics and proliferating its ambitious promises. Elite unity was firm, leaving little opportunity for protesters to gain high-profile allies. Yet campaigners were also cognizant of the fact that the Games' celebratory environment carved out a unique opportunity to gain the attention of bystander publics, to score recruits, and to secure mainstream media attention. To be sure, security forces were heavily armed and committed to nipping deviations from the Olympic script, but they weren't eager to flex their repressive muscles under the hot glare of the global media spotlight. As in Vancouver, Olympics boosters did their best to depict activists as a gaggle of incorrigible whiners. London mayor Boris Johnson opened up his pre-Games column in the *Sun* by going on the offensive, "Oh come off it, everybody—enough whimpering," he wrote. "Cut out the whining. And as for you whingers, put a sock in it, fast. We are about to stage the greatest show on earth in the greatest city on earth."[11]

Not everyone was willing to jam footwear down their gullets. Campaigners cobbled together a redoubtable collection of allies, drawing from grassroots activist circles as well as NGOs and the arts community. These groups were brought together by four central grievances: (1) the high price tag for the largely taxpayer-funded Olympics, (2) the role of corporate sponsorship, (3) the seizure of space for Olympics purposes, and (4) Olympics-induced security measures.

The Counter Olympics Network (CON) served as an organizational clearinghouse bringing together diverse groups. CON held periodic planning meetings in the lead-up to the Olympics. Games Monitor and Our Olympics forged an online presence that helped disseminate information about the history of the Olympic Games as well as upcoming protests and events. Occupy London and Youth Fight for Jobs persistently juxtaposed government-driven austerity with five-ring extravagance. Groups like Save Leyton Marsh challenged Olympic organizers' seizure of public space. Meanwhile, the UK Tar Sands Network, the Reclaim Shakespeare Company (RSC), and Greenwash Gold kept their eye on the corporate prize, zeroing in on Olympics sponsors with questionable green credentials, in particular BP, Dow Chemical, and Rio Tinto. The Defend the Right to Protest campaign focused on civil-liberties issues, as did the Newham Monitoring Project, which started a community legal observer program that trained dozens of local people in effective strategies and protocols for cop watching. Kerry-anne Mendoza of Our Olympics described activism as a "rainbow coalition of discontent" that wasn't based in any particular ideology, but possessed more of a moral and intellectual current that addressed a "democratic deficit." Partway through the Olympics she said, "I very much feel like we're in day one of this thing in historical-time terms. I feel like this is just starting."[12]

At the Counter Olympics Network's open meetings, groups like Space Hijackers, War on Want, and No to Greenwich Olympic Equestrian Events (NOGOE) functioned like affinity groups in a de facto spokescouncil formation, with each organization sending a representative or two in order to coordinate actions. In a sense, CON shepherded extant political concerns that were exacerbated by the Olympics. As with Vancouver, this was more of a *moment* of movements than a *movement* of movements. Activist Isaac Marrero-Guillamón was explicit about this: "I don't think you can say there's a movement against the Olympics in London—there are different groups doing projects and trying to link those projects together. It's a very monadic structure—very loose, very networky."[13]

Whereas protest in Vancouver tended to be more brass-knuckle serious and reliant on traditional mobilizations, activism in London was notable for its propensity to go with the celebratory grain, using humor and wit in an effort to connect with a wider audience. This was influenced in part by heavy-handed police actions in the lead-up to the Olympics. Activists were cognizant of the dialectic of resistance and restriction. Before the Games began, Jess Worth of the UK Tar Sands Network and the Reclaim Shakespeare Company told me, "Given the police crackdown that there already has been and will continue to be in the run-up to the Olympics, I think as activists we're having to be quite creative as to how and where and when we do our interventions. We're looking at other ways to do this, through subvertising, culture jamming, greenwash-exposing—stuff that isn't running into the path of the Olympic torch run because that's going to be incredibly tough."[14] In fact, most of the Olympics-induced activism in London occurred *before* the actual Olympics, while only a few actions were carried out during the duration of the Games, which played out between 27 July and 12 August 2012.

Activists in London purposefully aimed to engage everyday people, even Olympics aficionados. As Emily Coats, also of the UK Tar Sands Network, said, "With the Olympics it is really important to not just focus on those people who are already critical. We need to be reaching the average Londoner who's feeling put out" by everyday inconveniences brought on by the Games.[15] Part of this outreach entailed making the activists' stance vis-à-vis sports crystal clear. Not a single activist among the dozens I interviewed assumed an antisport stance. Agent Monstrio of the Space Hijackers captured the general view among activists, saying, "It's not a protest against sport but what's done in the name of it."[16] CON's David Renton—an avid runner and supporter of Liverpool Football Club—told me that actually his love of sports inspired him to make his Olympics activism "my activist priority." He was careful to point out, "I have absolutely no conflict or tension or complaint about the athletes whatsoever," adding, "One thing we often get wrong on the left is that we're often seen as anti-humor, anti-party, anti-fun."[17]

Spiraling Costs, Overestimated Benefits

When it came to funding the London Olympics, antagonism surfaced at the bid's outset. While boosters unremittingly heralded the ostensible economic benefits the Games would generate, critics pointed to a dearth of historical and empirical evidence, asserting the funding structure would socialize the fiscal risks. As with previous Games, pro-Olympics commentators overestimated the positive economic impacts, while underplaying the costs.[18] London's bid document confidently proclaimed, "Every sector of the economy will benefit from the staging of the Olympic Games."[19] But London's bid estimated outlays at £2.37 billion ($3.8 billion), whereas by 2007 that figure had ballooned to £9.3 billion ($15 billion), two-thirds (£6.2 billion, or $10 billion) of which were derived from central-government grants. As the costs catapulted, so did the public's share; the National Audit Office noted that the taxpayers' portion had almost tripled while the private-sector's contribution had shrunk to less than 2 percent of the Games' overall cost.[20] The National Lottery was called upon to contribute more than £2 billion ($3.2 billion) to the Olympic cause.[21] This diverted monies that would otherwise be distributed to communities across Britain that were getting hammered by the economic downturn. Campaigners argued that numerous worthy causes were penalized by the decision to use lottery funds to prop up the Games. London-based photojournalist and campaigner Mike Wells said, "I like sport, but I find it very difficult to find anything good in the London Olympics. At best it could be seen as a harmless yet expensive distraction—at worst a massive form of theft."[22]

The rosy fiscal predictions embedded in London's candidature file were swiftly thrown into doubt. A mere year and a half after securing the Olympic bid, the House of Commons Committee on Media, Culture, and Sport reported that costs were firing skyward: "Despite previous assurances that budgets were sound, it is now clear that costs are going to be significantly higher than forecast in the bid document."[23] The committee was actually quite matter-of-fact about the inflation of costs: "It is inevitable, as has been the case with previous Games, that the Games will, quite simply, cost the UK significantly more than the outline cost in the original bid."[24] Tasked with Olympics oversight, the committee asserted that the bid's cost figures were "already seriously outdated" and that despite the government's assurances to the contrary, "*it was always likely that these would escalate over time.*"[25] Even supporters were getting nervous about the cost overruns. While questioning Olympic minister Tessa Jowell in front of the House of Commons Committee for Media, Culture, and Sport, MP Alan Keen said, "There are two things I am sure you will agree with: it would be difficult to find a more laid-back Member of Parliament than I am, nor one who is more enthusiastic about sport, but I have to say I am beginning to get extremely anxious about this."[26] Nevertheless, the committee optimistically hedged, "There will be an economic benefit to be gained from hosting the Games, but it may not be quite as large as people expect."[27] But this all depended on how "economic benefit" was measured—a contentious metric in Olympic studies.[28]

In 2008 Ken Livingstone, then London's mayor, openly confessed he had deliberately duped government officials into supporting the London Olympics as a ruse for developing East London: "I didn't bid for the Olympics because I wanted three weeks of sport. I bid for the Olympics because it's the only way to get the billions of pounds out of the Government to develop the East End." He added, "It's exactly how I played it to ensnare the Government to put money into an area it has neglected for 30 years."[29] The ethics of such hoodwinkery aside, lowballing Olympics cost estimates has become standard Olympic practice, a point activists emphasized repeatedly. Campaigner Julian Cheyne ran an independent cost tally that put the total at £13 billion ($21 billion).[30] A Sky Sports investigation calculated the price tag to be £24 billion ($38 billion).[31]

The discrepancy from the commonly cited £11.4 billion ($18.3 billion)—which added operating costs to the £9.3 billion figure—arose from the inclusion of public transport upgrades. Mayor Livingstone hinted that this would be part of the London legacy, but the costs were left off the official Olympics balance sheet. In this way, activists argued, boosters misleadingly understated Olympic costs while simultaneously trumpeting—and socializing—them. The *Economist* succinctly laid out the tradeoffs involved: "By combining the games with a regeneration project, Britain has added to the costs of both. . . . Without the games, though, the regeneration would take a lot longer. The 2012 Olympics are, in effect, a gamble on reviving the capital's poorest districts. But the stake is mostly the whole country's money, and money is short."[32]

Olympics critics Julian Cheyne and Martin Slavin emphasized that the much-heralded Stratford City project was to be built regardless of whether Britain hosted the Games. There was already a regeneration program in gear, but the Olympics were rolling in to take the credit.[33] Indeed, a careful reading of government documents demonstrates that sizable infrastructure investments were vital to Olympics success, but also that many of the projects that boosters claimed as Olympic-inspired were actually already underway. The Department for Culture, Media, and Sport reported in 2007: "The Candidature File identified $11.5 billion/£7.18 billion of investment in road and railway improvements. *This investment was committed independently of the Games* and includes projects which were to proceed regardless of whether London won the bid."[34] Yet Olympic Delivery Authority (ODA) chief executive David Higgins made a point of highlighting the improvements to transportation infrastructure that the Lower Lea Valley would get, thanks to the Olympics, "bringing economic and social benefits that go far beyond 2012, and far beyond sport."[35] The tendency was to ignore such transport costs when selling the bill to the public while at the same time adding improved infrastructure to the ledger of Olympic benefits at the end of the day. This is a prime example of what Olympic scholars John Horne and Garry Whannel identify as a "hidden subsidy," which creates a scenario whereby "the host city picks up a large tab."[36]

Such nuance was lost often on politicians who had staked a great deal on the success of the Games. When in the weeks prior to the Olympic

IMAGE 7 Medal stand at Youth Fight for Jobs "Austerity Games," 23 July 2012. Courtesy of Jules Boykoff.

opening ceremony Prime Minister David Cameron claimed the Games would generate £13 billion, critics quickly demanded he provide evidence.[37] Instead, he remained vague yet insistent, leading many to believe he had pulled the numbers from thin air. *Guardian* columnist Simon Jenkins wrote, "Such bogus claims are normally associated with communist apparatchiks." Yet many still viewed the Games as a success—even critics like Jenkins described the Games as "a breath of fresh air in an otherwise bleak summer."[38] The "breath of fresh air" narrative coated over the cost overruns. Two months after the Games concluded, British media reported that the London Olympics had arrived some £377 million ($603 million) under budget. To the chagrin of fiscally minded activists, lost in the storyline was the fact the Games actually cost more than four times what the original bid estimated.[39]

Media also proliferated the plotline that the Olympics were pivotal in the British economy's slight third-quarter uptick in GDP. Yet the Office for National Statistics asserted that, aside from a small boost provided by ticket sales (many of which had actually transpired prior to the third quarter), the economic growth from the "Olympics effect" was essentially unquantifiable.[40] By early 2013, economic analysts were talking about the "strong possibility" that Britain would be hit with "a triple-dip recession" thereby jeopardizing its AAA credit rating.[41]

Activists were well aware of the sharp contrast between a two-and-a-half-week party on one hand, and hard-to-swallow government austerity policies on the other. On 23 July 2012 Youth Fight for Jobs hosted the "Austerity Games 2012" in order to spotlight the juxtaposition. Their goal was to have fun and get a bit of exercise, too. Events included a "100-meter Race to the Bottom" as well as the "Hardship Hurdles," the "Deficit Discus," and—a crowd favorite—the "Toss a Tory Shot Put." While athletes participated in these events, organizers interspersed snappy, tongue-in-cheek commentary to help keep the focus on the politics, suggesting ideas for the millions on how to fight the millionaires. Meanwhile, a team wearing white T-shirts with big black lettering that read "Trust Me I'm a Banker" figured out ways to break the rules in each event, cagily using their advantage to maintain their big-bucks edge. It was political theater with a dash of sport.[42] Organizer Suzanne Beishon told me, "We're not anti-Olympics, but we wanted to ask what the Olympics should really be about and have some fun at the same time. The Austerity Games was a protest, and it captured a bit of the atmosphere around the Olympics, but it also had a political message to it, and it worked really well." She added, "We want to do similar events that inject politics in a fun, humorous way." Beishon stressed that they would not abandon holding protests and meetings but that this more humor-oriented approach complemented their straight-up political work.[43]

The London Games Brought to You by . . . Controversy

Since the mid-1980s corporate sponsors have attached themselves barnacle-like to the Olympic ship. Behind the rhetoric of internationalism and goodwill, these firms wish to gain access to new market demographics and to associate themselves with the Games' overwhelming popularity. Beneath the warm glow of the Olympic flame, corporations hope to glimmer. This has been a successful business strategy for companies across the world. The process has also wedged open an opportunity for activists to take aim at these corporations on the global stage, jumping scale with their extant campaigns. In London, campaigners gained their strongest foothold with such anticorporate activism.

On the eve of the Olympics, British media revealed that about £1.4 billion ($2.25 billion) of the Olympics' £11.4 billion ($18.3 billion) budget sprang from the coffers of corporate sponsors. Eleven Worldwide Olympic Partners (Acer, Atos, Coca-Cola, Dow, GE, McDonald's, Omega, P & G, Panasonic, Samsung, and Visa) supplied the IOC with approximately £700 million ($1.1 billion), with each firm furnishing about £63 million ($100 million). Meanwhile, lower-tier corporate partners provided £700 million more in cash, goods, and services.[44] London 2012 Olympic Partners—Adidas, BMW, BP, British Airways, BT, EDF, Lloyds TSB—reportedly contributed £40 million ($64 million) apiece. Meanwhile, "London 2012 Olympic Supporters"—Adecco, ArcelorMittal, Cadbury, Cisco, Deloitte, Thomas Cook, and UPS—each kicked in £20 million ($32 million). "London 2012 Olympic Providers and Suppliers" included Eurostar, G4S, GlaxoSmithKline, Heineken UK, Holiday Inn, Rio Tinto, and Ticketmaster, among others. They provided approximately £10 million ($16 million) apiece, much of it in goods and services.[45] Assuming these numbers are accurate—the IOC considers this "confidential commercial information"—corporate sponsors were responsible for roughly 12 percent of the overall cost of the London Games, with taxpayers left to pay a bulk of the remaining 88 percent.[46]

Corporate sponsors and their allies within the Olympic movement enjoy significant preferential treatment. In London they had access to some 250 miles of VIP driving lanes, which they shared with athletes and medical staff, whereas the general population was excluded from what became derogatorily dubbed "Zil lanes" (in reference to fast lanes expressly for politburo bigwigs in the Soviet Union).[47] Corporate sponsors even snapped up 10 percent of the coveted slots in the Olympic torch relay.[48] They also received a quarter of all tickets to sporting events. This paved a path to scandal when huge blocks of seats remained empty at a wide range of sports events. For the millions of everyday people who had followed the rules to secure tickets only to be turned away, the vacant seats were a symbol of Olympic privilege run amok.[49] Corporate-sponsor emissaries were also invited to what London mayor Boris Johnson termed "a gigantic schmoozathon," a high-stakes smorgasbord of capitalist hobnobbing.[50] Moody's Investors Service delineated who would profit from Johnson's schmoozathon—what the firm referred to as "corporates." Their report, issued a few months before the start of the London Games, succinctly stated, "Moody's expects that corporate sponsors will benefit most from the Games." After all, the 2012 Summer Games were "a huge marketing opportunity for corporates."[51] Indeed, corporate sponsors benefited from their investment. London 2012 Olympic Partner Adidas secured record numbers in 2012, thanks in part to the Olympics, topping 14.5 billion Euros ($19.3 billion).[52]

Another benefit to becoming an official Olympics sponsor was a temporary exemption from the UK corporation tax and income tax. In a sense, the Olympics refashioned parts of London into a de facto tax haven where tax-free profits were the order of the day. Foreign nationals who "carry out an official function or work for a London 2012 Partner"—including sponsors, athletes, journalists, and IOC officials—were not taxed on their income. This amounted to more than £600 million in forgone tax revenues.[53] This led to one of the most successful activist campaigns at London 2012—a symbolic action with material outcomes. After the corporate tax breaks became public knowledge—thanks in large part to an article that appeared in the *Ethical Consumer* magazine—the UK-based group 38 Degrees organized an online campaign designed to compel companies to forgo their tax breaks.[54] After thousands of netizens signed an online petition, fourteen prominent Olympic sponsors agreed to waive their tax-free status: Acer, Adidas, Atos, BMW, Coca-Cola, Dow, EDF Energy, GE, McDonald's, Omega, P & G, Panasonic, Samsung, and Visa.[55] Once McDonald's and Coca-Cola succumbed, their corporate-sponsor peers began to follow suit. The campaign benefited from a favorable political opportunity structure whereby the general public viewed corporations with newfound skepticism after the 2008 economic collapse. The remarkable success of this effort—what Jennifer Earl and Katrina Kimport would describe as a fully online "e-movement"—points to the promise of keyboard activism in particular instances when propitious political opportunity structure exists.[56]

While corporate sponsors positioned themselves to cash in on the Olympic halo effect, activists argued that most of them were anything but angels. They claimed the IOC has concocted a scenario whereby the very worst of the corporate world have the incentive to become Olympic sponsors. Dave Zirin calls this "corporate sin washing"—using the Games to cozy up to consumers so they'll forgive them their trespasses.[57] In particular, campaigners vigorously attacked Olympic sponsors for their ecological impacts, accusing them of using the Olympics to greenwash their dodgy reputations.

The term *sustainability* is notoriously vague. This allows companies to claim to be ecologically minded while doing the bare minimum, if anything—this is the essence of greenwashing. On the activist side of the equation, simply encouraging people to purchase environmentally friendlier goods leads to what Heather Rogers derisively dubs "lazy environmentalism" and "armchair activism," a process that transmogrifies citizens into consumers.[58] In this way, pressing for sustainability can simply reinforce—and even validate—the wider power relations that actually undercut ecological remediation.

Each Olympics is obliged to claim the mantle of the "greenest Games ever," and London was no exception. In support of London's bid, then–prime minister Tony Blair vowed the Games "would drive the environmentally-friendly regeneration and rejuvenation of East London."[59] London's candidature file hailed sustainability as "integral to every aspect of London 2012's vision for the Games."[60] It promised to build "a legacy for the environment," achieving sustainability through green building and the creation of greenspaces.[61] Toward that end, it created a Commission for a Sustainable London 2012 (CSL) to monitor London 2012's green activities. It also began a "sustainability partner" sponsorship program that included

BP, BMW, BT, Cisco, EDF Energy, and GE.[62] Both endeavors generated significant political dissent.

The CSL was formed in early 2007, bringing together an array of environmental experts whose job was to ensure that the London Organizing Committee of the Olympic Games (LOCOG) was living up to its public promises and policies. While its scope was admittedly narrow, it wasn't simply LOCOG's green-hued rubber stamper. In October 2011 CSL issued a report finding that when it came to the sustainability of official Olympic consumer goods, "London 2012 has been successful in changing the behaviour of the industry, but needs to seize the opportunity to change the behaviour of the consumer." The report revealed that full public disclosure of supply-chain locations was lacking—Adidas was the only sponsor that was divulging the location of factories producing London 2012 gear.[63] Still, many activists were frustrated by the CSL's unwillingness to address bigger-picture ecological concerns or to speak critically about London 2012's six sustainability partners.

Turns out one of the CSL's own commissioners shared this frustration. In early 2012, Meredith Alexander, who had served as the lead commissioner for supply-chain management on the aforementioned report, resigned, citing a public statement from the commission that ignored the Bhopal gas spill and made Dow appear to be a socially responsible company. She explained, "When you look at the list of [top-level corporate] sponsors, I find it impossible to reconcile who is chosen as a sponsor with any idea of ethical or moral choice. I have never seen any evidence that the Olympic values come into play when sponsors are chosen."[64] In June 2012, the CSL seemed to reach a similar conclusion. It recommended that in the future the sustainability-partner program should be "much more explicit in their commitments, so the partner 'earns' the right rather than just paying for it." In other words, the commission implicitly admitted that standards for becoming a sustainability partner were nonexistent.[65] In a way, the commission validated the critiques of people like Alexander who viewed the program as a pay-to-play charade.

Alexander believed that, to address sustainability matters meaningfully, a wider remit was required. She asserted, "The objective is to make the Olympics as sustainable *as possible*. The objective isn't to make the Games sustainable, and the reason for that is a giant event like this, with all the energy use, all the air travel, all of the associated impacts, you could say it's not inherently sustainable."[66] In an effort to make big-picture lateral connections, Alexander went on to spearhead the Greenwash Gold campaign, an undertaking that brought together three groups—Bhopal Medical Appeal, London Mining Network, and UK Tar Sands Network—in order to shine a spotlight on the environmental misdeeds of Olympic sponsors. Activists produced three short, snappy, animated films on BP, Dow, and Rio Tinto, and asked people to vote on who deserved the gold medal for greenwashing.[67] With the Deepwater Horizon oil disaster along the Gulf Coast fresh in the public mind, BP was a prime bull's-eye for greenwashing. Campaigners targeted Rio Tinto—the mining company that provided metal for the Olympic medals—for polluting communities from Quebec to West Papua.[68] On 16 April 2012, they held an event at the Amnesty International UK building where they screened the three videos and followed them with testimonial panels of people from around the world—from Bhopal to Utah, from Mongolia to Mississippi—who were affected by the actions of the three companies. Speaking in many languages, eco-victims described in powerful terms how BP, Dow, and Rio Tinto had changed their lives for the worse.

Yet, organizers were wary of being labeled doom and gloomers. Meredith Alexander told me,

> What we're talking about is obviously incredibly serious. We're talking about global climate change, which is going to devastate the planet. We are talking about indigenous communities being destroyed. We are talking about pollution leading to deaths. These are not happy subjects. And I think the sort of po-faced, it's-all-so-dreadful approach appeals to some people who are already in that space and already interested and concerned. But actually for a lot of people, we're competing for their attention with all kinds of things, and humor is a really strong way in.[69]

This tension animating activist practice—grappling with dire situations while trying to engage people on friendly terms—was prominent in London. Oxford-based poet-activist Danny Chivers captured the quandary at the heart of anticorporate action vis-à-vis the Games: "The Olympics are a real opportunity to challenge the corporate sponsors. So, how do we challenge them without looking like massive spoilsports?"[70]

BP earned extra attention from activists for its sponsorship of the Royal Shakespeare Company, which featured international programming astride the Games as part of the Cultural Olympiad. BP's ecological misdeeds birthed the Reclaim Shakespeare Company, a collection of self-described "anarcho-thespians" who used the Olympic platform to press toward their goal of stripping the oil behemoth of its credibility in art circles. BP was cornering the arts-sponsorship market, inking long-term deals with the British Museum, the National Portrait Gallery, the Royal Opera House, and the Tate, and it appeared the Royal Shakespeare Company was next on their list.[71] Blending humor, creativity, and pluckiness, RSC campaigners carried out a series of pre-Games actions that captured the zeitgeist of Olympics activism in London.

On 23 April 2012, William Shakespeare's 448th birthday, RSC made its first storm-the-stage intervention. As RSC participant Danny Chivers wrote in *London Late,* the alternative newspaper published during the Games, the troupe was "brought together by a shared love of the Bard and a loathing of badly behaved oil companies."[72] Each guerrilla performance was tailored to the play that followed, with activists carefully crafting their presentations replete with a dash of Shakespearean language and lingo. At their world premiere, the guerrilla actors clambered onto the hallowed stage where, dressed in Shakespearean garb, Richard Howlett delivered a soliloquy detourning the Bard for activist purposes:

> What country, friends, is this?
> Where the words of our most prized poet
> Can be bought to beautify a patron
> So unnatural as British Petroleum?

After delivering a tongue-lashing to BP for the ecological devastation it had wrought, Howlett declared, "and yet":

> They wear a painted face of bright green leaves,
> Mask themselves with sunshine.
> And with fine deceitful words
> They steal into our theaters, and our minds.
> They would have us sleep.
> But this great globe of ours is such stuff as dreams are made on.
> Most delicate, wondrous, to be nurtured
> For our children and theirs beyond.
> Let not BP turn these dreams to nightmares.
> Fuelling the Future? Thou liest malignant thing!

Do we sleep?
I find not myself disposed to sleep.

Howlett concluded his eloquent denunciation with, "Let us break their staff that would bewitch us! Out damned logo!" at which point he tore the BP logo from the back of the program and encouraged others in attendance to do so as well.[73] The RSC's debut was met with both bemusement and applause. Many in the crowd ripped out their BP logos. For Howlett, crafting a well-written diatribe and delivering it with crisp precision was vital for both respecting and engaging the theater crowd—"we hope they have some respect for how we're doing it rather than just ranting and raving," he told me.[74] Chivers added, "It's important that we don't set ourselves up as the anti-fun opposition."[75] The work of the RSC is notable for its conscious decision to go with the celebratory flow, punching sideways at the target, implicitly following the words of poet Emily Dickinson—"Tell all the Truth but tell it slant."[76]

Humor was crucial to the interventions. RSC's jocular approach "relaxed the atmosphere," Howlett stated. "Getting the audience to laugh at BP is a great thing."[77] Chivers said, "If we're going to enter a space of entertainment, we need to be entertaining. . . . Maybe if we can make them laugh a bit, and be challenging to BP while engaging the audience, we can get them to think about the BP sponsorship." He ticked off the ways humor was important to RSC: "It can be a fantastic way of making a connection to the audience straightaway. It's also a way of defusing potentially hostile situations. And it helps for engaging activists—people have joined us because they think it looks like fun."[78]

But RSC's performances were not always greeted with appreciation. At times they were booed or met with icy murmurs, as when they inadvertently gate-crashed a BP sponsorship party where the energy company's employees had assembled with Royal Shakespeare Company higher-ups for a night of theater and schmoozing. Howlett said of the jeers, "I quite liked that because it gave me the sense that we were using the theater as a forum for discussing issues of the day, and people are showing their feelings about that. In Shakespeare's day, when people went to the theater, they threw stuff if they didn't like it. It was this bawdy, loud place where people expressed themselves and the actors on stage would've been much more aware of that. So I quite liked that we were reinvigorating that idea of how the theater could be."[79] The Reclaim Shakespeare Company advanced an "ethical spectacle" while ratcheting up their efforts to concrete, achievable goals. Not only did activists wish to strip the varnish from the unearned green sheen BP was getting from the Olympic Games, but they also wanted to get the Royal Shakespeare Company to ditch BP and adopt ethical sponsorship practices. Theatergoers and workers within the theater made up the primary target audience. The wider public was also in the troupe's sights, in the hope people would apply outside pressure on the theater company to get them to rethink their BP sponsorship deal. As such, the group launched a web site—BP or Not BP—to coincide with the first intervention. They catalogued their protests online and used social media—primarily Facebook and Twitter—to extend the performances outward, giving them a second life beyond the finite theater audience.[80] These social-media interventions constituted what Paolo Gerbaudo calls "tactical communication" that is rippling with both practical information as well as "an emotional sense of togetherness" that binds geographically dispersed protesters.[81]

Activists deliberately alternated between contained and transgressive contention. They put forth an inside-outside strategy whereby they engaged with actors and theater workers, getting many of them—including the prominent thespian Mark Rylance—to sign a letter in the *Guardian* that was timed as a one-two punch with the first intervention at the Royal Shakespeare Theater in Stratford-upon-Avon. The letter commemorated Shakespeare's birthday before arguing, "what should be an unabashed celebration of Shakespeare's continued relevance to our world has been sullied by the fact that the festival is sponsored by BP." The signees supported the idea that the Royal Shakespeare Company was "allowing itself to be used by BP to obscure the destructive reality of its activities." They suggested "an end to oil sponsorship of the arts" and demanded "more responsible ways to finance this country's cultural life, for our own and future generations."[82]

After the initial action in Stratford-upon-Avon, the troupe struck four more times, including in late June at the Roundhouse Theater in Camden before *Comedy of Errors* and the following day at Riverside Studios before a performance of *Romeo and Juliet in Baghdad*. All the RSC's actions took place before the Olympic Games. This was strategic. Jess Worth said, "We decided not to do something during the Olympics because we thought nobody would notice, since everyone would be focusing on the Olympics, and partly because we didn't really want to do any activism connected to the Olympics during the Olympics in case we got shot." After a moment she added, "I think if we'd felt like we could have a serious impact by doing some kind of protest during the Olympics, we would have done one. So I don't want to overemphasize how the police put us off. It's not the only reason. We just realized this was largely going to be a media campaign. The best time to wage the campaign was in the months leading to the Olympics rather than [during] the Olympics themselves."[83] The group intervened one final time before the Games started, infiltrating the British Museum's *Shakespeare: Staging the World* exhibition, where about a dozen performers carried out a skit highlighting BP's purported duplicity. Museum security expelled the protesters, but not before their pop-up performance drew a sizable crowd.[84] RSC continued their actions after the Games concluded, working behind the scenes with actors and Royal Shakespeare Company insiders to help institute ethical sponsorship policies. Howlett said, "I see our role as urging people in theater who have political consciences to take a stand."[85] According to the *Independent,* a Royal Shakespeare Company spokesperson noted the theater has not renewed sponsorship with BP, a hopeful development for activists.[86]

One anticorporate action that was actually sanctioned by Olympic officials occurred on 27 July 2012, the day of the opening ceremonies. The target was Games sponsor, Dow. Bhopal Medical Appeal organized a die-in with members of Drop Dow Now joining in solidarity. For months the BMA's Colin Toogood worked behind the scenes with authorities like Mark Lewis, head of London 2012 security at Westfield Shoppingtowns, to obtain permission to carry out the protest.[87] Olympic security escorted activists into a small, secluded space blocked off from most pedestrian traffic where about fifty people engaged in a die-in at the gates of the Olympic Park, while activists held a press conference as well as a moment of silence for victims of Bhopal. The action was strategically situated in front of one of the large Dow ads. Police were "very accommodating," said participant Bridget Botelho.[88]

According to Toogood, BMA did some strategic jurisdictional shimmying to gain approval for their protest: "The reason we got to protest is because we didn't ask for one, we told them we were going to do it, and we did this with a letter from some solicitors. We addressed it to the Metropolitan Police, and copied in LOCOG and Westfield [mall]. So, we were challenging the police to object and the police didn't have any particular grounds or agenda to reject, partly because that piece of land is private." He added, "What we had insinuated without being too clear was if we didn't get that protest, we were going to call a judicial review on the infringement of our democratic rights." He revealed with a chuckle, "We actually didn't think we'd get the protest, and really what we wanted was the judicial review, so the protest was sort of the worst case scenario. But it's not that bad of a worst case."[89]

Toogood was cognizant of the fact that his group was playing into the good-protester–bad-protester dynamic: "They were holding us up at the ones who were a goodie example. So, it worked well for them, but it worked well for us too. I don't have a problem with that. The fact is we had a demonstration at the gates of the park on the opening day and nobody else did." While the symbolic action did not score a lot of media attention, it did earn a segment on Channel 4 as well as some articles in the foreign press. Toogood remarked, "We didn't get the sort of press we might have liked, but having said that, a year before if you would have told us we'd do something that would make Channel 4 news, we would have bit your hand off." When asked to look back on the Bhopal Medical Appeal actions, Toogood said, "I couldn't be more pleased with it. It's played out better for us than it's played out for Dow in terms of public relations. It has been a complete disaster for them."[90]

Targeting Dow was no simple task. The *Wall Street Journal* complicated Toogood's appraisal by pointing out that although Dow might be "a magnet for criticism" due to its ties Bhopal—not to mention its development of napalm—it had different goals from consumer-oriented firms like Coca-Cola and McDonald's that aimed to use their Olympic sheen to attract customers. Instead, Dow used the London Olympics to secure pole position for future Games-related infrastructure deals, to entertain and impress current clients, and to portray itself as an appealing place for current and prospective employees to work. Image construction was paramount, and for the purposes of stimulating business-to-business deals, not consumer interest.[91] This was Johnson's schmoozathon in action, well out of the public eye and thus the reach of dissident citizens, and it points to the challenge that sits at the core of the dialectic of resistance and restriction.

Space Games

To stage the Games, Olympic authorities needed to produce space in particular ways. Often this entailed hailing a state of exception that justified seizing public space and converting it into Olympic zones of exclusion. As we saw earlier, VIP driving lanes reserved for the "Olympic family" created what Lefebvre would identify as "spatial contradictions" that crystallize political conflicts: "it is only *in* space that such conflicts come effectively into play."[92] In London, spatial contradictions became a flashpoint for dissent.

While Jacques Rogge quite remarkably claimed that he and other IOC members "are working-class people," actual working-class London taxi drivers mobilized to challenge the VIP driving lanes, claiming that preferential treatment was not only inherently unfair, but detrimental to their livelihoods.[93] Beginning in fall 2011, unionized cabbies deliberately clogged the roads in protest, demonstrating both their collective disgust and their potential power. On 9 September 2011 they flash-mobbed the hotel where LOCOG higher-ups were meeting, choking up traffic for just under an hour. Led by the United Cabbies Group, the taxi drivers protested their unrequited efforts to communicate with LOCOG.[94] Taxi drivers—including those from London's iconic black cabs and the Rail, Maritime, and Transport Workers union—continued to protest the exclusive lanes throughout the Olympics. On the day of the opening ceremony they carried out a sizable slowdown, for example.[95] But battles in London over Olympic space preceded these efforts, too.

Three episodes highlight spatial contention in the lead-up to the Games: (1) the demolition of Clays Lane Estate, (2) the use of Leyton Marsh as a temporary basketball facility, and (3) the conversion of Greenwich Park into an equestrian venue. In all three instances activists were unsuccessful in blocking Olympic plans—they were overmatched. In part this derived from their inability to mobilize resources and to gain wider public support, but the protesters' ineffectiveness also highlights the power asymmetry between the Olympic juggernaut and grassroots activists. The political terrain was wildly uneven. The Games were like a freight train that flattened the opposition.

The Geneva-based Center on Housing Rights and Evictions (COHRE) has long tracked displacement resulting from mega-events like the Olympics.[96] The 2008 Beijing Summer Olympics—where more than 1.5 million people were displaced to make way for the Games—forced COHRE to work in overdrive.[97] Not so in London. Nonetheless, for the East Londoners who were removed from their homes and relocated across the city, the disruption brought on by the Olympics was no small matter. Activist Julian Cheyne, who was displaced from his home in Clays Lane Estate in

Newham borough, remarked, "You are swept aside—it's just like a juggernaut."[98] It was, he said, "a very stressful situation," adding, "The only reason Clays Lane was demolished was because of the Olympics."[99]

Clays Lane was an East London housing estate that was compulsorily purchased in mid-2007 to make way for Olympics construction. Prior to its demolition, it was a thriving housing cooperative and home to a wide range of people—about 450 in total—including numerous vulnerable individuals for whom the cooperative served as a support network. Even before London had secured the Games, the London Development Agency (LDA) had identified Clays Lane as first-rate real estate. In 2003, Gareth Blacker, the LDA's head of property and development said, "If we do the site assembly we're proposing to do, we're creating a prime opportunity for the property."[100] Antidisplacement activists argued it was not "a prime opportunity" for everyday Londoners but rather for high-flying property developers. While this dynamic—gentrification with an assist from the Olympics—plays out similarly in other host cities, the scale of displacement was relatively minimal in London. In total, about one thousand people were dislodged. In addition to the Clays Lane residents, approximately five hundred students were displaced from a student estate; a travelers' estate was also disbanded.[101] Aside from the inconvenience of having to move, many noted they lost community when they were forced to disperse; also, by being plopped at the top of housing lists, they effectively bumped others down who had been previously waiting.[102] Activists attempted to organize, but the long-term campaign of solidarity that was required proved elusive; the unity of residents fractured as the battle against Olympics authorities dragged on.[103]

In truth, Games boosters telegraphed their master plan. London bid promoters confidently asserted, "The face of the capital would be changed forever by the Games."[104] Many critics agreed. But rather than the socially productive greentopia envisioned by LOCOG, activists saw the impending gentrification of their neighborhoods. Estelle du Boulay, director of the Newham Monitoring Project, an East London-based antiracist organization, told me, "There is a reality to these sports events when they land on your town, they basically overturn the community life that is already there and the progress that was happening organically. This is a huge project of gentrification. There's a lot of money in this project and we don't see it coming back to local communities." In fact, the Newham Monitoring Project was forced to relocate from Stratford after rents shot up in advance of the Olympics. She continued, "It all just feels like it was a terrible spin and we'll be feeling the impact of this for years afterwards. It will widen the gap between the rich and poor in the borough."[105] Anti-Olympics activist and photojournalist Martin Slavin argued this was all possible in East London because "the invisible hand of the market had long disappeared over the horizon."[106] This left London's residents vulnerable to the machinations of Olympic-style urban development. In the Games' wake, the battle continued, as London authorities moved to demolish the Carpenters Estate in Stratford, which sits near the border of the Olympic Park. Local councilors aimed to raze the estate to facilitate the expansion of the University College London.[107]

In nearby Waltham Forest, activists staged another strategic skirmish. Save Leyton Marsh was a collection of East London residents and Hackney Marsh users that formed in response to the Olympic Delivery Authority's announcement in December 2011 that it planned to construct a temporary basketball training facility on Leyton Marsh to be used during the Olympic Games. With assists from the Lea Valley Regional Park Authority (LVRPA) and the Waltham Forest Council, the ODA seemed unstoppable. But that didn't prevent Save Leyton Marsh from conducting a vigorous campaign that worked both inside and outside the corridors of institutional power.

Although supporters call it London's lung, Leyton Marsh was built on top of a landfill site that was chock-full of World War II mysteries. Excavating the marsh to make way for Olympic construction promised to be an ecological conundrum. Undaunted, the ODA pressed ahead, promising, "the site will be fully restored to its existing condition. The temporary buildings will be removed, the roadways and hard surfacing broken up for recycling and any topsoil that was removed will be re-laid and seeded."[108] For those with concerns, the ODA set up a construction hotline and e-mail account. A series of public meetings were also scheduled. Yet activists who participated in the process felt as if it were a scam and that the decision to plunge ahead with the Olympic blueprint was a foregone conclusion. Activist Fizle Sagar summed up her perception of the Olympic officials' overall attitude: "What are you little people bothering about?"[109]

The authorities' precooked plans were in high relief in early February 2012 when the Waltham Forest Council met to discuss the planned basketball courts. Activists from Save Leyton Marsh carefully stacked and packaged their facts, presenting them in formal testimony while also lobbying officials behind the scenes. A comprehensive environmental impact statement had not been filed by the authorities, which campaigners felt was necessary for such a large project. Yet the Council passed the plan four to three, sparking jeers and shouts of "shame" from the gathered denizens. It appeared neither facts nor unanswered questions could dent the council's foregone plot.[110] Save Leyton Marsh activist Charlie Charman told me the problem is that "they're almost immune from any sort of democratic input. It's totally dysfunctional"[111]

Activists believed more was at stake than simply the building of a temporary basketball facility. They viewed the LVRPA's actions as a foretaste of the privatization feast to come, a small land grab that would open the door to more enclosures of public space in the name of private use and profit. Government entities in Britain such as the LVRPA are under increasing fiscal pressure, with some wishing to expand their revenue intake. Under their expansive remit of "recreation," development of the marshes in the name of engendering fiscal responsibility is not a far-flung notion. In fact there is precedent for this: riding stables that were installed on Hackney Marsh, which began with a strong public-service component for locals, ended up becoming a place where wealthy people from afar pay to board their horses. And in a bout of turf creep, the stables incrementally added buildings. As Save Leyton Marsh activist Vicky Sholund said, "It's not their land, but they've taken it."[112] Charman added, "The concern is not actually pure privatization, but these public bodies are behaving as if they're corporate entities because they follow the same models now. They behave as if they were a private company."[113]

Activists had these bigger-picture processes in mind as they moved ahead with their campaign. In March 2012, as construction kicked into gear, activists tried to block the access road to prevent trucks from bringing building supplies to the site. They didn't have the numbers available to cover the road 24-7, which minimized their success. But all that changed in late March when activists from Occupy London joined the fight, setting up camp astride the basketball facility and largely bringing construction to a halt. The LVRPA secured court injunctions to prevent further building delays. A little more than two weeks later, police broke up the encampment, in the process arresting six activists on public-order offenses. Melanie Strickland of Occupy London, who herself showed up at Leyton Marsh to lend a hand, said, "People put their bodies on the line in solidarity to block the lorries. They were criminalized for doing what is right."[114]

An ODA spokesperson told the *Guardian* they were concerned with what they deemed "unlawful disruptive action" that was undercutting construction. The spokesperson played the fiscal card, stating, "These setbacks have incurred extra costs to the taxpayer" and vowed to "return the ground to its previous state."[115]

The ODA didn't stop there. When activists tried to use legal means to challenge Waltham Forest Council's decision to build the basketball facility, they were denied judicial review by an administrative court. To add monetary injury to insult, the ODA and Waltham Forest Council made the rare move of trying to recover their legal costs from engaging the judicial review process. The council claimed £4,500 ($7,200) in legal costs while the ODA sought an additional £20,000 ($32,000). Activists viewed these purported costs as not only astronomical, but dubious, too. Such cost recovery efforts are also extremely rare—campaigners suspected they were politically motivated and an effort to intimidate them. "The ODA has been using this all along," said Sholund, "threatening people with costs of one sort or another to stop them doing anything. And it's effective because most of the people challenging them haven't got money."[116] In the end, the basketball facility was built for the Games. But activists didn't view their efforts as wasted. "I think it's good we did try," Sholund told me "because I think we have been a thorn in their side."[117] Their legacy is that the local council and the LVRPA learned that locals will not take bullying lying down. Authorities have been put on notice that these groups are not going down without a fight. The Olympics ended up bringing together a group of activists that are set on continuing their work together. Through the struggle, locals made allies across the city, and learned lessons they believe will come in handy down the line. "We think this is a long-term thing," said Sholund. Sagar added, "We've all met each other, and now because of our experience we feel we've stayed the course and now we feel [that] this energy and this knowledge we have shouldn't just dissipate after the Olympics."[118]

One final example of an activist effort to stop the seizure of space for Olympic purposes occurred in Greenwich Park, where LOCOG planned to hold Olympic equestrian events. Greenwich Park is a UNESCO World Heritage Site and the oldest enclosed Royal Park. From LOCOG's point of view, benefits included its location near the Olympic Park, the panoramic view of London that would serve as a TV-ready backdrop, and the fact that constructing a temporary venue would leave no "white elephants" behind.

Enter NOGOE—No to Greenwich Olympic Equestrian Events—which raised an array of environmental concerns.[119] NOGOE argued that holding the events in the park would damage trees (some more than three hundred years old), rare grassland habitat, protected wildlife species, and the area's archaeology (for example, Saxon burial mounds and a Romano-Celtic temple site).[120] NOGOE also criticized the LOCOG consultation process, questioned whether the relatively small park could handle the throngs that were expected for the event, and accused organizers of localwashing: using Greenwich Park to infuse the Games with a high heritage quotient. And, as Patrick Wellington noted in the January 2010 issue of the *NOGOE Newsletter,* there was a class dynamic thrumming beneath the surface of the protests: "All this to be done on behalf of a minority elite sport of the wealthy in one of the poorest boroughs in London."[121]

Eventually the activists delivered more than thirteen thousand signatures of protest to a number of targets including the IOC, then-prime minister Gordon Brown, the mayor of London, and UNESCO.[122] They also proposed an alternative: holding equestrian events in Windsor, where the picture-perfect Windsor Castle could be a backdrop. Despite the group's efforts, in March 2010, the Greenwich Council approved the park for equestrian use. In July 2011, NOGOE attended a test event to engage in what the *Guardian* described as "polite protest," donning signs that read "Get thee to Windsor forthwith ye dunderheads" and "Stop horsing around in Greenwich Park." NOGOE's Rachel Mawhood told the *Guardian,* "We think we still hold the moral high ground," adding that Greenwich Park "has never been built on before. It is a public park surrounded by areas of high deprivation. It's the backyard for thousands of people living in cramped estates. People have said it looks unrecognisable and like an open prison."[123]

When I asked her whether, in retrospect, she would modify her statement, Mawhood said, "No, I wouldn't change a syllable. LOCOG was utterly delinquent in Greenwich Park." Mawhood parted company with NOGOE in spring 2012 but continued to fight tenaciously against holding equestrian events in Greenwich Park. A one-person watchdog force, she sent countless, meticulously researched missives to authorities, pressing them to be as environmentally responsible as possible. After the Games she told me, "Operationally, LOCOG's biggest mistake was to try to ignore the statutory water and sewerage provider's planning conditions. Not surprisingly, when a few weeks before the start of the Olympics Thames

Water discovered LOCOG's unorthodox water-supply arrangements, they did everything to protect their shareholders' investment and their assets." Mawhood blew the whistle on this dodgy scenario: "I suspect that Thames Water held LOCOG and the Government to ransom by charging a punitive amount—tens of millions—to supply a very small amount of water to LOCOG's development in the Park." While Mawhood was indefatigable, her efforts got little traction either with LOCOG or in the media. She asserted, "activism is severely circumscribed when the 'free' press won't investigate and report and inform, for fear of losing its press accreditation to Olympics events. I do worry that that has set a precedent that we may come to regret."[124] In the following chapter I explore media coverage of London activism in detail.

One criticism that emerged from activist circles in all three instances of Olympic-induced seizure of public space was that the process for disputing such actions was top-down, unreceptive, and unaccountable. Critics consistently contended the Olympic planning process was an elite escapade devoid of meaningful public input. Julian Cheyne called the Clays Lane consultation process an "eyewash program" where "everything is completely done from the top, and everything is tailored to make it appear that there's some kind of communal representation."[125] Residents in the host boroughs whose lives were affected by the Olympics were sidelined. It wasn't so much that the planning process happened *with* activists and East London community members as it happened *to* them. CON activist David Renton said the Olympics "feels like a disembodied event that has very little roots in London . . . like all sorts of decisions are being made about making the Olympics the right kind of spectacle. And this kind of spectacle isn't even about showing off athletes, it's about showing off businesses."[126] Such sentiment is echoed in academia. Graeme Hayes and John Horne assert that civil society has "rarely been factored into the definition of the Games or Games projects. The role of civic organizations and publics is one of implementation and support, not one of definition and decision."[127]

"Spectacular Security"

The production of space is vital to the Olympic project, and essential for activists willing to challenge the ever-shifting geographies of power. As geographer David Featherstone puts it, "Subaltern groups construct agency through specific negotiations of power relations and through reconstituting spatial relations."[128] State forces also "construct agency" in the Olympic moment, not only by seizing space and producing it in accordance with celebratory Olympism, but also by ratcheting up security measures to ensure the smooth functioning of the Games. While activists aim to provoke an "ethical spectacle" that encourages the public to look at the Games both anew and askance, authorities attempt to construct what Philip Boyle and Kevin Haggerty call "spectacular security." With "the spectacle of security," Olympic policing officials "must strike a fine balance so that it is not *too* spectacular" whereby it might "disrupt the circuits of capital and consumption."[129]

London's bid book stated reassuringly that the city would "provide a low-risk environment as Host City for the Olympic and Paralympic Games in 2012."[130] However, within hours of learning it would host the Games, London suffered a coordinated terrorist attack on its subway system and a double-decker bus. The *New York Times* described commuters who were "were plunged into the nightmare of a subterranean bloodbath."[131] This brutal attack—one of the worst terrorist attacks in British history—crystallized the threat of terrorism as one of the key themes after the Munich Olympics of 1972. While the bombings never seriously threw London's successful Olympics bid into doubt, they did encourage the government to ramp up its surveillance and policing in advance of the Games. Yet the security forces, whose primary charge is to quash terrorism, can also be swerved to squelch, or at least intimidate, political activists.

This two-pronged nature of security was highlighted by Olympic officials themselves. In late 2011, Chris Allison—Scotland Yard's assistant commissioner and the national coordinator of Olympic security—briefed the London Assembly on policing costs for the Olympic and Paralympic Games. He singled out "four key risks to the Games"—terrorism, protest, organized crime, and natural disasters.[132] Emphasizing protest as a "threat" and then sandwiching it between terrorism and organized crime was unnerving for activists. As the Games approached, Allison's public pronouncements were laced with a bit more suavity. He assured civil libertarians that Scotland Yard would not crack down on protesters as long as they remained within the law, acknowledging, "They have a right to peacefully protest."[133] He set forth the good-protester–bad-protester dynamic, asserting, "If you want to protest, speak to us beforehand so we can manage your right to peacefully and lawfully protest." He went on to warn, "But if as an individual we think you are going to disrupt the Games in some way, then I am telling you that we will take whatever action we can within the law to prevent you from disrupting the Games."[134] As we shall see, Olympic security officials engaged in preemptive policing to contain dissent.

To the chagrin of activists, the Olympics brought considerable militarization of London's public sphere. The Ministry of Defense stationed Rapier and Starstreak surface-to-air missiles in various locations across London, including atop apartments in residential neighborhoods. During the Games, the city's airspace was patrolled by Typhoon fighter jets and Puma helicopters, replete with trained snipers who had the option to use lethal force.[135] The Royal Navy docked its largest warship—the *HMS Ocean*—along the River Thames.[136] The Metropolitan Police acquired more than ten thousand plastic bullets and set up mobile stations to facilitate swift deployments and bookings.[137] The BBC reported that Olympic security had obtained a long-range acoustic device (LRAD), a military-grade weapon battle-tested in war zones and big brother to the MRAD purchased for Vancouver 2010.[138] In addition, more than eighteen thousand military personnel policed Games venues, thanks to the fact that in the weeks prior to the opening ceremony, G4S, the private security firm entrusted to supply bag checkers and other security personnel, announced it would fall short. The world's biggest private security firm was supposed to supply more than ten thousand guards for Olympic venues as stipulated in its £284 million ($458 million) contract.[139] The troops literally had to be called in to make up for the shortfall, giving the Games a more military sheen. Much of the hardware was removed after the Games, but networks of security practice remain, normalizing the martial-metropolitan approach to securing urban space.[140]

A five-thousand-volt electrified security fence was pegged to the perimeter of the official Olympic area, but Olympic security also concerned itself with the rest of London. Police targeted Olympics activists, ostentatiously filming campaigners as they entered a Counter Olympics Network meeting in April 2012. Three months before the London Olympics commenced, Scotland Yard organized "dispersal zones" where police could bar those they deemed to be engaging in antisocial behavior.[141] These zones remained in place a full three months after the Games. Estelle du Boulay of the Newham Monitoring Project told me that in the state of exception created by the Olympics, local police were "rolling out more draconian measures and more attempts to increase the power of the police." She said that in the year running up to the Olympics, "We've seen a different kind of policing, a harder form of policing against our communities, and just a far greater police presence on the ground. It's been quite an intimidating presence."[141] Olympics security practices dovetailed with what the Met had been calling "total policing," a new policy unfurled in the wake of the London riots of 2011.[143] To du Boulay, the total-policing approach "seems to be a smoke-screen for a tougher type of policing, for things that police have wanted to bring in for a long time."[144] While total policing was always shrouded in ambiguity—perhaps as much a brand as a policy—there was a decidedly preemptive dimension to it. The policing of Olympics-related dissent in the lead-up to the Games highlights such early-stage, preventative policing.

The Space Hijackers are a group of self-proclaimed "anarchitects" based in London. In their manifesto they explain, "We oppose the hierarchy that is put upon us by Architects, Planners and owners of space."[145] Since 1999 they have been engaging in humor-based, antistate subversion that aims to refashion space for political purposes. Composed of numerous "agents," they organize rollicking frolics designed to put the "fun" in "fun-damentally opposed to capitalism" while simultaneously blurring the lines between politics, art, and activism.[146] Agent Maxwell explained, "For us, it's about how public space is increasingly heavily securitized and a lot of that has to do with the privatization of public space. . . . It's about trying to reclaim space that has been taken over by powerful interests for the ben-efit of a wealthy minority, and we try to challenge who that space is being taken from and given to. We're trying to re-imagine what you can do in the space."[147] Agent Monstris added, "We're all frustrated cosmonauts or astro-nauts" interested in "physical space, virtual space, mental space, political space, sexual space. The idea is to turn it on its head and to look at things in a very different way that will engage people. Because when you start talking about 'the politics of public and private space,' most people will turn off and start falling asleep."[148] Agent Square Mile chimed in, "Part of the fun is devising the projects that are playful and thoughtful at the same time, and that are an absolute pleasure to do. The things we protest are horrific, but if you just let that totally suck you down, then you have no energy to do anything. So you need to find ways in which you can energize yourselves and other people."[149]

In spring 2012 the group proclaimed itself to be "the Official Protesters of the London 2012 Olympic Games," starting a web page and changing its Twitter avatar. Shortly thereafter, Twitter suspended their account after

LOCOG complained they were violating brand-protection laws. Twitter wrote to the group, "We have received reports from the trademark holder, London Organising Committee of the Olympic Games and Paralympic Games Ltd [LOCOG], that your account, @spacehijackers, is using a trademark in a way that could be confusing or misleading with regard to a brand affiliation. Your account has been temporarily suspended due to violation of our trademark policy."[150] This started an online firestorm that ultimately led to the reinstatement of their account. Tongue in cheek, the group reported, "Eventually after tense negotiations Twitter allowed us access back to our account, along with the hundreds of new followers that we had gained. We would like to thank Locog and the IOC for this Official Recognition and look forward to working with them to facilitate further protest in the future."[151] The incident highlights the tradeoffs involved in Mark Andrejevic's "digital enclosure"—the use of social media allows for enhanced discursive mobility, but also facilitates surveillance and repression.[152] Nevertheless, the group was on to new anti-Olympic adventures.

Space Hijackers received missives from the Metropolitan Police asking them to relay their protest plans so that the Met could facilitate the demonstrations—these requests went ignored. Two weeks before the Games, the Space Hijackers voyaged to the Olympic site and Westfield shopping mall where they measured the range of their megaphone, simulated speed dashes away from security personnel, and appraised potential supplies for barricade building and projectile tossing. On their web site they reported, "As Official Protesters we wanted to ensure that provisions had been made not only to facilitate our protests, but also that any non-brand-compliant protesters would be safely removed from the area."[153] They were accosted by mall police along the way but used humor to deflect their inquiries. As Agent Maxwell said, "When you draw in the police with humor, you do get a different response, I think. When you draw them into your joke, you change the parameters of the conversation. It makes for a more convivial and less tense process, and it means you can negotiate more." After all, he said, "It does make people look silly if they can't take a joke."[154] Savvy engagement with policing officials allowed the group to carve out tactical space in which to operate, and their use of wit attracted positive media attention. They gained participants along the way, people who wanted to protest but to have fun, too.

While the police's preemptive efforts didn't slow down the Space Hijackers, they did affect other campaigns that had the Olympics in

IMAGE 8 Greenwash Gold award ceremony at Trafalgar Square. Courtesy of Sally Brady.

their sights. A week before the London 2012 opening ceremony, activists from the Greenwash Gold campaign took to Trafalgar Square to award the gold, silver, and bronze for corporate greenwashing. As mock representatives from Olympic sponsors Rio Tinto, BP, and Dow stood on the stand to receive their medals—as determined by online voting—they were doused with lime-green custard, symbolizing greenwashing. Police swooped in and arrested seven participants on suspicion of criminal damage, apparently for littering the public square with custard. No one from what became known as "the Custard 7" was actually charged with any crime. Yet their bail conditions restricted their movement and thus curtailed their political freedom. One activist's bail prohibited entrance into Trafalgar Square, Wimbledon, Wembley Football Stadium, Horse Guards Parade, Hyde Park, and Lords Cricket Ground because "It is feared that" the individual "will attend these sites to commit further offences due to the fact that they are being used for Olympic venues."[155] The Custard 7 was mandated to return to the police station in late September *after the Paralympics concluded.* In the end, officials dropped their case just before the activists were due to be charged, but the bail conditions had done their job of keeping them away from most Olympic-related venues. The police tactic of arresting activists on questionable grounds without leveling formal charges temporarily demobilized some of the most committed campaigners at a vital moment, forcing them to carefully monitor their movements for fear of stepping on the wrong parcel of politicized turf. Not only did this limit free expression, but it also surreptitiously squelched the possibility of solidarity work. For instance, Greenwash Gold activists couldn't attend a subsequent protest by the group No Sochi 2014 because the event took place on the edge of Hyde Park.

Preemptive policing also suppressed the efforts of Critical Mass, a group of bicyclists who had been peaceably convening in London since April 1994. An established example of "leaderless" activism, Critical Mass rides occur throughout the world as a way of challenging the hegemony of the automobile while promoting exercise, bike safety, and good cheer.[156] On the night of the opening ceremony—choreographed by superstar British film director Danny Boyle for £27 million ($44 million)—Critical Mass cyclists took to the streets for their comparably low-budget monthly ride. However, part way through the excursion, police employed Section 12 of the Public Order Act 1986 to try to prevent the bikers from crossing north of the River Thames. The law states police can intervene to stop a public procession if they reasonably believe it "may result in serious public disorder, serious damage to property or serious disruption to the life of the community."[157] The Met did this despite the fact that the House of Lords ruled in 2008 that the relevant sections of the Public Order Act requiring prior notice did not apply to Critical Mass. By all accounts, the ride was peaceful and not a threat to public order or the "life of the community."[158] Activists also pointed to the irony that the cyclists were enacting the very health legacy the Games ostensibly aimed to create.

Police kettled and arrested 182 people, using a heavy hand—and even CS gas—in the process. Fabian Flues, who participated in the ride and narrowly escaped arrest, described getting kettled by police before officers "started running towards us and just grabbing people and so everyone got into a panic. There were police officers coming from all sides, and they were jumping on people and throwing them off their bikes."[159] Agent Rachmetoff

from the Space Hijackers, who was one of the Critical Mass arrestees, dead-
panned, "Due to poor planning by the Olympics, they scheduled their
opening ceremony on the same night as Critical Mass." When police saw
Rachmetoff's "official protester" T-shirt he was snatched and yanked into
the police kettle where he was eventually arrested. "That was good recognition of our brand," he dryly noted.[160] Again, activists were arrested but not
charged (only a few of the 182 received formal charges). And again, draconian bail conditions were imposed, which forbid the arrestees from going
within one hundred yards of any Olympic venue and from entering the
borough of Newham with a bicycle.[161] Kerry-anne Mendoza, who was also
arrested, called this trend of preemptive suppression "political policing."
She said, "I'm not charged with any criminal offense, yet the police are able
to restrict my freedom to move, my freedom to assemble, my freedom to
partake in peaceful protest, and without ever having put me before a court
to decide if those infringements on my civil liberties are justified based on
law." She added "The police are getting into the habit now of using bail
conditions without charge as a means of restricting the ability of people to
dissent."[162] In March 2013, five of the nine cyclists who went to trial were

IMAGE 9   Poster for Counter Olympics Network mobilization. Courtesy of Counter Olympics Network.

found guilty, receiving minor penalties and fines, but not before the activists expended their time and resources in a defensive stance.[163]

Scotland Yard's use of Section 12 of the Public Order Act 1986 is a classic example of what the late Alexander Cockburn described as "emergency laws" and measures that "lie around for decades like rattlesnakes in summer grass."[164] When activists in London took to the streets, the rattlesnakes popped their heads up and sank their fangs into the nearest ankle. After learning about how police had extended the "dispersal zone" order in Stratford for an additional three months, Occupy London activist Harjeet Kaur commented, "That rattlesnake is morphing into a King Cobra."[165] This is the Olympics-inspired state of exception writ large. Activists repeatedly voiced their concern. Kevin Blowe of the Newham Monitoring Project told me "The rights of free speech shouldn't disappear just because of a sporting event." He remarked, "The paranoia around the Olympics and the broader sense of wanting to have this almost sterile, incident-free, entirely orchestrated Olympic Games is driving the use of those policing powers."[166] The question is whether the Olympics will serve as a historical hinge swinging toward a future where these temporary measures become the new normal, where the exception becomes the rule.

Coda in the Capital

On 28 July 2012, the day after the opening ceremonies for the London Summer Olympics, activists gathered at Mile End Park in East London for a mobilization and march under the banner "Whose Games? Whose City?" Organized by the Counter Olympics Network, the demonstration attracted around one thousand people. The march snaked through Bow, along the way passing Bow Quarter Tower where surface-to-air missiles were ratcheted to the roof. Curious military personnel peered over the tower wall to find people chanting, "Hey ho Seb Coe, Get Your Missiles Out of Bow!" Others chanted, "Seb Coe, Get Out / We Know What You're All About / Missiles, Job Losses, Olympics for the Bosses." Meanwhile there was heavy police presence, including the light-blue-clad police liaison officers who amiably chatted up the crowd, vacuuming up whatever information they could.

Spearheading the march were activists from Disabled People Against Cuts (DPAC), a steadfast collection of campaigners, many of them in wheelchairs, who had been vociferously protesting the ever-fraying social safety net while the British government chose to lavishly fund the Olympics. A specific source of DPAC's ire was Atos, a Worldwide Olympic Partner. Prior to the Games, the multinational IT company carried out "work capability assessments" for the British government that led to thousands of sick and disabled people having their social support axed. Of the more than 700,000 assessments carried out by Atos, 40 percent appealed their findings, with 38 percent of those appeals successful. In an eight month period in 2011, 1,100 claimants died after they were denied benefits and placed in a "work-related activity group." As big-time beneficiaries of Britain's neoliberal outsourcing strategy, Atos had won more than £3 billion ($4.6 billion) in government contracts.[167]

The march culminated at Wennington Green where speakers from various groups gave brief speeches. Antimissile activist Chris Nineham captured the spirit of many concerned citizens when he remarked, "The local people think the idea of stationing high explosives in residential sites is a completely irresponsible and stupid thing to do. They should never have done it and they should never do such a thing again."[168] All in all, it was a peaceful event, not in the least bit spiky. CON organizer Cheyne said that to use disruptive tactics "in a sense rather misses the point, because you may end up simply having more repression at the end of it, and more annoyance at the end of it, and make it harder to construct a sensible alliance for the future."[169]

This mobilization was the largest demonstration during the actual Olympics. CON's David Renton spoke for many when he said, "Our failure has been that we haven't kept up the momentum of protest through the duration of the Games."[170] Political activists did not disrupt the smooth veneer of the Olympic spectacle. Compared to Vancouver, activists got off to a late start, and they were relatively disconnected. Police put activists on their back foot, demobilizing many through the cagey—if questionable— use of restrictive bail conditions and by intimidation through intensive militarization and the conflation of activism and criminality. Numerous activists told me that such policing tactics stultified dissent. Activist Kerry-anne Mendoza's comments were representative of this thread of thought: "You're seeing the criminalization of activists and the social stigma being applied by the authorities, by the government, and by the media all at the same time, which absolutely does have an effect on the way that protesters are listened to by their fellow citizens."[171]

Numerous activists I interviewed highlighted the fact that Twitter and Facebook allowed them to convey information at great speed, but no one explicitly breached the emotional possibilities of social media, and only a handful explicitly acknowledged the downsides. While the perils of the digital enclosure were foregrounded in Vancouver, they ghosted in the background in London. Notwithstanding the aforementioned efforts of the Reclaim Shakespeare Company, a great deal of the social-media work done by anti-Olympics activists in London was more informational than emotional. In studying the Egyptian rebellion, the *indignado* protests in Spain, and Occupy Wall Street, Gerbaudo found that the most effective use of social media rode two simultaneous tracks: fomenting personal, emotional connections and facilitating information-drenched public dialogues. The construction of *"emotional tension"* and the advancement of *"emotional attraction"* are vital to translating online activity to offline action. If he is correct in his assertion that social media can provoke the *"emotional condensation* of the people around a common identity,"* then activists in London could have made better use of Twitter and Facebook to foster emotional connection with the cause.[172] Although numerous activists in London pointed to the positive possibilities of social media, few articulated their disadvantageous flipside. To be sure, Agent Maxwell noted that social-media interventions "can become background noise" since the social-media juggernaut never stops. And, he surmised, something actually happens to information once it is transmitted: the social-media process "seems to fetishize—if you've seen it on Twitter, it's become a thing" of the past.[173] Also Mendoza deftly pointed to the crux of Gerbaudo's contention that social media must inspire on-the-ground dissent in public space. She told me:

> There are people, I think, who divert all their attention to social media and feel like because we've Tweeted, we've expressed our dissent. And that's to take nothing from those people who are doing that. I would rather they were Tweeting their dissent than not doing their dissent at all, but I think the bottom line is that we do actually need people on the streets visible to the authorities that are putting through these laws, that are putting through these policies of austerity, they need to see us. We need to get in the way, disrupt the traffic, literally bring the country to a stop for a moment so that people can in that pause, say, "Do you realize what's happening to our country?" and have that heard. That doesn't happen as effectively on Twitter because you're essentially talking to people who agree.[174]

Yet, activists deploying social media were also talking to the authorities who were interested in squelching their dissent. While I asked nearly every activist I interviewed in London for their assessment of social media in the emergent repertoires of contention, very few offered a critical appraisal that involved the surveillance capacities of the police and corporate entities.

The political opportunity structure that activists faced in London was not propitious. The summer was a perfect storm of patriotic nationalism. First there was Queen Elizabeth's Diamond Jubilee celebrating her sixtieth year on the throne. This was followed by soccer's intensely nationalist European Cup, and then the Olympics where "Team GB" did remarkably well, earning a serious medal haul. This amounted to a wet blanket of conservatism that pervaded British discourse and put a damper on dissent. Such conditions decreased the possibility of activists achieving the crucial aspects of collective action such as mobilizing support from potentially sympathetic bystander publics. And campaigners were never fully able to carve out the tactical freedom to pursue social-change goals. Instead they were perpetually on the defensive.[175]

Nonetheless, to a degree, activists in London employed humor effectively to spotlight the Olympic underbelly. Agent Maxwell of the Space Hijackers described the use of wit as a one-two punch: "First, it's for the people who are involved and secondly, it's for the people you're trying to talk to." He continued:

> It's just much more fun to do funny, silly things, basically. On the other side of it, you're able to talk to a lot more people than you otherwise might be able to if you were a bit more earnest. Humor is a double-edged sword sometimes. If you say something in a sarcastic way, it's almost as if you have to have two conversations with people. The first one is where you're telling them the silly joke where you get their attention. And the second one is when they say, "Okay, so what's your actual point?" And that's when you say, "Okay, that was our joke, but this is what we really mean." Sometimes people can feel a bit defensive like you're trying to take the piss out of them, like they're the butt of the joke. It's delicate to be sure that the humor is constructed in such a way that your target audience doesn't feel like they're the butt of the joke. Then joke is always the target of your action, and that's something we find challenging at times.[176]

The counter-Olympics campaign in London points to both the advantages and limits of humor. If creating a tantalizing spectacle is not connected to material gains or large mobilizations that forge a path for social change, then in a way it's just vapor.

Humor-oriented interventions helped press toward a number of pre-conditions of collective action, allowing campaigners to maintain solidarity while attracting a few new recruits. The actions also nurtured activist leaders, as certain people stepped up to head specific actions, meetings, and campaigns. Activists' relationship to the mass media was complicated: on one hand they were able to generate relatively favorable media coverage, but on the other hand they were unable to obtain sustained media attention that was critical of the Games.[77] The interrelation between Olympics activists and the mainstream media will be taken up in full in the following chapter.

4

Media and the Olympics

———————————————●

The Olympics have become one of the glitziest global media extravaganzas. Over the years, the fees for media rights to cover the Games have ballooned as have the sheer number of journalists from around the globe who attend the Games to cover them. Merely 11 reporters covered the 1896 Olympics in Athens, whereas approximately 20,000 journalists descended on the international media center in London for the 2012 Summer Games.[1] The BBC alone allocated 765 journalists to cover the event full-time, surpassing the number of athletes on Team GB by more than 200. It justified its immense output of journalistic humanpower by suggesting that covering the Olympics fulfilled its remit for public service by bringing together people and nations. Meanwhile NBC sent a whopping 2,800 people to London to report on the Olympics.[2] Other media organizations from around the world flock to the Games to cover events for their home countries and—thanks in large part to the Internet—for global audiences, too. A great deal of this coverage is straight-up sports fare, and much of it in the predictable rhythms of victory and defeat. However, in the lead-up to the Games, mass-media outlets often offer news consumers significant coverage that explores the political and economic complexities of hosting the Olympics. As we have seen, the Olympic Games provide activists with a unique opportunity to express their dissent. In this chapter I examine mainstream press coverage of activism vis-à-vis the Vancouver Winter Olympics and London Summer Games. The exceptionality of the Games is reflected in media coverage of activism, which in many ways diverges significantly from coverage of other protester efforts.

The news media influence political discourse surrounding the Games, giving the public cues about what issues are important. Helen Jefferson Lenskyj notes, "The mass media undoubtedly play a central role in keeping the Olympics in the news and disseminating information on Olympic issues."[3] Media outlets help set the political agenda through both the amount of coverage they offer and the types of portrayals—or frames—they ante up. As mentioned in chapter 1, activists and their adversaries engage in "framing contests" whereby political actors attempt to persuade the general public, political elites, and the media that their political beliefs are the correct ones. Such contestation is bounded by the political opportunity structure of the time and geography. The mass media serve the pivotal role as the referee in this discursive battle. In short, when it comes to the Olympic Games, media absolutely matter.

Covering Dissent in Vancouver

Activists in Vancouver knew that for many people, the Olympics rank high on the happy meter, earning approval ratings that politicians would envy. The Olympics' popularity complicated the task of openly discussing—and indeed critiquing—the political-economic underbelly of the Games. Yet campaigners pressed ahead, attempting to portray the Games as a corporate juggernaut whizzing through town at taxpayer expense and promising public debt and social dislocation in its wake. Activists engaged in a framing contest with Olympic officials and their boosters. Nicolien Van Luijk and Wendy Frisby note that Olympic supporters put forth "three dominant logics" to frame the issue in their favor: Olympism, security, and sport-based nationalism. Meanwhile, protestors "reframed these logics with two main counter-logics of civil liberties and corporatization."[4] As we have seen, dissident citizens carried out an array of mediagenic protest actions leading up to and during the Olympic Games. A closer look at press coverage of these actions reveals some baseline patterns of how the media tend to cover Olympics-induced dissent.

John Horne and Garry Whannel assert, "In the build up to any Olympic Games the media coverage is often focused on two central questions: 'will it go over budget?' and 'will the facilities be ready in time?' The answer to both questions is usually 'yes.'"[5] Indeed, in the case of Vancouver, the answers to both questions were affirmative. The Games had gone far over budget, a fact that activists emphasized to their advantage. Yet Vancouver organizers had learned from previous Olympic construction debacles—such as Montreal in 1976 where Olympic infrastructure building went down to the wire—and completed its facilities well in advance of the opening ceremony, rendering moot that potential avenue of criticism.

To collect a dataset of articles, a research assistant and I carried out a Lexis-Nexis search from January 29 (two weeks before the opening ceremonies) through March 1 (the day after the closing ceremony), using the search terms "anti-Olympic" or "Olympic" and "protest." We drew from six prominent, influential newspapers, three in the United States—the *New York Times,* the *Washington Post,* and *USA Today*—and three in Canada—the *Vancouver Sun,* the *Vancouver Province,* and the *Globe and Mail.*

In covering Olympic activism at the 2010 Winter Olympics in Vancouver, two prominent patterns emerged. First, US coverage was anemic and strikingly superficial, offering only nine relevant articles in the three national-level press outlets. Furthermore, the US press by and large adopted what Christopher Shaw calls "the Olympic frame," which foregrounds the notion that the Olympics inspire world peace and kindle global compassion and understanding while tiptoeing around the political complexities that animate activist resistance. Shaw asserts that the IOC—abetted by local organizing committees and the media—has unstintingly reproduced this frame for decades.[6]

The Olympic frame redounded through US coverage of the 2010 Winter Games. The US press coverage that did emerge was strikingly superficial. The *New York Times* parachuted journalists into Vancouver to capture images of the intense poverty in the Downtown Eastside—Canada's poorest postal code—without sufficiently explaining *why* such poverty exists.[7] Meanwhile, *USA Today* chalked up the Olympics' inauspicious start—a lack of snow, the tragic death of a Georgian luger—to a "run of terrible luck." Olympics activism was reduced to "a daily dose of glass-smashing protesters in the downtown streets." Blending cliché and rote analysis, the newspaper also pointed to "the unflinchingly optimistic spirit of the host nation" and quoted an academic who expounded on "the kindness and demeanor of the Canadian people, the beauty of their city and constant reminder that sports can indeed unite diverse people."[8] The *Washington*

Post ran a story about US figure skater Johnny Weir, who alleged receiving threats from animal activists because of his penchant for wearing fur. The skater was offered space to air his accusations, while the purported antifur activists were not sourced. Weir said, "All these crazy fur people. Security-wise, to stay in a hotel would be very difficult. There have been threats against me. I didn't want to get hurt." The article then pivoted to a discussion of activism on the streets, describing the vandalism of the Heart Attack march without explaining why stores like Hudson's Bay Company might be targeted. The article only noted, "The protest was organized by the Olympic Resistance Network to 'disturb business as usual' on the first day of the Games. The network is an umbrella group for a dozens [*sic*] of causes surrounding the Games, ranging from environmental concerns to economic issues."[9] As a whole, the US press abdicated its responsibility to cover dissent north of the border, punting the possibility to the Canadian media.

Media coverage in the host city, on the other hand, was complex and relatively robust. Over the time period under consideration, the *Vancouver Sun,* the *Vancouver Province,* and the *Globe and Mail* produced seventy-six articles. These articles formed the second significant pattern of coverage—three sequential phases: (1) pre-Olympic stories that included space for dissent; (2) articles appearing once the Olympics began in which journalists slipped into the well-worn ruts of activist denunciation, and; (3) articles appearing toward the end of the Games that praised the police and championed the Olympics as a success.

In the first phase of Canadian coverage of Olympic dissent, activists managed to successfully piggyback off the Games to bring attention to their ideas and issues. Before athletes skied the slopes and hit the halfpipes, activists were relatively successful in placing their issues under the media spotlight. Protesters benefited from the attention the Olympics brought to Vancouver, often achieving substantive coverage. A *Globe and Mail* article featured the advocacy of Rev. Ric Mathews who suggested a radical repurposing of Olympic funding for intractable social issues.[10] The *Vancouver Province* wrote about a creative "border guide" intervention where activists offered tips for getting across the border with less hassle (one tip was to don a Canadian hockey jersey).[11] The *Globe and Mail* reported positively on another innovative action where activists wrapped yellow crime-scene caution tape around a building where Prime Minister Stephen Harper was making an appearance, noting that East Vancouver MP Libby Davies publicly supported the act.[12] Outspoken Olympics critics like Harsha Walia were afforded space on the op-ed pages of the *Vancouver Sun* to present substantive criticism while discussing a logical yet "rapidly creeping sense of dread" as the Games swerved into town.[13]

Journalists turned to anti-Olympics campaigners for insight and analysis. Alissa Westergard-Thorpe of the Olympic Resistance Network told the *Globe and Mail,* "Our impact will be to have our voice heard, to try and counter some of the corporate sanitization of Vancouver. . . . The most we can hope for is to disrupt the corporate image control."[14] In that, the activists succeeded, at least before the Olympic cauldron was lit, which is no small task on the corporate media terrain. Activists benefited from years of organizing and the media's inability to resist the sharp juxtaposition between Olympic affluence and abject poverty. The 2008 economic collapse also created a context where so-called public-private partnerships were questionable, as the government was forced to swoop in and rescue faltering corporate developers. These contradictions were too much for the media to ignore—they opened up spaces of dissent. As columnist Gary Mason put it in an essay for the *Globe and Mail,* "You don't have to be a disciple of dissent to be dismayed at the amount of money being spent on security for the Vancouver Olympics."[15]

In the second phase of coverage the press demonstrated that old journalistic habits die hard, or at the least that the professional norms and values of journalism carry weight. Once the Olympic Games began, media coverage changed and dissent's news hole shriveled. The Canadian media clicked into autopilot, resorting to boilerplate protest coverage, with activists branded as violent, whiny, disruptive malcontents putting forth a dizzying array of complaints. A Simon Fraser University criminology professor summed up the general sentiment in the press when he wrote in the *Vancouver Sun* that "it's time to join the party. None of our issues of concern are going to disappear from the political agenda, and raising them now as part of an anti-Olympic agenda—confronting the dedication, effort, and joy of athletic excellence—seems to be little more than a display of misplaced anger or sulky self-indulgence."[16] The idea that activists were undercutting hard-working athletes pervaded the media narrative.

In addition to this, the characterization of "misplaced anger" became commonplace after the previously described diversity-of-tactics protest event on February 13—dubbed by activists as the "2010 Heart Attack"—that resulted in broken plate-glass windows at corporations like the

Hudson's Bay Company. Rather than exploring what "diversity of tactics" meant or why corporations might be targeted for protest, the media, by and large, took the road more traveled, repeatedly equating the vandalism with "violence." Full-throttle denigration of activists was also common. After the Heart Attack March, which was designed to clog the arteries of capitalism, the *Vancouver Province* described the window-smashers as "hateful morons" and "goofballs" who "didn't even do a decent impression of genuine anarchists." The author added, "These people weren't legitimate protesters."[17] The *Globe and Mail* reduced march participants to "[a] loosely organized group of 'thugs' from central Canada promoting anarchy" although the article also gave space for Westergard-Thorpe to explain that Hudson's Bay was not a random target since it "has a long history of violent colonialism."[18] Meanwhile, the *Vancouver Province* forwarded the thesis that "[t]he problem in Vancouver is that the protest movement has been hijacked by pea-brained anarchists and other perpetual malcontents, such as the window-smashing clowns who marred the second day of the Olympics. These punks not only spoil the Games for others, they force Canadian taxpayers to fork out millions for extra security and threaten the very existence of our fragile democracy."[19] A letter writer echoed the *Province* narrative, calling protesters "cowardly losers in masks busting windows." While he claimed to be sensitive to the critique of Olympics overspending, he wrote, "once it was a done deal it was time to get on board."[20]

Vancouver Sun columnist Stephen Hume got particularly exercised over the window smashing, labeling the glass breaking "acts of violence." He also painted a bright line dividing "good protesters" and "bad protesters," claiming that smashing windows and then fleeing was "on the same moral continuum as those who try to get their way by heaving bricks through people's windows at midnight, by writing poisonous hate mail, phoning anonymous threats or secretly maiming a farmer's livestock or killing someone's pets to make a point." Hume even went as far as to compare anti-Olympics protesters to the Ku Klux Klan, concluding that the activists' "specious attacks on one group's civil liberties, purportedly in defence of someone else's" was a "sorry human tradition" that deserved unabashed denunciation.[21] Although activist Westergard-Thorpe asserted in the *Globe and Mail,* "Property damage is not the same as physical violence," her proposition was drowned out by a chorus of condemnation that argued the exact opposite.[22]

In the spirit of deprecation, Doug Ward of the *Vancouver Sun* rebuked the "violent tactics of the black-bloc anarchists, a fringe subculture within a fringe political sub-culture" before highlighting how such tactics "splintered the unity of the far-left anti-Olympic protest against the 'Olympic industry'" and "further marginalized the Olympic Resistance Network."[23] The newspapers never entertained the possibility that agent provocateurs infiltrated the march, even though police openly admitted they were covertly joining activist groups.[24] This despite the Vancouver Integrated Security Unit's refusal to promise the British Columbia Civil Liberties Association it wouldn't infiltrate the movement or break the law disguised as activists. And it was only activists who were portrayed as "violent," not the police who used batons and other physical means to subdue protesters. Nor was structural poverty and its attendant misery ever framed as "violence."

As we have seen, the violence label was supplemented with flat-out name-calling, which was in full swing before any glass was smashed. The *Vancouver Province* dubbed anti-Olympics activists as "radical fringe groups" and "hardcore nutters."[25] The *Vancouver Sun* portrayed the Olympic Resistance Network as a "churlish and sophomoric" group whose dissent "is not only farcical but gratuitous, a lame excuse to feed its insatiable appetite for complaint."[26] On top of this, protesters were regularly accused of whining. As Barbara Yaffe put it in the *Vancouver Sun,* "Can't the whiner and grumble-bunnies hold their tongues even on a special occasion, and allow Harper to relax and cheer on the home team?"[27] In an op-ed titled "Stop Whining: Just Enjoy the Games" Hume caricatured activism as "an insufferable grump" who is "mewling about the Winter Games." The Games were happening in Vancouver, so "Complaining about the inevitable and the unchangeable is just a self-indulgent waste of energy and it gets boring real fast." Therefore, expressing dissent about the Olympics meant "trying to make the experience as unpleasant as possible" for everyone.[28] When protesters condemned so-called safe assembly zones or free-speech zones, instead calling them "protest pens," the journalists dismissed activists for complaining since the areas didn't provide any outward "evidence of coercion."[29] This misses the point that all of Canada is supposed to be a free-speech zone. Section Two of the Canadian Charter of Rights and Freedoms guarantees "fundamental freedoms" like free expression, freedom of association, and freedom of peaceful assembly.

Protesters were also portrayed as having a laundry list of disconnected, single issues. They were "a magnet for countless causes."[30] An op-ed for the *Globe and Mail* commented about Westergard-Thorpe, "Any temptation to admire her dedication to the cause was negated by the fact that it was nearly impossible to discern what the cause is. Interpreting ancient Sanskrit might be easier."[31] The media tended to view the interconnection of dissident grievances as a sign of weakness rather than solidaristic strength. While anti-Olympics demonstrators were sometimes given the chance to articulate their criticism, the Canadian media regularly offered ample space to critique the critics, and often without affording activists a chance to respond. For instance, the *Vancouver Sun* published a single-source story featuring a Vancouver city councilor who shredded the protesters' agenda.[32]

In the third phase of Canadian press coverage of Olympics activism, journalists praised the work of security officials and assured readers that the Olympics were a success for Canada as a nation. As the Games came to a close, a "Good Cop, Bad Protester" dynamic emerged with a dash of Canadian nationalism. Activists' concerns over civil liberties were depicted as overblown and all for naught. After observing that "[i]n the absence of terrorism, the $900-million security force had time to help local police in responding to domestic protests," the *Globe and Mail* noted that after the Heart Attack March, "the protests failed to attract much attention."[33] Security forces, on the other hand, glided down the press-paved road of appreciation, with the *Vancouver Sun* asserting the Vancouver Police Department "won a gold medal" for their restrained conduct.[34] Although police were besieged by "an onslaught of visitors and protesters,"[35] they remained "gentle"[36] and "admirably restrained."[37] One essay in the *Vancouver Province* even featured a letter of thanks written by a protester to police, which ostensibly said, "I have never been surrounded by so many gentle men in my life. . . . Your men were continuously insulted and spat upon, screamed at. At no time did I see any of them respond with anything but civility and politeness. Thank you is simply not enough to show you my gratitude, respect and, above all, admiration."[38] It's hard to imagine a more positive portrayal of the police being written by the Vancouver Police Department public relations office.

As one might expect, the press rallied to defend the Olympics as a success for the host city and the country more broadly. The fact that the Canadian hockey team won gold helped generate a positive assessment, but the plaudits extended beyond the rink. Under the headline "Scoffs and Sneers Can't Break Our Cheers: Games Win Gold," the *Vancouver Sun*'s indefatigable Games booster Stephen Hume wrote, "instead of the nadir of disaster some predicted and a few wished for . . . the Vancouver Games have been an apex event" and "a remarkable unifying force in a country of often fractured and regionalized national identity."[39] Others made the claim that the national unity extended to Canada's Aboriginal population, which was described as keen on the way the Games played out. The *Globe and Mail* reported, "while there have been a few angry native protesters, with placards saying, 'No Olympics on stolen land,' the face overwhelmingly shown to the world has been happy." To many First Nations people this seemed like a conspicuous airbrushing, but it gelled with the predominant media narrative that the Games were a unifying success.[40] In this swirl of affirmative news coverage the Canadian press missed the fact that alternative media and social media were playing a key role in the unfolding of protest. The mainstream press never mentioned the crucial organizing being done out of the VIVO Media Arts Center. And it ignored the crucial, blow-by-blow documentary work of the Vancouver Media Co-op. The press also disregarded the Olympic Resistance Network's transnational connections to the broader Global Justice Movement. As such, the media overlooked what Jennifer Earl and Katrina Kimport describe as the "dramatic potentialities" of online activism in terms of the important "possibilities of low-cost participation in and production of protest" that free protesters from the historical handcuffs of physical copresence.[41] In a sense, the mainstream media missed an essential element of the activist scoop.

Coverage of the Games in Vancouver highlights the US press's penchant for circumventing dissent as well as a qualitative longitudinal pattern. Building from this foundation, it is important to carry out systematic quantitative analysis to ascertain satisfying answers to central questions: What are the predominant frames that media employ when covering Olympics-related dissent? Also, which sources do media turn to for information? After all, these sources influence which frames predominate. Did pro-Olympics boosters colonize media space? Were Olympics critics afforded discursive space to voice their grievances? Below I carry out systematic analysis that uncovers the dominant frames employed by the press in covering protest and dissent at the 2012 London Olympics. I also determine whose views dominated the news. But first, let's take a closer look at some key concepts from media studies.

Framing, Journalistic Norms, and Indexing

As mentioned in chapter 1, media framing is the process by which journalists organize the whirling swirl of empirical reality into consumable news packages. In this research stream, journalists place figurative picture frames around the ever-moving target of events and actions, thereby focusing our attention on particular issues, ideas, and individuals while obscuring what lies outside the frame. Through such framing processes journalists yield *media frames* that organize events and issues into a consumable information packet for the general public. As defined in chapter 1, frames are consistent, coherent bundles of information that journalists provide to instill real-world events with structure and meaning. Media frames organize issues and offer interpretive cues, pointing both backward at what happened and forward to what it all means. Thus, frames are analytical constructs with normative implications, which is highlighted by Robert Entman's definition of framing: "selecting and highlighting some facets of events or issues, and making connections among them so as to promote a particular interpretation, evaluation, and/or solution."[42] Media frames are not neutral.

When political actors engage in framing contests they are more successful if they are able to pass their claims through two filters: cultural resonance and journalistic norms. If a group's or individual's claims resonate with established political culture, they are more likely to be converted into a media frame, especially if they cohere with the journalistic norms and values that guide news production (more on these norms in a moment). Therefore activists often attempt to represent themselves in ways that chime with the predominant octaves of political history and that are sufficiently compelling to journalists and their ingrained newsmaking predilections, organizational dictates, and temporal pressures.

In this process of news production, journalists are of vital importance, as they decide what is culturally resonant and what is not. As both public processors of information and as producers of media frames, they create interpretive representations of reality that are rooted in the norms, values, and routines of newsgathering. These norms constitute a vital filter in the frame-construction process, influencing what becomes news as well as the ways the content of that news gets shaped.

Previously, a coauthor and I have delineated "first order norms" as personalization, dramatization, and novelty, highlighting that personalities, conflict, and newness are baseline generators of political news. This means when conflict exists between well-known political personalities, media coverage is almost sure to ensue and that the cliché "if it's not new, it's not news" still maintains relevance in contemporary journalism. These concatenating norms not only trigger the "second order" norm of balance—telling "both" sides of the story—but also the authority-order norm, whereby journalists turn to authority figures as sources who assure the public that sociopolitical issues will be addressed in short order.[43] The tendency to turn to authority figures—or, "official sources"—for their political opinions is a deeply ingrained facet of news coverage as is the related tendency towards indexing, whereby media coverage is bracketed—or indexed—according to the range of views and policies found within the corridors of institutional power. In other words, the discursive bandwidth, as demarcated by the media, correlates with the amount of disagreement among policymaking elites.[44] This, in a feedback loop of sorts, is related to the "first-order" norms of dramatization and personalization.

Although mass-media scholars typically apply indexing to foreign-policy issues,[45] in this chapter I argue the concept is also relevant to intermestic affairs like the Olympics since the Games have causes and consequences that are interwoven into both domestic and international affairs.[46] In other words, I extend the concept's use, carrying out source analysis on the terrain of Olympic studies. By deploying the media-studies concept of indexing—or linking "story frames to the range of sources and viewpoints within official decision circles, reflecting levels of official conflict and consensus"—I am able to gauge who is allowed into the conversation and who is left out, and how this selection process affects the creation of media frames.[47]

Methodology

The empirical data for this study derive from eight influential newspapers in the United Kingdom and United States. The four prominent British newspapers span the political spectrum, from the right-of-center *Daily Mail* and *Daily Telegraph* to the left-of-center *Guardian* and *Independent*.[48] The US sources under consideration are the *New York Times, USA Today,* the *Wall Street Journal,* and the *Washington Post.* The Audit Bureau of Circulations listed the *Wall Street Journal, USA Today,* and the *New York Times* as the top three most circulated daily newspapers in the United States in early 2012. The *Washington Post* appeared in the number eight slot on the list, and was included in this analysis to get representation from the US capital, given the nationalist stakes of the Games.[49] The influence of these newspapers goes beyond direct readership: many television outlets and other print publications take their cues from these agenda-setting newspapers. Newspapers also tend to cover the Olympics more as a news event than simply a set of entertainment stories.[50] While television has played an important role in the popularization and proliferation of the Olympics, newspapers are also a vital source of primary historical data, though not one that can be uncritically accepted at face value.[51] The eight newspapers in this study have also made the transition to the Internet, making their articles available online in differing degrees.

In order to capture coverage in the lead-up to the Games, the actual Olympics, and the aftermath, the time frame stretched from 1 June 2012 (a full six weeks before the Olympics) through 26 August 2012 (two weeks after the Games concluded). The databases were Lexis-Nexis (for the *New York Times, USA Today,* and the *Washington Post*), ProQuest (for the *Wall Street Journal*), and the newspapers' websites (for the *Daily Mail,* the *Daily Telegraph,* the *Guardian,* and the *Independent*). In order to capture the breadth of Games coverage, the search term was "Olympics."[52] After securing a wide pool of articles, a research assistant and I whittled down the dataset to only include articles that dealt with Olympics politics in some way; we excluded articles that solely covered sport.

Table 1 summarizes the breakdown of the dataset for articles on London 2012 Olympics politics. US sources contributed a third (33 percent) of the articles, while the host country's newspapers churned out two-thirds of the overall coverage (67 percent). Of the US press, the *New York Times* (11 percent) and *Wall Street Journal* (10 percent) led the way, while in Britain, the *Telegraph* (22 percent) and *Independent* (20 percent) offered the most articles, with the *Guardian* (18 percent) close behind.

As Reg Gratton notes, "The media do more than report on the events and performances of the Games; they also make numerous judgments about the host country and its society and how well the Games have been organised."[53] The articles on Olympics politics broke down into ten distinct themes: (1) Olympics economics; (2) corporate sponsor politics; (3) policing and security; (4) feminism, sexism, and gender equality; (5) infrastructure readiness; (6) the politics of tickets to events; (7) geopolitical relations; (8) media issues, both mainstream media and social media; (9) Olympic

Table 1
Dataset for Olympics Politics, London 2012

Source	Number of articles	Percentage of dataset
New York Times	247	11%
USA Today	127	5%
Wall Street Journal	237	10%
Washington Post	163	7%
Daily Mail	156	7%
Guardian	414	18%
Independent	463	20%
Telegraph	503	22%
Total	2,310	100%

legacy; and (10) activism and protest. A research assistant and I analyzed the 2,310 news articles in order to isolate articles that mentioned protest or activism. This included union activism, the efforts of grassroots activists, and athletes who engaged in protest.[54]

Of the articles on the politics of the Olympics, only 151 included two sentences or more about activism or protest. This translated to 6.5 percent of the overall dataset. Table 2 breaks down the minidataset of articles on protest by media outlet. While US newspapers provided 33 percent of Olympics politics coverage, they only contributed 11.5 percent of the protest-related articles.

Table 2
Dataset for Activism and Protest, London 2012

Source	Number of articles	Percentage of dataset
New York Times	6	4%
USA Today	4	3%
Wall Street Journal	7	4%
Washington Post	1	0.5%
Daily Mail	18	12%
Guardian	36	24%
Independent	48	32%
Telegraph	31	20.5%
Total	151	100%

A research assistant and I then created and independently read a thirty-one-article minisample, noting all emergent frames. For the sake of parsimony, we compacted related tropes, resulting in four predominant frames: the Principled Grievance Frame, the Disruption Frame, the Criminality Frame, and the Freak Frame. We also coded for the Amalgam of Grievances Frame, due to the frame's prevalence in previous media coverage of dissent.[55] After achieving inter-coder reliability we analyzed the 151 news articles that covered activism and dissent. In the discussion of each frame below, I offer the frame definitions we employed when coding.

Media Coverage of Protest and Activism in London

In covering Olympics stories that in some way involved protest and activism, the British and US media deployed two dominant frames: the Principled Grievance Frame (54 percent of all articles) and the Disruption Frame (47 percent of all articles).[56] The most widely used frame—the Principled Grievance Frame—affirmed the legitimacy of the activists' claims, placing them within the scope of acceptable political discourse. As we shall see, even the Disruption Frame—that activists could interrupt the smooth machinations of the Olympics with their dissent—was not always used in purely deprecatory fashion. Nevertheless, two denigrating frames did emerge in the data: a Criminality/Corruption Frame (9 percent) whereby activists were depicted as engaging in illegality or malfeasance and a Freak Frame (3 percent) whereby protesters were portrayed as outside the mainstream in terms of outward appearance or ideology. In other words, these activists were described as culturally incongruent. Quite remarkably, though, not a single story contained what social-movement scholars call an Amalgam of Grievances Frame whereby activists are alleged to hold a hodgepodge of loose-knit grievances that translates into a lack of a unified message.[57] This absence is notable, especially in light of the fact that anti-Olympics groups like the Counter Olympics Network featured numerous, disparate strands of activism spanning different issues and holding diverse goals. Overall, these findings—in their generally affirmative orientation toward activism—diverge markedly from previous research on union activism and grassroots activism where activists were more commonly deprecated, delegitimized, and therefore undermined.[58] Figure 4.1 summarizes the results. Below I will explain these anomalous findings by highlighting the political context of the London 2012 Olympics and by offering specific examples of each frame as it appeared in the press.

Principled Grievance Frame

The Principled Grievance Frame was the most common frame in this study, with more than half the articles (54 percent) describing the activists' grievances—or allowing activists to do so themselves—without immediately undercutting the claims or outright dismissing them. In other words, with this frame, the ideas and opinions of activists were nestled comfortably between the media-generated brackets of permissible discourse.

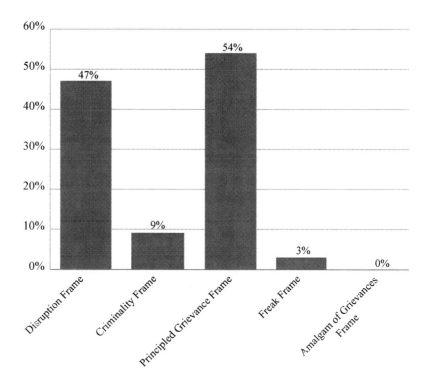

FIGURE 4.1 Framing Activism: The predominant frames deployed by UK and US media sources covering political activism in the context of the London 2012 Games. Compiled after analyzing articles from the *Daily Mail*, *Daily Telegraph*, *Guardian*, *Independent*, *New York Times*, *USA Today*, *Wall Street Journal*, and *Washington Post*.

To understand the predominance of this frame, it is important to note that many of the articles in the dataset covered union activism. There was a plethora of high-profile labor actions in the lead-up to the Games. The month before the Olympics started, thousands of bus workers with the Unite union threatened to strike unless they received a £500 bonus. Meanwhile, London Underground workers with the Rail, Maritime, and Transport Workers union (RMT) voted to strike. In July, the National Farmers' Union threatened to pour their milk down the drain, potentially affecting the supply chain for the Olympic Games, to protest the sharp cut in the price-per-liter paid to farmers. The Public and Commercial Services Union (PCS) represented warders at the National Gallery who threatened to strike, beginning the first day of the Games. Representing border officials at Heathrow Airport, PCS also threatened to strike over working conditions and the privatization of the civil service. As mentioned in the previous chapter, taxi drivers engaged in numerous actions on a parallel track, deliberately clogging the roads in order to spotlight the special Olympic driving lanes—so-called Zil lanes—that were set up for Olympic officials, athletes, and corporate sponsors to the detriment of maximum taxi mobility.

In *Framed!: Labor and the Corporate Media,* Christopher Martin asserts, "When the news media cover labor, they don't do so by communicating 'neutral' facts but by telling us stories about labor, especially stories that shape and reflect our culture's commonsense ideas about labor, management, and capital." Furthermore, he argues, news media forge "a 'common ground' narrative between labor and management positions" by angling in on labor relations from the perspective of the consumer, thereby replacing the public sphere—where citizens can engage in rational, critical debate—with the consumer sphere where the needs of the commercial consumer reign. In doing so he posits that "the procapitalist function of the mass media predictably involves antiunion sentiment because organized labor necessarily infringes on the decision-making power of capital and may inhibit capital's profit margins."[59] At the 2012 Olympics, even more was in play than the high-stakes, ever-present battle between labor and capital. In London, labor actions were bound up in a complex process involving nationalism and the recuperation of a tarnished imperial ruling order. Commentators and politicians wondered aloud whether the Games could re-burnish Britain's formerly hegemonic status on the global stage. This context lent more weight to the union's power to disrupt everyday life in the name of improving working conditions, one of the few leverage points the labor movement has retained in the face of its long-term diminishment. Yet, by and large, aside from the right-wing *Daily Mail*, the media proliferated very little "antiunion sentiment."

In fact, despite the unions' explicit threats to disrupt the glossy machinations of the Olympics, union activists were largely depicted with the Principled Grievance Frame. This cuts against the grain of Martin's finding that in covering major labor stories in the United States, the corporate mass media often use the "consumer is king frame" whereby uninterrupted consumption is paramount to a healthy economy and the "collective action is bad frame" whereby union activities undermine the consumer economy.[60] In London, the Principled Grievance Frame trumped these common, deprecatory tropes.

This happened in part because, thanks to the Olympics, elected officials and government bureaucrats were hamstrung. They were not free to dismiss the possibility of a strike, since they would be harshly criticized for not solving the underlying labor issues if the Olympics were affected. They were also not able to publicly denounce the unions for fear of inflaming them to the point of striking, thereby creating travel gridlock at the Games. After all, local officials were already trumpeting the idea that the Games would bring heavy traffic and a jam-packed London Underground. In the lead-up to the Olympics, London mayor Boris Johnson's voice regularly boomed over the loudspeakers at Tube stations across the city, promising dire congestion on public transportation and urging riders to either make alternative plans or travel during off hours. Also, once London bus workers accepted a bonus in mid-July and called off their strike—less than two weeks before the Games commenced—other workers had additional leverage at the table.[61] Union spokespeople stressed the fact once one union got a raise for its Olympics-induced increase in workload, it seemed perfectly reasonable that others should, too. Also, journalists made space for lucid union leaders—and occasionally the rank and file—to articulate the reasons why workers deserved a better deal.

Athletes protesting the Olympic Charter's Rule 40 were also frequently depicted using the Principled Grievance Frame. Rule 40 prevents athletes from advertising their own corporate sponsors if they are not approved Olympic partners. The rule reads: "Except as permitted by the IOC Executive Board, no competitor, coach, trainer or official who participates in the Olympic Games may allow his person, name, picture or sports performances to be used for advertising purposes during the Olympic Games."[62] According to LOCOG, Rule 40 was designed "to protect against ambush marketing; prevent unauthorized commercialisation of the Games; and to protect the integrity of athletes' performance at the Games." Therefore, "the IOC places certain limits on how a Participants' [*sic*] image can be exploited during the Games Period."[63]

The rule applied in London from 18 July through 15 August where it drew the ire of numerous prominent athletes. US track star Sanya Richards-Ross, who won gold in Athens 2004 and Beijing 2008 before emerging triumphant in the 400-meter dash in London, became a de facto spokesperson for the athlete activists. Sounding reasonable and logical, she stated, "People see the Olympic Games, when athletes are at their best but they don't see the three or four years before when many of my peers are struggling to stay in the sport. The majority of track and field athletes don't have sponsors. In the sport, a lot of my peers have second and third jobs to be able to do this. We understand that the IOC is protecting its sponsors but we want to have a voice as well."[64] Athletes took to Twitter to voice their displeasure, with US 100-meter hurdler Dawn Harper sending out a photo of herself gagged with a piece of tape that had "Rule 40" on it. Other track stars like Nike-sponsored Nick Symmonds and Jamie Nieto also used social media to critique the rule, with many writing under the hashtag #wedemandchange or #rule40.[65] The fact that big-name athletes publicly protested Rule 40 triggered the personalization, dramatization, and novelty norms, thereby making their efforts newsworthy. Additionally, these athletes' desire for even more commercialism went with the neoliberal grain, thereby making their claims culturally congruent. This was no John Carlos–Tommie Smith moment. This was a group of athletes who knew their window of opportunity for cashing in on Olympics fame was small and shutting by the day. And yet, these athletes founds themselves tucked firmly in Andrejevic's "digital enclosure"—emboldened to express their dissent through interactive media like Twitter but also hemmed in by the surveillance capacities inherent to using the technological tools of "the digerati."[66] Plus, athletes were flirting with danger, as the IOC's social-media guidelines for the London Games expressly prohibited tweets that did not "at all times conform to the Olympic spirit and fundamental principles of Olympism as contained in the Olympic Charter."[67] Rule 40 is part of the Olympic Charter.

Damien Hooper, an Aboriginal boxer from Australia, also generated some attention through his actions. He stirred up political controversy when he entered the ring for his match against USAmerican Marcus Browne wearing a T-shirt featuring the Aboriginal flag. Many viewed this as a contravention of the IOC's Rule 50: "No kind of demonstration or political, religious or racial propaganda is permitted in any Olympic sites, venues or other areas."[68] The Australian Olympic Committee publicly chastised the twenty-year-old boxer, and the IOC chose to let the National Olympic Committee deal internally with Hooper rather than dole out punishment. Hooper defended himself, saying, "I'm Aboriginal, representing my culture, not only my country but my people as well. I'm very proud and that's what I wanted to do and I'm happy I did it. I was just thinking about my family and what mattered to me. It made my whole performance a lot better."[69] Yet he also agreed to not wear the shirt into the ring in future bouts. Journalists gave Hooper latitude, thanks to his age and the fact that he opted to back down and not continue to don the shirt. The IOC's soft touch contributed to the notion that the breach of Olympic protocol was a minor nuisance—not a major disruption—emanating from cultural pride, not radical politics. The IOC's approach also chimed with its predilection for multiculturalism and its stated goal to become more inclusive when it came to indigenous and Aboriginal involvement in the Games. This bundle of factors translated into a Principled Grievance Frame rather than a Disruption Frame or Freak Frame.

The press also applied the Principled Grievance Frame to a raft of small protests aimed at visiting luminaries from countries with dodgy human-rights records or histories featuring the oppression of ethnic or political minorities. For instance, just before the opening ceremonies, Tamil dissidents living in exile in the UK staged demonstrations over the planned presence of Sri Lankan president Mahinda Rajapaksa at the Games. The president was accused of atrocities in the 2009 war that defeated the Tamil Tigers. The article featured two grassroots activists who were allowed to lay out their critique without rebuttal. One said, "There is credible evidence that his government is responsible for ethnically motivated crimes against humanity and continuing persecution of other ethnic and religious groups in Sri Lanka. Just this week we released a report showing how government institutions such as the police and military under his command are involved in a systematic network of politically motivated disappearances as well as abduction for ransom." The article did not question or undercut these assertions, placing them within the boundaries of acceptable discourse.[70] President Alassane Ouattara of the Ivory Coast similarly faced protesters upon arriving in London for the Games. Demonstrators were depicted as sensible and forthright, although pro-Ouattara voices were able to counter the president's negative depiction, if in vague terms.[71]

Yet when it came to applying the Principled Grievance Frame to protesters with foreign roots, the press had its limits. A spate of stories that appeared in the *Daily Mail* and the *Telegraph* in late June 2012 alleged that a band of disgruntled "hooligans" from Argentina planned to travel to London with a flag for the Falkland Islands. After "receiving intelligence" that visiting Argentineans intended to "use the Games to highlight an Argentine campaign for sovereignty over the islands," they also reported that Argentine athletes might "put on a black power-style protest" like Carlos and Smith did in 1968. The British authorities went to the IOC asking for assurance that athletes would not be allowed to engage in symbolic political acts at the Games. Olympic officials and unidentified representatives from the Foreign and Commonwealth Office were given the opportunity to speak out again such alleged plans, though not a single Argentinean was interviewed.[72] In the end, these supposed thugs and fist-pumping athletes never materialized.

Disruption Frame

The Disruption Frame appeared in 47 percent of the articles in the protest dataset. The Disruption Frame was coded when journalists described activist actions as disturbing or potentially interfering with the Olympic Games or the lives of regular, law-abiding (and nonprotesting) citizens. As mentioned previously, the former is reasonable, since the unions' (sometimes explicitly stated) strength came from the possibility of interrupting the smooth flow of the Games. However, the latter is less sensible, since disrupting the lives of the general populace was not a stated objective of the unions or any grassroots activist group. The context of the Olympics created a unique scenario whereby the media's use of the Disruption Frame was not necessarily a deprecatory frame; whereas usually it is when applied to activists.

Because of the state of exception inherent to hosting the Olympics, the Disruption Frame often employed by the media to make sense of labor actions carried more heft than the run-of-the-mill "consumer frame" utilized during normal political times. If the Olympics went awry on the world stage, so went the media narrative, then Britain could be badly embarrassed. The *New York Times* highlighted this line of thought. In a preview piece for the Games, the newspaper alluded to union strikes before asserting, "every day seems to bring a new humiliation in the tragicomedy that is the XXX Olympiad."[73] British officials were sensitive to such "humiliation" and spoke out forcefully to dissuade workers from striking, arguing such strikes would be "greatly disruptive" as London mayor Boris Johnson so frequently intoned.[74] The *Telegraph* led with headlines like "London Braced for Fresh Travel Chaos as Tube Workers Vote for Strike," while the *Independent* followed suit: "London Bus Strike Causes Travel Chaos."[75] The *Wall Street Journal* reported that the possible strike at Heathrow "threatens to cause chaos at Britain's borders as thousands of tourists arrive for the Olympics."[76] Home Secretary Theresa May described the possible strike at Heathrow as "shameful," arguing, "[t]hey are holding a strike on what is one of the key days for people coming into this country for the Olympic Games. I believe it is not right for them to hold a strike. They will risk damaging people's enjoyment of coming through into the UK."[77]

Predictably, the right-wing *Daily Mail* was especially critical of union activity, frontloading the Disruption Frame and adding a dash of disdain. Bus workers "caused travel misery" in London with their walkout.[78] An editorial argued that "a handful of sour union militants" viewed the Olympics as "a chance to bring maximum shame on our country, in pursuit of their selfish demands."[79] The newspaper also ran an attack piece against RMT leader Bob Crow, painting him as a union fat cat living a life of extreme privilege. The article led with a description of Crow "watching the sun set with a beer in hand" while "relaxing on a river cruise." Crow was pegged as a "hardline union leader" who was "plotting strikes that could disrupt the Olympics." The newspaper added, "The RMT boss . . . has been accused of holding the country to ransom with threats of Tube and rail strikes during the Games."[80] A *Telegraph* editorial titled "The Olympic Strike Will Bring Shame on Britain" picked up the ransom motif, writing, "The attempt by Mark Serwotka and the Public and Commercial Services Union to hold the Olympic Games to ransom is worthy of contempt." The essay concluded, "ministers must try their hardest to bring Mr Serwotka to heel (or, failing that, to prevent any disruption). But even if he succeeds in tarnishing the Olympics, he and his fellow union barons should know that their disgraceful actions will not be forgotten—or forgiven."[81] The *Wall Street Journal* piled on the ransom trope, stating, "the willingness of the Tube workers' union to hold Londoners to ransom with strike threats over its demands for Olympic bonuses" was even higher on the debacle meter than G4S's security fiasco.[82]

Stories featuring the Disruption Frame also presented a significant amount of he said/she said, balanced reporting with a union spokesperson on one side and a government official on the other. Coverage of union activism was strikingly similar across ideologically divergent newspapers, which points to the importance of the professional norms of journalism.

Criminality/Corruption Frame

Fewer than one in ten (9 percent) articles in the dataset featured the Criminality/Corruption Frame. On one hand, this frame puts activists and their actions in the news, and some campaigners live by the mantra that any coverage is good coverage. On the other hand, this frame depicts activists as engaged in a wide range of criminal activity—from criminal suspicion to public-order violations—that necessitates police intervention. The frame can conflate activism and criminality in the public sphere.

In some previous research on media coverage of activism, the Criminality Frame was widely employed.[83] But in coverage of London 2012, this frame was relatively infrequent because of the fact that very few political activists were arrested for—let alone charged with—criminal activity. London Olympics campaigners were tactically tame, forgoing transgressive contention and instead embracing contained contention that relied on well-established tactics within a legalist strategy. Protesters faced a complex political opportunity structure. On one hand, they needed to carry out creative actions that could attract the attention of the media in a city saturated with political activism. On the other hand, they had to be careful not to alienate sympathetic bystander publics with over-the-top actions that challenged a remarkably popular event where national pride was at stake. The same creative actions that might generate media interest—thanks to the professional norms of journalism—could backfire in the form of the Criminality Frame (if arrests ensued) or the Freak Frame (as discussed below). In the ever-present gamble over tactics and strategy, activists by and large took the conservative path, aiming to organize events that were family-friendly but not necessarily media-friendly.

There were two prominent episodes of contention vis-à-vis the Games that generated activist arrests, both of them described in the previous chapter: (1) the Greenwash Gold mock award ceremony in Trafalgar Square the week before the Olympics commenced, and (2) the Critical Mass cycle ride on the night of the opening ceremonies. With the arrests of environmental and social-justice activists as part of the Greenwash Gold campaign, the use of the frame was logical. But even as the frame was applied, activists were afforded the opportunity to challenge the wisdom of the arrests while lobbing critiques at the corporate targets of their ire. Former CSL member Meredith Alexander, who helped organize the protest, told the *Guardian,* "Dow, BP and Rio Tinto are spending millions to tell the public how sustainable they are. We did a 15-minute piece of theatre to reveal the truth and as a result of this piece of theatre 25 police officers turned up and six people were arrested. It is an Olympic-sized overreaction."[84] The Critical Mass cycle ride on 27 July resulted in more than 180 arrests, triggering the Criminality Frame. The *Telegraph* described how cyclists "clashed with officers" of the law who "intervened when participants allegedly breached regulations restricting their route."[85] Citing Section 12 of the 1986 Public Order Act, police snatched cyclists from their bikes, detained them on buses, and eventually processed them at a local police station. Yet some outlets, in covering the arrests, allowed activists to weigh in to critique police tactics. The *Wall Street Journal,* in an informative article that placed the arrests in the wider context of Olympics protests, quoted the Counter Olympic Network's Steve Rushton, who said, "Tonight the police criminalized cycling—cyclists were assaulted and arrested by the bus load. It's ironic that cyclists featured so heavily in the actual ceremony, too, while their real-life counterparts were being arrested just nearby."[86]

Sometimes the press employed the Criminality Frame through enthymematic reasoning or argument whereby the journalist made a number of assertions in succession while leaving a gap in the assertions that invited the reader to fill in the missing link. In other words, by creating an enthymeme—a syllogism with an unexpressed premise that leads to a logical yet unstated conclusion—the journalist led the newspaper reader to believe campaigners were engaging in corruption or criminality.[87] For instance, in a *Guardian* article about Scotland Yard's plans to make preemptive arrests in order to prevent disruptions to the Games, Assistant Commissioner Chris Allison was quoted extensively about squelching criminal activity before pivoting immediately to a discussion of protesters.

While he offered assurances activists would not be preemptively targeted, he laid the enthymematic trap: "If you want to protest, speak to us beforehand so we can manage your right to peacefully and lawfully protest," he said. "But if as an individual we think you are going to disrupt the Games in some way, then I am telling you that we will take whatever action we can within the law to prevent you from disrupting the Games, because you don't have the right to do it."[88] One Occupy London activist was not satisfied, laying bare the enthymeme: "The definition of protest currently seems to be synonymous with disruption and criminality," she told the newspaper. The *Independent* echoed this sort of enthymematic reasoning, writing, "The Met said it would not allow any demonstration to interfere with Olympic athletes or spectators." The article then quoted the paternalistic line from Scotland Yard: "We want anyone who wants to protest to come and speak to us so we can work together to ensure that their point can be made. What people do not have the right to do is to hold a protest that stops other people from exercising their own rights to go about their business."[89]

Freak Frame

When journalists employ the Freak Frame they focus on the nonmainstream values, beliefs, and opinions of dissidents, as well as their age and appearance. With this frame, the more radical elements of the movement—in terms of both outward appearance and ideology—are often transformed into a synecdoche for the entire movement. In covering activism at the London Games, the press only used the Freak Frame 3 percent of the time; compared to previously studied activist groups, this is relatively rare use of this deprecating frame. The aforementioned tactical conservatism of counter-Olympics organizers helps account for the relative dearth of this frame. In describing the mobilization and march of 28 July, Counter Olympics Network spokesman Julian Cheyne told *USA Today,* "It was very peaceful, and that makes it probably very boring for the media to cover. We've never advocated violence or bad behavior of any kind."[90] In a way, the Counter Olympics Network organizers, in attempting to come across as family friendly, forfeited addressing the vital journalistic norms of novelty and dramatization—as Cheyne himself implicitly noted—which could account for the group's minimal coverage as well as a lack of the Freak Frame.

One protest that was neither "family friendly" nor "boring"—at least not to the *Daily Mail,* the only outlet to cover the event—was a topless demonstration carried out by four Ukrainian feminists from the group Femen. Scantily clad activists splattered themselves in fake blood—to challenge the "bloody" Islamist regimes they felt the IOC too readily supported—and painted slogans like "No Sharia" on their bare upper torsos. Yet this article presented basic information about the group, offering a list of causes for which it advocates as well as quotes about its philosophy from its Facebook page.[91]

Who Did the Media Invite to the Discursive Dinner?

In order to track which sources the media turned to for analysis and commentary, I tallied up the individuals who were either directly quoted or paraphrased in the articles, slotting them into the following categories: activists (union members/leaders, grassroots activists, and athlete activists), government officials (elected and government bureaucrats), Olympic officials, representatives from private companies, security and policing officials, media personalities, pundits, and others. The results are summarized in figure 4.2.

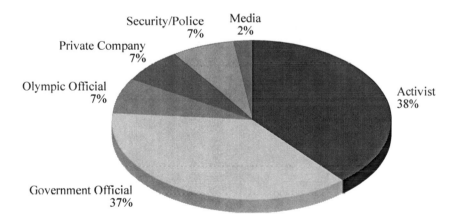

FIGURE 4.2 Media Sources: A breakdown of sources the mass media turned to for analysis and commentary. Compiled after analyzing articles from the *Daily Mail, Daily Telegraph, Guardian, Independent, New York Times, USA Today, Wall Street Journal,* and *Washington Post.*

The go-to sources for the press outlets under study were activists and government officials.[92] Activists were quoted or paraphrased 158 times in the 151-article dataset, accounting for 38 percent of all sources. Meanwhile, journalists turned to government officials 156 times, or 37 percent of the sources. The relatively high number of activists can be attributed in part to the fact that in this chapter I zero in on stories that featured at least two sentences about protest or activism. Also, campaigners often—though not always—brought novelty, drama, and personalization to the table. The prevalence of government officials can be chalked up to drama and conflict as well as the media's authority-order penchant whereby journalists consult authority figures who assure us everything will work out all right. The fact that activists and government officials appeared in nearly equal numbers points to use of the balance norm. And the primacy of activists undercuts the indexing hypothesis—at least for this small slice of protest-related Olympics coverage—in that the range of views admitted through the news gates exceeded the public authorities and "official sources."

Figure 4.3 takes a closer look at the activist sources, which broke down into three groups: union representatives (54 percent of activist sources, 20 percent of all sources); grassroots activists (35 percent of activist sources, 13.5 percent of all sources); and athlete activists (11 percent of activist sources, 4.5 percent of overall sources).[93] Union leaders and rank and file were cited at a significant clip: one of every five sources. RMT

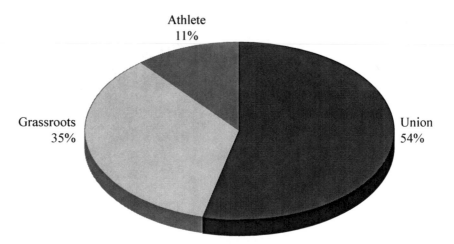

FIGURE 4.3 Activism Sources: A breakdown of activist sources. Compiled after analyzing articles from the *Daily Mail, Daily Telegraph, Guardian, Independent, New York Times, USA Today, Wall Street Journal,* and *Washington Post.*

union leader Bob Crow was quoted numerous times, as was Unite's Peter Kavanagh and Mark Serwotka of PCS. Grassroots activists from the Counter Olympics Network and Occupy London also made their way into the news. Sanya Richards-Ross was the most frequently quoted athlete activist. Of the government sources that journalists turned to for comment, 62 percent were elected officials (23 percent of all sources) and 38 percent were bureaucrats (14 percent of all sources). Elected officials were quoted more than any other source: 97 times in 151 articles. The media frequently turned to Boris Johnson, David Cameron, Jeremy Hunt, and Theresa May. Among government bureaucrats, Transport for London officials and Labor Transport spokespeople were frequent contributors, brought in to balance comments from union officials.

The IOC largely stayed above the fray, leaving protest enforcement and commentary to local Olympic police and security forces, as well as elected officials. Olympic officials made up only 7 percent of all sources. Among LOCOG's ranks, Lord Sebastian Coe was a recurrent commentator, assuring the general public that the Games were on track and promising a successful Olympics. But he was also put on the hot seat for Olympic brand micromanagement, with the *Independent* quoting him responding to a question about whether one could appear at an Olympics event in a Pepsi T-shirt even though Coca-Cola was an official Olympic sponsor: "No, you probably wouldn't be walking in with a Pepsi T-shirt because Coca-Cola are our sponsors and they have put millions of pounds into this project but also millions of pounds into grassroots sport."[94] Private companies composed 7 percent of all sources. For instance, Nick Buckles, chief of G4S, was forced to respond to his firm's failure to provide the promised 10,400 security officials, telling parliament the debacle was a "humiliating shambles."[95] Security and police officials composed another 7 percent of media sources, with Scotland Yard officials frequently consulted on policing issues vis-à-vis protests. Member of the media made up 2 percent of all sources, with one imbroglio involving a BBC presenter who was accused of emulating Fox News for his aggressive, leading questioning of Jeremy Hunt.[96] Pundits were rarely turned to for comment, comprising only 1 percent of all sources.[97]

In his seminal work on press coverage of the Vietnam War, media scholar Daniel Hallin found that "dissenters appeared in stories primarily about dissent itself while official spokespeople appeared in stories which reported the actual news."[98] Such subtle marginalization prevents dissident citizens from injecting alternative viewpoints into the discursive arena. Coverage of Olympics-related activism in London conformed to Hallin's finding, with activism or protest being the topic of 77 percent of the articles (116 out of 151). Another nine stories were Olympics overviews in which activism or protests were mentioned, while another seven were stories about security that alluded to protests or possible protests. Quite remarkably, numerous stories about political activism failed to source a single activist.[99] In sum, discussion of protest was largely cordoned off from hard-news media coverage of the Olympics—recall that of the 2,310 articles covering London Olympics politics, only 151 featured protesters (6.5 percent); and as we have just seen, a strong majority of those articles were *about* dissent. If we are to believe E. E. Schattschneider that "*the definition of the alternatives is the supreme instrument of power*," then activists did not wield much discursive power on the mediascape in the United States and United Kingdom.[100]

Of Patterns and Possibilities

The patterns of US and UK press coverage of Olympics-related protest and activism derive in part from the norms and values of news production. Yet, as Horne and Whannel point out, as the Olympic Games approach, "newsworthy possibilities depend on the specific location and political developments at the time." They go on to note, "In terms of news management by the organizing committee, the months leading up to the Games, are the most perilous period, in which negative stories can easily turn into front page dramas."[101] Indeed the run-up to the Games was "the most perilous period," but LOCOG's high-profile blunders did a great deal to open up space for dissent. For instance, the idea to place surface-to-air missile launch pads atop residential apartment buildings—and then notifying residents of this development by sliding an informational brochure under their front doors—set the table for the levelheaded dissent of the "Stop the Olympic Missiles" campaign.[102] Corporate sponsors' own goals also opened up avenues for activism. When information emerged that Adidas, the official apparel supplier for London 2012, was producing goods in factories with questionable working conditions—paying laborers thirty-four pence an hour—the door opened for activists from War on Want. Campaigners like Murray Worthy were able to articulate politically poignant contradictions to the *Telegraph:* "What's really shocking is at a time [Adidas] are spending £100 million alone on the sponsorship deal with the Olympics, never mind the additional deals with the athletes, that similar amounts of money are not being spent on real improvements in workers' rights."[103]

In the lead-up to the Games, critics inside and outside the mainstream media wedged open discursive possibilities. The mass media often reflect and reproduce social relations, but they can also assist activists in their quest to challenge the macroarrangements of power. This occurs in accordance with Ruud Koopmans and Paul Statham's concept of "discursive opportunity structure," or the conditions that shape "which ideas are considered 'sensible,' which constructions of reality are seen as 'realistic,' and which claims are held as 'legitimate' within a certain polity at a specific time."[104] In London the discursive opportunity structure was relatively propitious for campaigners. In the lead-up to the Games, British media covered Olympic missteps with sharp-toothed criticality.

Media across the political spectrum hammered away at potential problems and questionable maneuvers by Olympics honchos. The right-of-center *Daily Mail* and *Daily Telegraph* tended to zero in on questions of spending and underestimating costs, while left-of-center outlets like the *Guardian* and the *Independent* focused more on civil liberties, the militarization of the public sphere, and allegations of greenwashing. Critics chipped out political space through their scathing statements about the Games, bequeathing an opportunity to activists. Alternative media like *Red Pepper* and *Open Democracy* also helped create feasible forums for dissent. Nonetheless, London Olympics activists did not take full advantage, converting the auspicious discursive opportunity structure into boots-to-pavement dissent. On the eve of the Games, *USA Today* wrote, "Protesters are expected to be plentiful," a sentiment echoed in the *Guardian,* which posited there very well "could be a summer of protest linked to the Olympics."[105] Yet these prognostications were largely incorrect—a carnival of Olympics-induced dissent never fully emerged.

The interplay between activists and the mass media often forges a scenario where campaigners feel compelled to amp up or escalate their tactics. Escalation is both a reaction to the ability of activists' opponents to adapt to previous tactics as well as the result of the mass media's unquenchable penchant for novelty. Political activists, who are almost always disadvantaged in terms of social status and resources, often try to make up for these limitations by engaging in unique, creative actions designed to win mass-media attention. Contained, sanctioned actions are less likely to garner such attention, while novel, conflictual, personality-driven events enhance the chances of media interest. This relationship with the media creates a dialectic of escalation whereby activists feel perpetually pressed to foment protest activities that are novel and attention grabbing enough to be newsworthy. Yet, this leads to a trade-off in that such actions can be easily dismissible as gimmicky, outlandish, or zany. Also, such actions can distract target audiences or trivialize the short- and long-term goals of campaigners, thereby setting the table for mass-media deprecation.[106] In London, activists opted to engage the zeitgeist of humor-oriented, go-with-the-grain activism that could slice a viable path between tactical escalation and mass-media deprecation. In some ways they succeeded, but as we have seen, in other ways, the approach lacked the power to whip up mass mobilizations that demonstrated power in the streets.

Activists may wish they had garnered higher quantities of press coverage, but the quality of coverage they did receive was relatively affirmative when compared with prior episodes of contention—union activism and grassroots activism alike—in a range of contexts. In part this owes to the vigorous union efforts to piggyback off Olympics, using the state of exception as an extra leverage point. The unions benefited most from the unique political opportunity structure the Olympics brought; grassroots activists could have done more with the discursive space. In the end, activists were able to piggyback off the event, but they did not manage to "piggyjack" it or seize the Olympic stage to deflect attention from the Games toward political issues that mattered to them.[107] This was a missed opportunity in that the Olympics have become a massive media extravaganza. Nearly thirty years ago Whannel dubbed the Games "the ultimate media festival," a moniker that's even more valid today.[108] As such, the framing contest between activists and their pro-Games political adversaries will continue as the Olympic juggernaut heads on to Sochi and Rio.

5

Looking Ahead through
the Rearview Mirror

────────────────●

In 2011 *Time* magazine proclaimed "The Protester" as its "Person of the Year," writing, "'Massive and effective street protest' was a global oxymoron until—suddenly, shockingly—starting exactly a year ago, it became the defining trope of our times. And the protester once again became a maker of history."[1] *Time*'s quick glossing over of the South African anti-apartheid movement and the Global Justice Movement's "Battle in Seattle" is questionable. But one thing the magazine gets right is that there has been a recent resurgence in militant public-space protest around the globe and that this activism is ricocheting in transnational fashion from public park to municipal square, with movements drawing energy and inspiration from dissidents in disparate longitudinal and latitudinal coordinates. But, as we have seen, protesting the Olympic Games is complicated; the dissident reawakening that crescendoed in 2011 did not automatically convert into full-bore activism at Vancouver 2010 and London 2012. Nestled at the nexus of sports politics and critical research on the Olympics, this book has been an effort to examine—in interdisciplinary and ethnographic fashion—the dynamics undergirding anti-Games activism in these two cities and to assess how it fits within the wider historical patterns of dissent.

The recent wave of global activism is, in the best of circumstances, rooted in the concept of *parrhesia,* a term that first appeared in the fourth-century work of Euripedes. Today translators commonly interpret it to mean "fearless speech." Those who engage in parrhesia do not veil their thoughts, but offer unvarnished versions of truth with as much lucidity as possible.[2] As such, Michel Foucault asserts, "the *parrhesiastes* is someone who has the moral qualities which are required, first, to know the truth, and secondly, to convey such truth to others."[3] Those engaging in parrhesia embrace criticality and wield it from the ground up, even as they risk their relative privilege in the name of disclosing truth, which they view as their duty. This demands courage despite the risk of danger, as the powerful usually do not take kindly to candid acts of the truth teller. For Foucault, parrhesia inflected the realm of politics as "a guideline for democracy as well as an ethical and personal attitude characteristic of the good citizen."[4] He was well aware that the public sphere was glutted with ersatz truth tellers engaging in what he called "negative *parrhesia*" or "ignorant outspokenness."[5] But the bona fide *parrhesiastes,* through their courageous actions in the face of large majorities or significant danger, jumpstart provocative dialogue in the effort to level the plane toward social justice.

Willingness to become a parrhesiastes despite the immense risks involved is rooted in Foucault's precept that "We are subjected to the production of truth through power and we cannot exercise power except through the production of truth."[6] Only a few Olympic athletes have stepped up to claim the mantle of parrhesia, producing truth in accordance with their deeply held beliefs, people like Muhammad Ali, Alice Milliat, John Carlos, Tommie Smith, and Peter Norman. In doing so they sacrificed polysemic athlete status on the altar of their political convictions. John Carlos, famous for his iconic medal-stand moment at the 1968 Summer Olympics in Mexico City, knows a whole lot about the courage it takes to assume a strong political stance at the Games under the unrelenting glare of the media spotlight. In May 2012, Carlos advised, "You have to be a troublemaker to make change."[7] But being a "troublemaker" means pressing against the well-oiled gears of the Olympic machine; athletes and non-athletes alike have a lot to lose in doing so. Yet, Carlos felt like he had no choice. Sounding like the paradigmatic parrhesiastes, he said he took his action "To set a standard. To have a society show its best face. To bring attention to the plight of people who were less fortunate. To wake up the consciousness of those who had let their conscience go dormant. And to encourage people to stand for what's right as opposed to standing for nothing."[8] In this book I have tried to highlight the fact that numerous everyday people have decided "to stand for what's right" and speak out against various aspects of the Olympic Games. For every parrhesiastes who comes to us in the form of a high-profile athlete, there are thousands who will toil in relatively anonymous fashion. We will not read their names in history books.

The decision of Carlos, Norman, and Smith to take action wreaked an acute personal toll on them. Although they were pilloried in the press at the time, history has been kinder to them. Even President Barack Obama publicly praised them: "I think to signify in that Olympics that there was more work to do, to acknowledge the injustices that were still taking place, I think that was a breakthrough moment in an overall push to move this country towards a more equal and more just society." He even said, "I think that what they did was in the best tradition of American protest."[9] As with 1960 Olympic champion Muhammad Ali—who today is roundly viewed as modern-day hero even though he was vilified while he engaged in parrhesia—the 1968 medal-stand dissidents have gained widespread admiration and respect. In short, we show a social-psychological tendency to think more fondly of activists the farther they get in the rearview mirror of history.[10]

But in the context of the Olympic Games, the moment dissident citizens take action—whether they are prominent athletes or everyday people—they can expect significant push-back due to the relatively adverse political opportunity structure they face. For anti-Olympics campaigners, political opportunity structure can be broken down into six central tenets: (1) the openness of the political institutions of the host city and country; (2) the solidity of elite alliances in support of the Games; (3) the presence or absence of elite allies for activists to work with; (4) the ability and willingness of security forces to clamp down on dissent; (5) the presence of international pressures that aid the activist cause; and (6) the receptivity of the mass media.

The cases of Vancouver and London demonstrate that while the host city may harbor relatively transparent political institutions, they often become noticeably opaque during the state of exception that the Olympics engender. Academics and activists alike have pointed out that the Games are an elite-driven process with scant opportunity for meaningful public participation. In *Megaprojects and Risk: An Anatomy of Ambition,* Bent

Flyvbjerg, Nils Bruzelius, and Werner Rothengatter note that megaproject boosters, either because of ignorance or a desire for efficiency, "often avoid and violate established practices of good governance, transparency and participation in political and administrative decision making." This translates to civil society being "typically kept at a substantial distance from megaproject decision making."[11] Researcher Iain Lindsay, who carried out ethnographic work in the Olympics-affected London boroughs, corroborates this assessment: "The entire process circumvents democratic rules and regulations and . . . offers little or no chance of accountability."[12] We certainly saw a buffer stuffed between decision makers and activists in both Vancouver and London. Being boxed out of decision-making processes complicates the job of activists. It forces them to rely on the application of pressure from outside the corridors of institutional power and makes them even more dependent on securing mass-media attention.

When the Olympics come to town, all that is hyperpartisan melts into air. Elites across the political spectrum unite in support, often altering the law of the land to bring it into sync with IOC dictates. Rule 50 of the Olympic Charter states, "The IOC Executive Board determines the principles and conditions under which any form of advertising or other publicity may be authorised."[13] In Britain, to align local law with this IOC rule, elected officials passed the London Olympic Games and Paralympic Games Act of 2006. This law strictly defined trademark infringement, delineating particular words that could not be used in close proximity "in relation to goods or services." To employ two of the following words together—"games," "Two Thousand and Twelve," "2012," or "twenty twelve"—was to violate the law. The act also outlawed using those four words in combination with any of these seven terms: "gold," "silver," "bronze," "London," "medals," "sponsor," or "summer."[14] The Olympic Delivery Authority engaged in aggressive brand policing, forcing one café to delete the "flaming torch breakfast baguette" from its menu and making a flower shop disassemble a decorative, tissue-paper window display in the shape of the Olympic rings. Even former IOC marketing sage Michael Payne accused the ODA of being overzealous, calling it a major "own goal" that went "too far."[15]

At the same time, the capacity of policing forces to engage in repression in order to preserve the security of the Games increases during the Olympic moment. In the context of the Games, elected officials of all stripes support militarization to protect the sanctity of the event. The Olympics present policing entities with a singular opportunity to revamp their stockpiles while forging new laws and rules that enhance their power. As a former head of criminal intelligence for the Hong Kong police said in the context of the 2008 Beijing Games, "I don't know of an intelligence-gathering operation in the world that, when given a new toy, doesn't use it."[16] Thanks to WikiLeaks—a relatively new political actor that has strategically rallied international pressure in an activist direction—we know that US government elites view the Olympics as a way to leverage security cooperation from host cities. When Brazil experienced power outages in 2009, the United States sniffed an opportunity. A cable from the US embassy in Brasilia read: "The newly heightened concerns about Brazil's infrastructure as a result of this blackout, combined with the need to address infrastructure challenges in the run-up to the 2014 World Cup and 2016 Olympics, present the United States opportunities for engagement on infrastructure development as well critical infrastructure protection and possibly cyber security."[17] Such "opportunities" also pave a trail for private security firms to cash in.

As we have seen, securing media attention in a time of widespread Olympic celebration is no simple matter. The media firms that pay for the rights to the Games have a built-in incentive to promote a problem-free Olympics. Other media outlets are not inclined to produce an abundance of coverage that taints the festivities. Plus, the Olympics are immensely popular, so it is a challenge for activists to gain political traction with the general public. The Olympics have become the world's premier multisport event, a dizzying exhibition of contestation and cooperation that brings together nations and cultures from around the world to compete on the track, the court, the field, and the slopes. Olympic historian Alfred E. Senn may well be correct when he asserts the Olympics "holds a firm and unique place in the consciousness of the world."[18] National Olympic Committees now outnumber United Nations member states, 204 to 193.[19] And gender-wise, the Games are an equal opportunity pleasure provider: polling data suggest the Games draw as much attention, if not more, from women as from men.[20] The Olympic Games are routinely—and in some cases fanatically—followed by large groups of people around the world. As mentioned earlier, the 2012 London Olympics became the most watched event in the history of US television, attracting more than 200 million viewers.[21] In the United Kingdom, a full 90 percent of the population tuned in to the BBC to watch the Games, more than 50 million viewers.[22] All this adds up to a less than propitious political opportunity structure for Olympics activists. Yet, politics can be finicky. Outbursts of activism can materialize in inauspicious conditions. And the heightened interconnectivity of protest sites in our contemporary moment may bode well for ramping up dissent against the seemingly implacable IOC.

The Games We Play

The Olympics present an idiosyncratic opportunity for political activists. Because the Olympics are such a grandiose juggernaut, they affect many issues that political activists care about, from displacement and environmental degradation to rampant public spending and the influence of corporations in society. As we have seen, challenging the Olympic Games is not your everyday activist escapade: campaigners benefit from unique opportunities they do not possess during other episodes of contention. When it comes to the dialectic of resistance and restriction, activists experience a complicated mix. On one hand they enjoy greater tactical freedom than usual, thanks to the protective glow of the global media spotlight and the possibility of piggybacking off the Games' popularity, using the Olympics as a firm platform for launching dissent to a wider audience. But on the other hand, campaigners face a revamped security infrastructure laser-focused on staging an incident-free Games. While Olympic security forces

IMAGE 10 Julian Cheyne passes alternative torch to activists from NoSochi2014 on 28 July 2012. Courtesy of Jules Boykoff.

stockpile weapons and exceptional measures to prevent terrorism that can also double as suppressors of dissent, the authorities do not wish to wield their power unduly while the whole world is watching. As we have seen, the enormous security architecture tends to stimulate its own iterative loops of resistance and activism as it raises civil-liberties concerns. The efficacy of campaigners is also complicated by the fact that the general population thinks highly of the Olympics, believing in its tenets of goodwill and internationalism while appreciating the remarkable athletic prowess vying for the gold.

I have argued in this book that anti-Olympics activism is less a "movement of movements" than it is a *moment* of movements. Anti-Olympics activism has not yet become a social movement, as it has not robustly sustained itself through time. Rather, such activism is a prime example of what Tarrow calls "event coalitions" whereby protesters join forces temporarily for a single event—the Olympic Games—but cooperation dissipates after the occasion passes. Protesters revert to their prior activities rather than continuing on with anti-Olympics dissent. At the tail end of the London 2012 Summer Games, activists from Britain, the United States, Russia, and Brazil came together to form the International Counter Olympics Network (ICON), so perhaps protesters will eventually be able to build a vibrant, durable movement. And in a symbolic act at the mobilization on 28 July 2012, Londoner Julian Cheyne passed the counter-Olympic torch—which CON had originally received from Canadian activists—to campaigners from No Sochi 2014. Yet despite the incipient efforts of ICON, anti-Olympics activism currently lacks consistent transnational panache.

In *Activism and the Olympics* I have tried to create what Featherstone calls "maps of grievance" for anti-Olympics campaigns in Vancouver and London. I do this in an attempt to theorize activist actions in a way that honors the unique spatiality that contributes to their ever-evolving political tactics, strategies, and identities.[23] Activists must navigate the extant political geography of power while trying to forge—via both antagonistic contestation and with-the-grain, humor-based actions—new, more equitable social relations. In the typology presented in chapter 1 we saw that when it comes to Olympic activism there are four types: (1) athletes protesting aspects of the Olympic Games; (2) athletes protesting wider sociopolitical issues; (3) nonathletes challenging the machinations of the actual Olympics; and (4) nonathletes using the Games to widen the audience for non-sports-related issues. In both Vancouver and London there was a notable dearth of athlete activists speaking out about politics, notwithstanding the challenges to Rule 40 discussed in the previous chapter. Thus my analytical attention has fallen on nonathlete political activists who argue the Games themselves are unfair or that the Games skew wider social relations in unjust directions. In particular I have focused on activists engaging in transgressive contention and direct action to confront the Olympic movement.

Vibrant, effective activism challenging the Games is complicated by the fact that campaigners face a "strategic incapacitation" policing model that targets transgressive protesters, exerts strict control over the use of public space, and enjoys access to military-grade weaponry and cutting-edge surveillance technology.[24] Given this political opportunity structure, activists have tended to rely more on creating a playful "ethical spectacle" that deploys humor to defuse police militancy, and employs horizontalism to undercut the perils of hierarchy.[25] Highlighting the importance of play, Benjamin Shepard asserts, "different kinds of social relations are produced when people play with politics and power."[26] While relatively horizontal, the activism in Vancouver and London was guided by leaders, offering additional support for Gerbaudo's contention that modern-day activists often engage in "choreographic leadership" that is "soft," emotional, and dialogical in character. While Gerbaudo tends to focus on how this type of low-key leadership is enabled by the deft use of social media, I assert in *Activism and the Olympics* that is best understood as an outgrowth of the dialectic of resistance and restriction. Activist leaders who become figureheads also become targets of repression and ridicule. We agree, though, that leadership in this context can be effective in the short term but needs to be bolstered in the long term, bricked into social movements with longevity and big-picture vision.[27]

The strategy of producing a participatory, radically democratic "ethical spectacle" runs astride the idea of carnival. Mikhail Bakhtin, in his exegesis on Rabelais, wrote, "Carnival is not a spectacle seen by the people; they live in it, and everyone participates because its very idea embraces all the people." It is "a special condition," liminal and vivid, that "is organized on the basis of laughter" and positioned in dialogical tension with spectacle.[28] In contrast to the spectacle's sharp division between actors and observers, the carnival provokes direct involvement. Later, in his work on Dostoevsky, Bakhtin, elaborated: "Carnival is a pageant without footlights and without a division into performers and spectators. In carnival everyone is an active participant, everyone communes in the carnival act."[29] Carnival is not a performance—it is lived experience where etiquette, hierarchy, and social separation are cast aside in favor of the eccentric, nonhierarchical, and "concretely sensuous."[30] Private life is collectivized, turned inside out and hung to dry on the social clothesline.

The Bakhtinian carnivalesque captures key elements within the zeitgeist of contemporary activism with its penchant for humor, relative horizontalism, low-key leadership, and jubilant seditiousness. Diametric to the Debordian spectacle's impenetrability, the carnival is participatory, albeit in certain respects performative as well. Humor- and satire-oriented political activism, notes Haugerud, "doesn't just mirror societal incongruities or imbalances; it also helps to define what is thinkable."[31] Indeed, Olympics activists in the twenty-first century have adopted humor, play, and fun as central organizing principles. Those who advocate jocularity and fun as vital to one's repertoire of contention recognize that activist play needs to be linked into organizational efforts with political endurance that make concrete demands. As Shepard puts it "the fun of social change works best as part of a holistic approach to organizing." This, he argues, "includes a clear goal or question, a great deal of research on an issue, accompanied by a coherent approach to communicating a goal, mobilization around it, a legal strategy, direct action to achieve it, and sustainability strategies to keep the campaign going."[32] Carnivalesque play is but one element that many view as necessary but few view as sufficient.

And relying on play and humor has potential downsides. Humor is necessarily subjective, which leaves it open to misinterpretation. Plus, it can quickly become hackneyed, fetishized, or a pallid substitute for crystal-clear policy demands. And play can always be trumped by heavy-handed repression.[33] In describing the political spectacle Debord wrote, "All that was once directly lived has become mere representation."[34] But in combating the spectacle with a humor- and play-oriented approach, activists could be accused of replacing "mere representation" with "mere entertainment." Many question whether carnival can be a real-deal force for political fight-back. For example, Terry Eagleton contends, "Any politics which predicates itself on the carnivalesque moment alone will be no more than a compliant, containable libertarianism."[35] In other words, these "protestivals," as Graham St. John calls them, may enact breathing alternatives to hegemony without necessarily being counterhegemonic.[36] Even so, when bolstered with political teeth and a dexterous set of strategies and tactics, the humor-oriented carnivalesque can pose real problems for power. Plus, as many protesters have pointed out in this book, it can be fun. This is where savvy activists can flip the Olympics on their ear, despite the uneven terrain of political opportunity structure.

For modern-day Olympics activists, online activities have assumed a vital role for organizing events, facilitating person-to-person communication, and creating educational opportunities. But this reliance on the Internet raises a host of other issues and pitfalls. This brings us back to Jodi Dean's "communicative capitalism," or "a political-economic formation in which there is talk without response, in which the very practices associated with governance by the people consolidate and support the most brutal inequities of corporate-controlled capitalism."[37] Dean argues that online messages and missives simply circulate content rather than demand response. Exchange value rules use value with a merciless fist. The idea that we can all create content—the "fantasy of abundance" as Dean terms it—deflects our attention from the brass-knuckle power relations that thrum behind our screens.[38] It also plays into "technological fetishism" that specializes in "capturing and reformatting political energies," converting efforts to engage politically into the anemic circulation of content.[39] This creates a vicious trap whereby we feel like we're engaged in struggle but really we're spinning furiously on a technological gerbil wheel. Thus, "Under communicative capitalism, communication functions fetishistically as the disavowal of a more fundamental political disempowerment or castration."[40] For Dean, the "promise of participation" becomes an "underlying fantasy wherein technology covers over our impotence and supports a vision of ourselves as active political participants."[41] Worse yet, keyboard activism provides us with a convenient alibi for spurning boots-to-pavement contestation.

The perils of "communicative capitalism" shine brightly in the context of Olympic activism. Anti-Olympics campaigning is by necessity shoestring and piecemeal, owing to the asymmetrical resource battle. Activist interventions are often relegated to flashy, one-off efforts that, while often fun and even funny, remain untethered from bigger efforts to mobilize viable alternatives and long-term campaigns that can grasshopper globally. As Dean puts it, "left activists seem ever more drawn to spectacular events that raise awareness, momentarily, but do little in the way of building the institutions necessary to sustain a new political order."[42] Activists foment a flurry of activity that does little to alter material reality. Many Olympics activists were well aware of the shortcomings of alternative and social media. London-based campaigner Isaac Marrero-Guillamón spoke of the positives—"Social media have been instrumental in extending the discussions that have happened face to face and in disseminating information"—but also explicated the downside: keen focus on such communications deflected attention from the hard work of organizing, mobilizing, and creating tactical havoc.[43] Yet, it should be noted that numerous scholars and activists have observed firsthand that a savvy digital repertoire of contention can contribute in a meaningful way to collective action.

Sochi 2014 Winter Games and the 2016 Summer Olympics in Rio de Janeiro

Because the Olympic Games have become such a multifaceted behemoth, they ramble into the path of numerous extant activist battles while spurring new ones. The regularity of social problems stemming from the Games drives Dave Zirin to sum up the Olympics phenomenon as "a familiar script replayed every two years, with only the language changing."[44] In 2014 the language will change to Russian. In February 2014, Russia will host the Winter Olympics in Sochi, a resort city nestled along the Black Sea. Since being awarded the Games, Russian officials have quietly fashioned a formidable political architecture to squelch dissent. To be sure, the persistent repression in the build-up to the Games is yet another chapter in the government's targeted repression of Russia's opposition movement. But ghosting in the background a less intuitive explanation looms: the Olympic Games. Quelling the political opposition is the omnipresent goal, but the Olympics and the 2018 soccer World Cup, which Russia will also host, are the vital backdrop.

Russian president Vladimir Putin led the crusade to secure the Games and is committed to staging them without incident, even if it drives up the cost. A half-year before the Games were to commence, costs had catapulted over $50 billion, making them the most expensive Olympics ever. Russia's state-owned development bank was already projecting losses in the billions.[45] Security alone would be extremely costly. In October 2012 Putin told security higher-ups that Russia would soon be hosting "very important political and sporting events" and that "it should be a matter of honor for law enforcement officials and special forces to ensure that these events take place in a normal, businesslike and festive atmosphere."[46] Russia is no civil-liberties paradise. Just ask Pussy Riot, the feminist punk-rock collective who had three members imprisoned after a provocative guerrilla performance at a Moscow cathedral in early 2012. But with the Olympics on the way, Putin has tightened his grip, signing into law an array of restrictive measures.

The Russian Duma has been busy blending dragnet with draconian. In summer 2012 it passed a law requiring NGOs that are "politically active" and receiving funding from outside Russia to register as "foreign agents." Then, in September, under the influence of the Federal Security Service, the Duma passed legislation with a capacious definition of "high treason." Critics fear it could be applied to any Russian—and certainly activists— who collaborate with foreign groups. One law targeting organized protest defines political activity as any effort to "influence state policy or public opinion." The Duma also ramped up fines for public "disorder." Even at permitted demonstrations, individuals can get hit with punishments of 20,000 rubles ($660) or up to fifty hours of community labor if "disorder" eventuates. The fines are even stiffer for unsanctioned rallies: more than $9,000 for participants and double that for organizers. Putin regularly conflates left-wing opposition leaders with terrorists, accusing them of inciting "mass disorder." Political protests are routinely labeled "extremist." Meanwhile, a new Internet law in Russia constricts free speech in cyberspace, green-lighting authorities to compile a secret blacklist that has already ensnared nearly two hundred web sites for their "offensive content."[47] In summer 2013, Putin signed a controversial antigay law that prohibits "propaganda" that supports "nontraditional" sexual orientation. Then, in August 2013 he issued a decree that banned non-Olympic "gatherings, rallies, demonstrations, marches and pickets" in Sochi between January 7 and March 21, creating a one-month buffer on either side of the Games.[48] All this put activists and NGOs on high alert.

On top of this, the region around Sochi is a political tinderbox. For starters, Sochi is the historic homeland for ethnic Circassians. The 2014 Olympics will occur on the sesquicentennial of the Circassians' forced removal by Tsar Alexander II. Today Circassians live in diaspora, mostly in Syria, Turkey, and Jordan, with other large pockets in exile in Lebanon and the United States. Many of them consider their 1864 removal an act of genocide. New Jersey-based Circassian Dana Wojokh asked me, "Would you have an Olympics in Darfur? Would you have an Olympics in Auschwitz? No, so why Sochi?"[49] Activists have jumpstarted a No Sochi 2014 campaign that took action at the London 2012 Games. On 29 July 2012, Sochi protesters gathered at the Albert Memorial in Kensington Gardens, directly in front of the Sochi House, the official Sochi 2014 Winter Olympics hotspot where for £30 (about $45 at the time) one could learn the "official" history of Sochi and details about Russia's upcoming five-ring mega-event. Outside the gates, No Sochi 2014 activists presented an alternative narrative that was erased from the official storyline: the genocide of the Circassian people. Interspersing chants and Circassian history, and wearing traditional Circassian garb, they presented their case to curious onlookers, four cooperative police officials, and a gaggle of international media.

Russia is beset with an array of intractable conflagrations nearby. Sochi sits minutes from the border of Abkhazia, the republic that split from Georgia, causing a spat with Russia. Then there's the high-profile conflict with Chechnya, as well as lesser-known squabbles with ethnic groups in the Russian North Caucasus, a veritable hornets' nest of long-term political discontent where an Islamist insurgency boils. Meskhetian Turks, North Ossetia, and South Ossetia all have their issues with the Russian state.[50] Tamara Barsik of the No Sochi 2014 campaign said, "Sochi is happening in a war zone. There's an Islamic insurgency happening less than 100 miles away. . . . The human security element is off the charts."[51] The Sochi 2014 Winter Olympics have aggravated opposition across the region.

In 2016 Rio will host the Summer Olympics. Games organizers raised activist eyebrows when they hired former IOC marketing guru Michael Payne to be Rio's senior strategy advisor.[52] As noted in chapter 1, Payne approvingly described the Olympics as "the world's longest commercial."[53] But despite Payne's penchant for privatization, Brazil has dumped large sums of public funding into the Olympic project—upwards of $27 billion—impelling everyday citizens and activists alike to question the government's fiscal priorities.[54] Rio has also enlisted the services of former New York mayor Rudy Giuliani's security firm for advice and consultation. Under Giuliani's guidance, Brazilian security forces are revamping their policing technology and weaponry.[55]

Activists in Rio have rallied to challenge the displacement that has occurred to make way for the 2014 soccer World Cup and the 2016 Summer Olympics. A number of favelas are being threatened with demolition. For instance, Morro da Providência—Rio's first favela and the recipient of significant state redevelopment funds—is under threat. This favela has existed since 1897; it is an established community with deep historical roots. Theresa Williamson and Maurício Hora, two activists taking on Olympics-induced eviction, wrote, "Rio is becoming a playground for the rich, and inequality breeds instability." Rather than pouring money into the Olympic machine while displacing longtime residents, they asserted, "It would be much more cost-effective to invest in urban improvements that communities help shape through a participatory democratic process. This would ultimately strengthen Rio's economy and improve its infrastructure while also reducing inequality."[56] Residents of Rio's Vila Autódromo have been organizing against the construction of a proposed highway that would slash directly through their neighborhood in order to facilitate Olympic and World Cup traffic.[57]

In June 2013, Brazil experienced an outburst of street protest linked to disgruntlement over what activists view as misfired spending priorities: funding the 2014 World Cup and 2016 Olympics instead of health and education initiatives. What started off as a dispute over a spike in bus fares in São Paolo led to a cascade of activism across the country. Hundreds of thousands poured into the streets and public squares to express their dissent, and activists used the fact that Brazil was hosting two mega-events as an effective motivational lever. Security forces responded with tear gas and reverberative grenades. Big-name soccer stars like David Luiz, Neymar, and Givanildo Vieira de Souza (also known as Hulk) spoke out in support of the protesters. Demonstrating class awareness, Hulk said, "I come from the bottom of the social ladder and now I have a good life. I see these demonstrators and I know that they are right. . . . We know that Brazil needs to improve in many areas and must let the demonstrators express themselves." Neymar promised "I'll get on the pitch inspired by this mobilisation."[58]

Suddenly the 2016 Olympics sat at the center of socio-political analysis. Matheus Bizarria of the nongovernmental organization Action Aid, told the *Guardian*, "It's totally connected to the mega-events. . . . People have had enough."[59] One poll found 77 percent of those residing in São Paolo supported the protest, which bodes well for the political opportunity structure of future collective action.[60] Meanwhile, Rio Olympic organizers plunged ahead with a "model venue exercise" that refined and streamlined the operational plan for the Games, and the IOC issued a statement that rehearsed its standard rhetoric: "The Olympic Games in 2016 will bring significant benefits to the whole population of Rio, improving the city in terms of transport, infrastructure and social housing, as well as bringing a considerable sporting legacy for Brazil."[61] The parameters were set for an activist battle to come.

Urban geographer and political activist Christopher Gaffney encapsulates many of the critiques that are surfacing in Rio: "As with most mega-events, development is highly uneven and tends to benefit private developers and construction interests while creating spaces of leisure for wealthy residents and the international tourist class. The increased security apparatuses that have become defining features of global-mega events effectively privatize public spaces in the city, installing surveillance mechanisms that continue operating long after the Games are over."[62] These criticisms jibe in various degrees with what we have seen in Vancouver and London. One could plausibly charge that publicly challenging the Olympics is a Panglossian affair. But with the Games affecting so many aspects of a host city's society—and often in ways that exacerbate the chasm between the privileged and the needy—it is hard to imagine anti-Olympics activism not cropping up in some form every time the Games touch down. The idea that the Olympic Games are apolitical is folly, a quixotic remnant of IOC brand identity. Because the Olympics are thrumming with politics, we should expect political fight-back in the foreseeable future.

New Wave Opiate of the Masses?

Olympics boosters argue the Games bring an array of positives to the public plate. The Olympics can foster diplomacy and bridge divisions of class and politics, jumpstarting conversations between people who would otherwise have little to say to one another. Many also argue that hosting the Games can help bring global attention to less-than-perfect democratic conditions, thereby setting the stage for improving them. But as we have seen, activists in Vancouver and London vociferously disagreed with such an approach. Instead, they contended, sports can often foster more calamity than amity while widening the gap between the haves and have-nots. Olympics critics argue international sports have proven conducive to flag-flailing hypernationalism that—in alignment with Orwell's sport-induced "orgies of hatred"—can occasionally rear its head as full-blown xenophobia.[63] Indeed, the modern Olympics have always tightroped the line between provoking nationalism and cultivating internationalism, or what boosters sometimes simply call Olympism.

But on the political left it is a standard-issue trope that sports take our eye off the political-economic prize, that they are a waste of time, an energy-sucker of dire proportions. In *Barbaric Sport: A Global Plague* Marc Perelman captures the essence of this position, arguing that "sport performs an apologetic function for the dominant mode of production and the system, in which it is not simply a mechanism of a geartrain but central to the machine." He goes on to contend, "Sport has become the new opium of the people, more alienating than religion because it suggests the scintillating dream of a promotion for the individual, holds out the prospect of parallel hierarchy. The element of 'protest' against daily reality that even religion (according to Marx) still retained is stifled by the infinite corrosive power of sport, draining mass consciousness of all liberating and emancipatory energy."[64]

In *Activism and the Olympics* I have eschewed this approach, arguing instead that critical engagement with the politics of sports can open up liberatory space for ethical commitment and principled action. Critical thinkers can embrace sports, pushing it to be better, more inclusive, more democratic, without simply being clueless dupes of capitalism. In fact, it's arguable that Marx himself would have rejected lockstep leftism of the antisports variety. Looking back at Marx's famous "opium of the people" passage one is struck by the sympathy nestled in his rebuke. For starters, he wrote, "The struggle against religion is therefore indirectly a fight against *the world* of which religion is the spiritual aroma." He noted, "Religious distress is at the same time the *expression* of real distress and also the *protest* against real distress. Religion is the sigh of the oppressed creature, the heart of a heartless world, just as it is the spirit of spiritless conditions. It is the *opium* of the people."[65] Far from offering an unbridled attack on religion, Marx viewed it as "the heart of a heartless world." To unthinkingly yank the heart from our collective chest would be to unnecessarily eviscerate our capacity for compassion. Same goes for sports, "the new opium of the people," as Perelman and his ilk would have it. To dismiss sports is to needlessly forfeit the common ground vital to meaningful political engagement. Naysaying in the name of the kneejerk. The Olympics afford an opportunity to plumb the practice of dissent, and we are remiss if we don't engage it in all its murky complexity. Sports are more than an opiate. Social change is more labyrinthine than linear.

Notes

Introduction

1. Manuel Vásquez Montalbán, *An Olympic Death,* trans. Ed Emery (London: Serpent's Tail, 1992), 48, 52, 34.
2. "Recap of Eric Heiden's 5 Olympic gold medals, Lake Placid 1980," YouTube, http://www.youtube.com/watch?v=XfpVqK3cswE.
3. Robert K. Barney, Stephen R. Wenn, and Scott G. Martyn, *Selling the Five Rings: The International Olympic Committee and the Rise of Olympic Commercialism* (Salt Lake City: The University of Utah Press, 2004).
4. Michael Payne, *Olympic Turn Around: How the Games Stepped Back from the Brink of Extinction to Become the World's Best Known Brand—And a Multi-Billion Dollar Global Franchise* (London: London Business Press, 2005), 95.
5. Karl Marx, *Capital: A Critique of Political Economy, Vol. 1: A Critical Analysis of Capitalist Production,* trans. Ben Fowkes (New York: Penguin Books, 1976), 163.
6. Jimmy Burns, *Barça: A People's Passion* (London: Bloomsbury, 1999).
7. Avery Brundage, "Circular Letter to Members of the IOC," Avery Brundage Collection, 1908–1975 (hereafter cited as ABC), Box 70, Reel 39, 30 August 1957, 3, International Centre for Olympic Studies, London, Ontario (hereafter cited as ICOSA).
8. Ibid., 2.
9. Michael L. Silk and David L. Andrews, "Sport and the Neoliberal Conjuncture: Complicating the Consensus," in *Sport and Neoliberalism: Politics, Consumption, and Culture,* ed. David L. Andrews and Michael L. Silk (Philadelphia: Temple University Press, 2012), 7.
10. Joshua I. Newman and Michael D. Giardina, *Sport, Spectacle, and NASCAR Nation: Consumption and the Cultural Politics of Neoliberalism* (New York: Palgrave Macmillan, 2011), 64.
11. Jules Boykoff, *Celebration Capitalism and the Olympic Games* (New York: Routledge, 2013).

12. Chuck Klosterman, *IV: A Decade of Curious People and Dangerous Ideas* (New York: Scribner, 2006), 238, emphasis in original.

13. George Orwell, "The Sporting Spirit," in *Shooting an Elephant and Other Essays* (New York: Harcourt, Brace & World, Inc., 1950), 152, 153–154.

14. Pew Research Center, "Winter Olympics Tops Public's News Interests," 24 February 2010, http://www.people-press.org/2010/02/24/winter-olympics-tops-publics-news-interests/.

15. Associated Press-Ipsos poll, 7–11 August 2008, available at http://www.pollingreport.com/olympics.htm.

16. Finlo Rohrer, "Saying No to London 2012," *BBC News*, 17 February 2005, http://news.bbc.co.uk/2/hi/uk_news/4272113.stm.

17. James H. Johnson, "Beethoven, and the Birth of Romantic Musical Experience in France," *19th-Century Music* 15 (1991): 23, 24, 27.

18. Tia DeNora, "Musical Patronage and Social Change in Beethoven's Vienna," *American Journal of Sociology* 97 (1991): 310–346.

19. Tia DeNora, *Beethoven and the Construction of Genius: Musical Politics in Vienna, 1792–1803* (Berkeley: University of California Press, 1997), 130.

20. John Sugden and Alan Tomlinson, "Digging the Dirt and Staying Clean: Retrieving the Investigative Tradition for a Critical Sociology of Sport," *International Review for the Sociology of Sport* 34, no. 4 (1999): 386.

21. More precisely, I carried out twenty-eight interviews with Vancouver activists and forty-two with people protesting the London Games. I made multiple trips to Vancouver from where I live in nearby Portland both before and after the Olympics. For the London Games, I was based in Brighton in the four months leading up to the Olympics, making frequent trips by train to the capital city. For the actual Games I resided in London.

22. Chris Gratton and Ian Jones, *Research Methods for Sport Studies* (Abingdon, UK: Routledge, 2001), 182–183.

23. Robert R. Sands, *Sport Ethnography* (Champaign, IL: Human Kinetics, 2002), 69.

24. Gratton and Jones, *Research Methods for Sport Studies,* 103; Daniel Burdsey, "That Joke Isn't Funny Anymore: Racial Microaggressions, Color-Blind Ideology and the Mitigation of Racism in English Men's First-Class Cricket," *Sociology of Sport Journal* 28 (2011): 270.

25. Richard Giulianotti, "Participant Observation and Research into Football Hooliganism: Reflections on the Problem of Entrée and Everyday Risks," *Sociology of Sport Journal* 12, no. 1 (1995): 7.

26. Michael L. Silk, David L. Andrews, and Daniel S. Mason, "Encountering the Field: Sports Studies and Qualitative Research" in *Qualitative Methods in Sports Studies,* ed. David L. Andrews, Daniel S. Mason, and Michael L. Silk (Oxford: Berg, 2005), 8.

27. Ibid., 10.

28. Burdsey, "That Joke Isn't Funny Anymore"; Daniel Burdsey, *British Asians and Football: Culture, Identity, Exclusion* (London: Routledge, 2007); Ben Carrington, "Cricket, Culture, and Identity: An Exploration of the Role of Sport in the Construction of Black Masculinities," in *Practising Identities: Power and Resistance,* ed. Sasha Roseneil and Julie Seymour (Basingstoke, UK: Palgrave, 1999) 11–32; Belinda Wheaton, "'Just Do It: Consumption, Commitment, and Identity in the Windsurfing Subculture," *Sociology of Sport Journal* 17, no. 3 (2000): 254–274.

29. Giulianotti, "Participant Observation and Research into Football Hooliganism"; Joshua I. Newman, "A Detour Through 'NASCAR Nation': Ethnographic Artic-ulations of Neoliberal Sporting Spectacle," *International Review for the Sociology of Sport* 42, no. 3 (2007): 289–308; Paul Watt, "'It's Not for Us': Regeneration, the 2012 Olympics and the Gentrification of East London," *City* 17, no. 1 (2013): 99–118.

30. Jacqueline Kennelly, *Citizen Youth: Culture, Activism, and Agency in a Neoliberal Era* (New York: Palgrave Macmillan, 2011); Brian Wilson, "Ethnography, the Internet, and Youth Culture: Strategies for Examining Social Resistance and 'Online-Offline' Relationships," *Canadian Journal of Education* 29, no. 1 (2006): 307–328; Luis A. Fernandez, *Policing Dissent: Social Control and the Anti-Globalization Movement* (New Brunswick, NJ: Rutgers University Press, 2008).

31. Helen Jefferson Lenskyj, *Olympic Industry Resistance: Challenging Olympic Power and Propaganda* (Albany: State University of New York Press, 2008); Helen Jef-ferson Lenskyj, *The Best Olympics Ever?: Social Impacts of Sydney 2000* (Albany: State University of New York Press, 2002).

32. Michael L. Silk, "Sporting Ethnography: Philosophy, Methodology, and Reflec-tion," in *Qualitative Methods in Sports Studies*, ed. David L. Andrews, Daniel S. Mason, and Michael L. Silk (Oxford: Berg, 2005), 85.

33. Kim V. L. England, "Getting Personal: Reflexivity, Positionality, and Feminist Research," *The Professional Geographer* 46, no 1 (1994): 82, emphasis in original.

34. Ben Carrington, "'What's the Footballer Doing Here?': Racialized Performa-tivity, Reflexivity, and Identity," *Cultural Studies <=> Critical Methodologies* 8 (2008): 426.

35. Ibid., 427, emphasis in original.

36. Ibid., 444.

37. Ibid., 442.

38. Kevin Gillan and Jenny Pickerill, "The Difficult and Hopeful Ethics of Research on, and with Social Movements," *Social Movement Studies* 11, no. 2 (2012): 138.

39. Sugden and Tomlinson, "Digging the Dirt and Staying Clean," 393.

40. Pierre Bourdieu, "Program for a Sociology of Sport," *Sociology of Sport Journal* 8 (1988): 155.

41. Ben Carrington, *Race, Sport, and Politics: The Sporting Black Diaspora* (London: Sage, 2010), 27.

42. Andrei Markovits and Lars Rensmann, *Gaming the World: How Sports Are Reshap-ing Global Politics and Culture* (Princeton: Princeton University Press, 2010), 8.

43. Joseph Maguire, *Power and Global Sport: Zones of Prestige, Emulation, and Resis-tance* (Abingdon, UK: Routledge, 2005), 159.

44. Carrington, *Race, Sport, and Politics*.

45. Richard Gruneau, *Class, Sports, and Social Development* (Amherst: The Univer-sity of Massachusetts Press, 1983).

46. Chris Gratton and Ian P. Henry, eds., *Sport in the City: The Role of Sport in Eco-nomic and Social Regeneration* (London: Routledge, 2001).

47. Jennifer Hargreaves, *Sporting Females: Critical Issues in the History and Sociology of Women's Sports* (London: Routledge, 1994); Michael A. Messner, *Out of Play: Critical Essays on Gender and Sport* (Albany: State University of New York Press, 2007); Michael A. Messner, *Taking the Field: Women, Men, and Sports* (Minne-apolis: University of Minnesota Press, 2002).

48. Alan Bairner, *Sport, Nationalism, and Globalization: European and North American Perspectives* (Albany: State University of New York Press, 2001).

49. David L. Andrews and Stephen Wagg, introduction to *East Plays West: Sport and the Cold War*, ed. Stephen Wagg and David L. Andrews (London: Routledge, 2007), 2.

50. Bourdieu, "Program for a Sociology of Sport," 153. While there has been an outburst of research, we should be mindful of Carrington's observation that being a sociologist who not only specializes, but also specializes in sport can lead to "double marginality." Carrington, *Race, Sport, and Politics*, 7.

51. Alan Tomlinson, "The Making—and Unmaking?—of the Olympic Corporate Class," in *The Palgrave Handbook of Olympic Studies*, ed. Helen Jefferson Lenskyj and Stephen Wagg, 233–247 (Basingstoke, UK: Palgrave Macmillan, 2012); Alan Tomlinson, "Carrying the Torch for Whom?: Symbolic Power and Olympic Ceremony," in *The Olympics at the Millennium: Power, Politics, and the Games*, ed. Kay Schaffer and Sidonie Smith, 167–181 (New Brunswick, NJ: Rutgers University Press 2000); Alan Tomlinson, "The Disneyfication of the Olympics?: Theme Parks and Freak Shows of the Body," in *Post-Olympism?: Questioning Sport in the Twenty-first Century*, ed. John Bale and Mette Krogh Christensen, 147–163 (Oxford: Berg, 2004).

52. Garry Whannel, "The Television Spectacular," in *Five-Ring Circus: Money, Power, and Politics at the Olympic Games*, ed. Alan Tomlinson and Garry Whannel (Sydney: Pluto Press, 1984); Garry Whannel, "The Rings and the Box: Television Spectacle and the Olympics," in *The Palgrave Handbook of Olympic Studies*, ed. Helen Jefferson Lenskyj and Stephen Wagg, 261–273 (Basingstoke, UK: Palgrave Macmillan, 2012).

53. Andrew Jennings, "The Love That Dare Not Speak Its Name: Corruption and the Olympics," in *The Palgrave Handbook of Olympic Studies*, ed. Helen Jefferson Lenskyj and Stephen Wagg, 461–473 (Basingstoke, UK: Palgrave Macmillan, 2012); Andrew Jennings, *The New Lord of the Rings* (London: Pocket Books, 1996).

54. Toby C. Rider and Kevin B. Wamsley, "Myth Heritage and the Olympic Enterprise," in *The Palgrave Handbook of Olympic Studies*, ed. Helen Jefferson Lenskyj and Stephen Wagg, 289–303 (Basingstoke, UK: Palgrave Macmillan, 2012); Kevin Wamsley, "The Global Sport Monopoly: A Synopsis of 20th Century Olympic Politics," *International Journal* 57, no. 3 (2002): 395–410; Kevin Wamsley, "Laying Olympism to Rest," *Post-Olympism?: Questioning Sport in the Twenty-first Century*, ed. by John Bale and Mette Krogh Christensen, 231–242 (Oxford: Berg, 2004).

55. Janice Forsyth, "Teepees and Tomahawks: Aboriginal Cultural Representation at the 1976 Olympic Games," in *The Global Nexus Engaged: Past, Present, Future Interdisciplinary Olympic Studies: Sixth International Symposium for Olympic Research*, ed. Kevin Wamsley, Robert K. Barney, and Scott G. Martyn, 71–75 (London, ON: International Centre for Olympic Studies, 2002); Christine M. O'Bonsawin, "'No Olympics on Stolen Native Land': Contesting Olympic Narratives and Asserting Indigenous Rights within the Discourse of the 2010 Vancouver Games," *Sport in Society* 13, no. 1 (2010): 143–156.

56. John Karamichas, "The Olympics and the Environment," in *The Palgrave Handbook of Olympic Studies*, ed. Helen Jefferson Lenskyj and Stephen Wagg, 381–393 (Basingstoke, UK: Palgrave Macmillan, 2012).

57. Lenskyj, *Olympic Industry Resistance*.

58. See Helen Jefferson Lenskyj, *Inside the Olympic Industry: Power, Politics, and Activism* (Albany: State University of New York Press, 2000); Lenskyj, *The Best Olympics Ever?*

Chapter 1   Understanding the Olympic Games

1. Avery Brundage, "Letter to Stanislaw Dabrowski," ABC, Box 179, Reel 103, 7 February 1969, ICOSA.
2. Sylvie Espagnac, "The IOC in Session in Salt Lake City," *Olympic Review* 27 (2002). 9.
3. Vanessa Kortekaas, "Business Diary: Sir Alan Collins," *Financial Times,* 27 September 2011, http://www.ft.com/cms/s/0/66acd994-e836-11e0-9fc7 -00144feab49a.html.
4. "Denver Triumph a 7-Year Effort," *New York Times,* 13 May 1970, 53.
5. For many of these letters, see ABC, Box 192, Reel 110, 1971, ICOSA.
6. "Colorado Drops Winter Games Bid," *New York Times,* 9 November 1972, 61.
7. B. Drummond Ayres Jr., "Invitation to Go Elsewhere," *New York Times,* 12 November 1972, E5.
8. Jerry Kirshenbaum, "Voting to Snuff the Torch," *Sports Illustrated,* 20 November 1972, http://sportsillustrated.cnn.com/vault/article/magazine/MAG1086771/ index.htm.
9. Richard D. Lamm, "Letter to Avery Brundage," ABC, Box 192, Reel 110, 22 November 1971, ICOSA.
10. Richard D. Lamm, "Letter to James Worrall," James Worrall Collection (hereafter cited as JWC), Box 15, Folder 1, 4 April 1972, ICOSA.
11. Al Nielson, "Letter to Mr. Avery Brundage," ABC, Box 192, Reel 110, 22 November 1971, ICOSA; Parkman Sayward, "Letter to Mr. Avery Brundage," ABC, Box 192, Reel 110, 19 November 1971, ICOSA; Sam W. Brown, Jr., "Letter to Mr. Avery Brundage," ABC, Box 192, Reel 110, 18 January 1972, ICOSA.
12. Avery Brundage, untitled document, ABC, Box 192, Reel 111, 8 May 1972, ICOSA.
13. B. Drummond Ayres Jr., "'Ski-Town' Split on Winter Olympics," *New York Times,* 6 November 1972, 43.
14. Kirshenbaum, "Voting to Snuff the Torch."
15. Ibid.
16. Ibid.
17. Mario Diani, "The Concept of Social Movement," *The Sociological Review* 40, no. 1 (1992): 13.
18. Sidney Tarrow, *Power in Movement: Social Movements and Contentious Politics,* 2nd edition (Cambridge: Cambridge University Press, 1998), 4.
19. Tom Mertes, "Grass-Roots Globalism," *New Left Review* 17 (2001): 108.
20. Konstantinos Zervas, "Anti-Olympic Campaigns," in *The Palgrave Handbook of Olympic Studies,* ed. Helen Jefferson Lenskyj and Stephen Wagg (Basingstoke, UK: Palgrave Macmillan, 2012), 533.
21. Sidney Tarrow, *The New Transnational Activism,* (New York: Cambridge University Press, 2005), 170–172.
22. Doug McAdam, Sidney Tarrow, and Charles Tilly, *Dynamics of Contention* (Cambridge: Cambridge University Press, 2001), 7–8.

23. Tarrow, *Power in Movement*, 103–104.

24. Jack A. Goldstone, "More Social Movements or Fewer?: Beyond Political Opportunity Structures to Relational Fields," *Theory and Society* 33 (2004): 338. Goldstone argues political protest and routine political participation are more complementary and mutually reinforcing than oppositional and dichotomous.

25. Isis Sánchez Estellés, "The Political-Opportunity Structure of the Spanish Anti-War Movement (2002–2004) and Its Impact," *The Sociological Review* 58, no. 2 (2010): 246–269

26. Doug McAdam, "Conceptual Origins, Current Problems, Future Directions," in *Comparative Perspectives on Social Movements: Political Opportunities, Mobilizing Structures, and Cultural Framings*, ed. Doug McAdam, John D. McCarthy, and Mayer N. Zald (New York: Cambridge University Press, 1996), 27.

27. Jules Boykoff, *The Suppression of Dissent: How the State and Mass Media Squelch US American Social Movements*. (New York: Routledge, 2006), 22; David S. Meyer, "Political Opportunity and Nested Institutions," *Social Movement Studies* 2 (2003): 17–35.

28. Goldstone, "More Social Movements or Fewer?," 355.

29. One of the earliest, sharpest, and most thoroughgoing critiques comes from Jeff Goodwin and James Jasper who argue that by focusing on the "political," POS has an inherent bias toward considering the state (thereby missing important nonstate actors); by highlighting "opportunity," theorists underanalyze the role of threat and repression; and by spotlighting "structure," scholars underplay cultural and strategic processes. This has led to "conceptual stretching" whereby POS comes to simply mean the larger political environment. See Jeff Goodwin and James M. Jasper, "Caught in a Winding, Snarling Vine: The Structuralist Bias of Political Process Theory," *Sociological Forum* 14 no. 1 (1999): 27–54.

30. Kirshenbaum, "Voting to Snuff the Torch."

31. Rohrer, "Saying No to London 2012."

32. Doug McAdam, John D. McCarthy, and Mayer N. Zald, "Introduction: Opportunities, Mobilizing Structures, and Framing Processes—Toward a Synthetic, Comparative Perspective on Social Movements," in *Comparative Perspectives on Social Movements: Political Opportunities, Mobilizing Structures, and Cultural Framings*, ed. Doug McAdam, John D. McCarthy, and Mayer N. Zald (New York: Cambridge University Press, 1996), 6.

33. William Gamson, "Bystanders, Public Opinion, and the Media," in *The Blackwell Companion to Social Movements*, ed. David A. Snow, Sarah A. Soule, and Hanspeter Kriesi (London: Blackwell Publishing, 2004), 245.

34. Robert D. Benford and David A. Snow, "Framing Processes and Social Movements: An Overview and Assessment," *Annual Review of Sociology* 26 (2000): 615–617.

35. Jules Boykoff and Eulalie Laschever, "The Tea Party Movement, Framing, and the US Media," *Social Movement Studies* 10, no. 4 (2011): 341–366.

36. Alex Wolff, "Commercial Meddling, Avarice Have Brits Grumbling Prior to Olympics," *Sports Illustrated,* 18 June 2012, http://sportsillustrated.cnn.com/2012/writers/alexander_wolff/06/18/london-olympic-complaints/index.html#ixzz1yDNupYMj. To be fair, in this instance, Wolff asserted activists stood on solid ground: "frankly, it's hard not to find sympathy for the critics."

37. Robert W. Entman, "Framing: Toward Clarification of a Fractured Paradigm," *Journal of Communication* 43 (1993): 55.

38. Ruud Koopmans and Paul Statham, "Ethnic and Civic Conceptions of Nation-hood and the Differential Success of the Extreme Right in Germany and Italy," in *How Social Movements Matter*, ed. Mario Giugni, Doug McAdam, and Charles Tilly (Minneapolis: University of Minnesota Press, 1999), 228.

39. Holly J. McCammon, et al., "Movement Framing and Discursive Opportunity Structures: The Political Successes of the U.S. Women's Jury Movements," *American Sociological Review* 72 (2007): 726.

40. Brett Hutchins and Janine Mikosza, "The Web 2.0 Olympics: Athlete Blogging, Social Networking and Policy Contradictions at the 2008 Beijing Games," *Convergence: The International Journal of Research into New Media Technologies* 16, no. 3 (2010): 281, emphasis in original.

41. International Olympic Committee, "The Olympic Movement in Society," Copenhagen: 5 October, 2009. http://www.olympic.org/Documents/Conferences_Forums_and_Events/2009_Olympic_Congress/Olympic_Congress_Recommendations.pdf, 18.

42. International Olympic Committee, "IOC Social Media, Blogging and Internet Guidelines for Participants and Other Accredited Persons at the Sochi 2014 Olympic Winter Games," Lausanne: 31 August, 2011. http://www.olympic.org/Documents/Games_London_2012/IOC_Social_Media_Blogging_and_Internet_Guidelines-London.pdf, 1–3.

43. W. Lance Bennett and Alexandra Segerberg, "The Logic of Connective Action: Digital Media and the Personalization of Contentious Politics," *Information, Communication & Society* 15, no. 5 (2012): 743.

44. Jennifer Earl et al., "Changing the World One Webpage at a Time: Conceptualizing and Explaining Internet Activism," *Mobilization: An International Journal* 15, no. 4 (2010): 429–433.

45. Jennifer Earl and Katrina Kimport, *Digitally Enabled Social Change: Activism in the Internet Age* (Cambridge, MA: The MIT Press, 2011), 1–14. They call this latter form of collective action "E-tactics."

46. Victoria Carty, *Wired and Mobilizing: Social Movements, New Technology, and Electoral Politics* (New York and London: Routledge, 2011), 91.

47. Glenn J. Stalker and Lesley J. Wood, "Reaching Beyond the Net: Political Circuits and Participation in Toronto's G20 Protests," *Social Movement Studies* 12, no. 2 (2013): 187, 191, 193.

48. Robert W. McChesney, *Digital Disconnect: How Capitalism Is Turning the Internet against Democracy* (New York: The New Press, 2013), 97.

49. See Matthew Hindman, *The Myth of Digital Democracy* (Princeton, NJ: Princeton University Press, 2009).

50. Mark S. Granovetter, "The Strength of Weak Ties," *American Journal of Sociology* 78, no. 6 (1973): 1376, emphasis in original.

51. Doug McAdam, "Recruitment to High-Risk Activism: The Case of Freedom Summer," *American Journal of Sociology* 92, no 1 (1986): 87.

52. Bennett and Segerberg, "The Logic of Connective Action," 748.

53. Ibid., 752.

54. I borrow these categories from Paulo Gerbaudo, *Tweets and the Streets: Social Media and Contemporary Activism* (London: Pluto Press, 2012), 7.

55. Clay Shirky, *Here Comes Everybody: The Power of Organizing without Organizations* (New York: Penguin Books, 2008), 22.

56. Ibid., 54.

57. Ibid., 310.

58. Summer Harlow, "Social Media and Social Movements: Facebook and an Online Guatemalan Justice Movement that Moved Offline," *New Media & Society* 14, no. 2 (2012): 225–243; Zeynep Tufekci and Christopher Wilson, "Social Media and the Decision to Participate in Political Protest: Observations from Tahrir Square," *Journal of Communication* 62 (2012): 363–379; Jeffrey S. Juris, "Reflections on #Occupy Everywhere: Social Media, Public Space, and Emerging Logics of Aggregation," *American Ethnologist* 39, no. 2 (2012): 259–279.

59. Malcolm Gladwell, "Why the Revolution Will Not Be Tweeted," *New Yorker,* 4 October 2010: 42–49, http://www.gladwell.com/pdf/twitter.pdf.

60. Evgeny Morozov, *The Net Delusion: The Dark Side of Internet Freedom* (New York: Public Affairs, 2011), 190, 203.

61. Ingrid H. Hoofd, *Ambiguities of Activism: Alter-Globalism and the Imperatives of Speed* (New York and London: Routledge, 2012), 11, 14.

62. Gerbaudo, *Tweets and the Streets*, 12.

63. Ibid., 40, 42.

64. Ibid., 44.

65. Gerbaudo, *Tweets and the Streets*, 159; Bennett and Segerberg, "The Logic of Connective Action," 743–744.

66. Benford and Snow, "Framing Processes and Social Movements," 615–617.

67. Boykoff, *The Suppression of Dissent*, 290.

68. Jules Boykoff, "Limiting Dissent: The Mechanisms of State Repression in the United States," *Social Movement Studies* 6 (December 2007): 281–310

69. Fernandez, *Policing Dissent*, 32.

70. Jennifer Earl, "Political Repression: Iron Fists, Velvet Gloves, and Diffuse Control," *Annual Review of Sociology* 37 (2011): 13.1–13.24; Jennifer Earl, "Tanks, Tear Gas, and Taxes: Toward a Theory of Movement Repression." *Sociological Theory* 21 (2003): 44–68.

71. Patrick F. Gillham, Bob Edwards, and John A. Noakes, "Strategic Incapacitation and the Policing of Occupy Wall Street Protests in New York City, 2011," *Policing & Society* (2012): 2.

72. Ibid.

73. Patrick F. Gillham and John A. Noakes, "'More than a March in a Circle': Transgressive Protests and the Limits of Negotiated Management," *Mobilization: An International Quarterly* 12, no. 4 (2007): 343.

74. Peter B. Kraska, "Militarization and Policing—Its Relevance to 21st Century Police," *Policing: A Journal of Policy and Practice* 1, no. 4 (2007): 501–513.

75. Avery Brundage, "Text of IOC President Brundage's Address of Memorial Services at Olympic Stadium on September 6, 1972," ABC, Box 249, Reel 144, 6 September 1972, ICOSA.

76. Jules Boykoff, *Beyond Bullets: The Suppression of Dissent in the United States* (Oakland: AK Press, 2007), 16–18.

77. Sze Tsung Leong, "Control Space," in *Mutations*, ed. Rem Koolhaas, Stefano Boeri, Sanford Kwinter, Nadia Tazi, and Hans Ulrich Obrist (Barcelona: Actar, 2001), 187.

78. International Olympic Committee, *Olympic Charter*, Lausanne, Switzerland: 9 September, 2013. http://www.olympic.org/Documents/olympic_charter_en.pdf, 93.

79. Robert F. Wheeler, "Organized Sport and Organized Labour: The Workers' Sport Movement," *Journal of Contemporary History* 13 (1978): 191–210; Kevin B. Wamsley and Guy Schultz, "Rogues and Bedfellows: The IOC and the Incorporation of the FSFI," 113–118, *Fifth International Symposium for Olympic Research*. Western Ontario University, 2000.

80. Lee Sustar and Aisha Karim, eds., *Poetry & Protest: A Dennis Brutus Reader* (Chicago: Haymarket Books, 2006).

81. Karamichas, "The Olympics and the Environment"; Minky Worden, ed., *China's Great Leap: The Beijing Games and Olympian Human Rights Challenges* (New York: Seven Stories Press, 2008); Jules Boykoff, "The Anti-Olympics: Fun at the Games," *New Left Review* 67 (January-February 2011): 41–59.

82. M. Patrick Cottrell and Travis Nelson, "Not Just the Games? Power, Protest and Politics at the Olympics," *European Journal of International Relations* 17, no. 4 (2011): 729–753; Margaret Keck and Kathryn Sikkink, *Activists Beyond Borders: Advocacy Networks in International Politics* (Ithaca: Cornell University Press, 1998), 220.

83. Pierre de Coubertin, *Olympism: Selected Writings*, ed. Norbert Müller (Lausanne: International Olympic Committee, 2000): 739–740.

84. Richard D. Mandell, *The Nazi Olympics* (Urbana and Chicago: University of Illinois Press, 1987).

85. de Coubertin, *Olympism*, 584.

86. Avery Brundage, "Remarks by Avery Brundage: 64th Session International Olympic Committee," ABC, Box 81, Reel 45, 24 April 1966, ICOSA.

87. Avery Brundage, untitled memo. ABC, Box 70, Reel 40, 18 March 1968, ICOSA.

88. Dave Zirin, *Welcome to the Terrordome: The Pain, Politics, and Promise of Sports* (Chicago: Haymarket Books, 2007), 126.

89. Alan Tomlinson, "Carrying the Torch for Whom?: Symbolic Power and Olympic Ceremony," in *The Olympics at the Millennium: Power, Politics, and the Games*, ed. Kay Schaffer and Sidonie Smith (New Brunswick, NJ: Rutgers University Press 2000), 170.

90. Lenskyj, *Inside the Olympic Industry*, 149.

91. Andy Miah, Beatriz García, and Tian Zhihui, "'We Are the Media': Nonaccredited Media and Citizen Journalists at the Olympic Games," in *Owning the Olympics: Narratives of the New China*, ed. Monroe E. Price and Daniel Dayan (Ann Arbor: The University of Michigan Press, 2008), 339, 343. The authors used the term in the context of exploring ambush media processes, meaning: "the process of capitalizing on the work of official media (hijacking) without intending an obvious corruption of that official journalism or any specific harm to it."

92. Monroe E. Price, "On Seizing the Olympic Platform," in *Owning the Olympics: Narratives of the New China*, ed. Monroe E. Price and Daniel Dayan, 86–114 (Ann Arbor: The University of Michigan Press, 2008). Price uses the term "piggybacking" rather than "piggyjacking."

93. Guy Debord, *The Society of the Spectacle*, trans. Donald Nicholson Smith (New York: Zone Books, 1995), 12.

94. Douglas Kellner, *Media Spectacle* (London: Routledge, 2003), 177.

95. Stephen Duncombe, *Dream: Re-Imagining Progressive Politics in an Age of Fantasy* (New York: The New Press, 2007), 126.

96. Angelique Haugerud, *No Billionaire Left Behind: Satirical Activism in America* (Stanford, CA: Stanford University Press, 2013), 191.

97. Ibid., 43.
98. Ibid., 190.
99. Pew Research Center, "Winter Olympics."
100. Hiestand, "An Olympics Ratings Analysis," *USA Today*, 24 August 2008, http://www.usatoday.com/sports/columnist/hiestand-tv/2008-08-24-olympics-ratings_N.htm.
101. "NBC's Olympics Coverage Was Most-Watched TV Event in US History," *Reuters*, 14 August 2012, http://www.guardian.co.uk/sport/2012/aug/14/nbc-olympic-coverage-most-watched.
102. Amy Chozick, "NBC Unpacks Trove of Data from Olympics," *New York Times*, 26 September 2012, B3.
103. John Plunkett, "BBC Olympics Coverage Watched by 90% of UK Population," *Guardian*, 13 August 2012.
104. CNN/ORC Poll, 7–8 August 2012, http://www.pollingreport.com/olympics.htm.
105. Thomas F. Carter, "The Olympics as Sovereign Subject Maker," in *Watching the Olympics: Politics, Power, and Representation*, ed. John Sugden and Alan Tomlinson (London and New York: Routledge, 2012), 62.
106. John Sugden and Alan Tomlinson, "Afterword,: 'No Other Anything . . .': The Olympic Games Yesterday and Today," in *Watching the Olympics: Politics, Power, and Representation*, ed. John Sugden and Alan Tomlinson (London: Routledge, 2012), 249.
107. This typology draws from a number of studies, including Jean Harvey, John Horne, and Parissa Safai, "Alterglobalization, Global Social Movements, and the Possibility of Political Transformation through Sport," *Sociology of Sport Journal* 26 (2009): 383–403; Larry Gerlach, "An Uneasy Discourse: Salt Lake 2002 and Olympic Protest," in *Pathways: Critiques and Discourse in Olympic Research*, ed. Robert K. Barney, 141–150 (London, Ontario, CA: International Centre for Olympic Studies, 2008); Cottrell and Nelson, "Not Just the Games?"
108. John Horne, *Sport in Consumer Culture* (New York: Palgrave Macmillan, 2006), 82.
109. Ibid.
110. Kellner, *Media Spectacle*, 74. Kellner explores how Michael Jordan is "a polysemic signifier."
111. There is evidence the national media in the United States are "hostile to substantive (issue-oriented) messages" from candidates, preferring the fluffy, which trends toward the polysemous. See Julianne F. Flowers, Audrey A. Haynes, and Michael H. Crespin, "The Media, the Campaign, and the Message," *The American Journal of Political Science* 47 (2003): 259–273.
112. "65 Athletes Support Boycott of Olympics on S. Africa Issue," *New York Times*, 12 April 1968, 28.
113. Harry Edwards, *The Revolt of the Black Athlete* (New York: The Free Press, 1969), 129.
114. Arthur Daley, "The Incident," *New York Times*, 20 October 1968, S2.
115. Brent Musberger, "Bizarre Protest by Smith, Carlos Tarnishes Medals," *Chicago American*, 17 October 1968, 43.
116. Douglas Hartmann, *Race, Culture, and the Revolt of the Black Athlete: The 1968 Olympic Protests and Their Aftermath* (Chicago: University of Chicago Press, 2003), 166.

117. See https://sites.google.com/a/olympismproject.org/olympism-project/; Peter Kaufman and Eli A. Wolff, "Playing and Protesting: Sport as a Vehicle for Social Change," *Journal of Sport and Social Issues* 34, no. 2 (2010): 170–171.

118. Eli Wolff, personal interview by author, 19 October 2012.

119. Payne, *Olympic Turn Around*, 169.

120. For years the IOC had taken South African sports officials at their word that they would not exclude people from their Olympic teams based on race if they could legitimately earn a spot on the team.

121. "Olympics Rebuff South Africans," *New York Times*, 28 January 1964, 36.

122. See Sam Ramsany, "Letter to the President of Organising Committee for the 21st Olympiad," JWC, Box 21, Folder 39, 31 May 1976. ICOSA.

123. Harvey, Horne, and Safai, "Alterglobalization, Global Social Movements," 392.

124. Douglas Booth, *The Race Game: Sport and Politics in South Africa* (London: Frank Cass Publishers, 1998), 61.

125. Rob Nixon, "Apartheid on the Run: The South African Sports Boycott," *Transitions* 58 (1992): 77.

126. Booth, *The Race Game*, 78–79.

127. Avery Brundage, "Letter to All IOC Members, All NOC Members, All International Federations," ABC, Box 70, Reel 40, 18 March 1968, ICOSA.

128. Booth, *The Race Game*, 111–112.

129. Sam Ramsany, "Letter to the President of Organising Committee for the 21st Olympiad," JWC, Box 21, Folder 39, 31 May 1976, ICOSA.

130. Dennis Brutus, "Letter to Mr. Duncan McSwain," JWC, Box D, Folder 87, 10 January 1970, ICOSA.

131. Lord Killanin, "Letter to Denis McIldowie," JWC, Box 21, Folder 39, 21 April 1976, ICOSA.

132. Bruce Kidd, "Letter to Mr. Harry Kerrison," JWC, Box 17, Folder 5, 22 March 1974, ICOSA.

133. Avery Brundage, "Cable to All Members of the IOC," ABC, Box 70, Reel 40, n.d., ICOSA.

134. By the 1980s, inside the IOC, members like Richard Pound were pressing for a stronger stand against apartheid. He later wrote, "I thought they were missing an opportunity to show that sport could find solutions to a difficult problem that had, to date, baffled the political leaders." See Richard W. Pound, *Inside the Olympics: A Behind-the-Scenes Look at the Politics, the Scandals, and the Glory of the Games* (Canada: Wiley, 2004), 123.

135. For instance, such as antisweatshop group Play Fair works to improve labor conditions for those producing gear for the Games in an effort to produce a sweat-free Olympics. See Jill Timms, "The Olympics as a Platform for Protest: A Case Study of the London 2012 'Ethical' Games and the Play Fair Campaign for Workers' Rights," *Leisure Studies* 31, no. 3 (2012): 355–372; See also http://www.playfair2012.org/.

136. IOC, "XII Olympic Congress," Paris, 1994, http://www.olympic.org/paris-1994 -olympic-congress.

137. International Olympic Committee, *Olympic Charter*, 15 June 1995, 13.

138. John Shaw, "The Budget and the Public Nag," *New York Times*, 10 May 1999, D4.

139. John Shaw, "Bondi Blues: Plan Elicits a Protest," *New York Times*, 9 May 2000, D8.

140. Miranda Devine, "Sun, Sand and Angry Hippies," *The Daily Telegraph (Sydney)*, 10 May 2000, 39.

141. Vanessa Walker, "Outnumbered Protesters Dig in for Battle of Bondi," *The Australian*, 9 May 2000, 3.
142. Lenskyj, *The Best Olympics Ever?*, 197.
143. Lenskyj, *Inside the Olympic Industry*, 140–153.
144. Robert K. Barney, "The Olympic Games in Modern Times," in *Onward to the Olympics: Historical Perspectives on the Olympic Games*, ed. Gerald P. Schaus and Stephen R. Wenn, 221–241 (Waterloo, ON: Wilfrid Laurier University Press, 2007), 238.
145. Lenskyj, *The Best Olympics Ever?*, 151.
146. International Olympic Committee, *Olympic Charter*, 1933, 12, http://www .olympic.org/Documents/OSC/Ressources/Bibliotheque/Olympic_Charter/ 1933%20-%20olympic%20Charter.pdf.
147. International Olympic Committee, "Olympic Rules," 1946, 27, http://www .olympic.org/Documents/OSC/Ressources/Bibliotheque/Olympic_Charter/ 1946%20-%20olympic%20Charter.pdf.
148. International Olympic Committee, *Olympic Charter*, 1950. 8, http://www .olympic.org/Documents/OSC/Ressources/Bibliotheque/Olympic_Charter/ 1950%20-%20olympic%20Charter.pdf.
149. Comité International Olympique, "Règles pour les Jeux Régionaux," "Rules for Regional Games," 1952, 7, http://www.olympic.org/Documents/OSC/ Ressources/Bibliotheque/Olympic_Charter/1952%20-%20olympic%20 Charter%20%20-%20Rules%20for%20Regional%20Games.pdf.
150. International Olympic Committee, "The Olympic Games: Charter, Rules and Regulations, General Information," 1955, 31.
151. International Olympic Committee, *Olympic Charter*, 1974, 51.
152. Ibid., 54.
153. International Olympic Committee, "Olympic Rules 1975 (provisional edition)," 35.
154. International Olympic Committee, *Olympic Charter*, 1978, 31.
155. International Olympic Committee, *Olympic Charter*, June 1991, 60.
156. International Olympic Committee, *Olympic Charter*, 2004, 101. In the 2007 *Olympic Charter*, this becomes Rule 51, which reads exactly the same as the 2004 Charter.
157. International Olympic Committee, *Olympic Charter*, 2013, 93.
158. International Olympic Committee, *Olympic Charter*, 1976, 63, http://www .olympic.org/Documents/OSC/Ressources/Bibliotheque/Olympic_Charter/ 1966%20-%20olympic%20Charter.pdf.
159. Lord Killanin, *My Olympic Years* (New York: William Morrow and Company, Inc., 1983), 10.
160. George Orwell, *A Collection of Essays* (New York: Harcourt Brace Jovanovich Publishers, 1946), 167.

Chapter 2   Space Matters

1. Sabine Bitter, personal interview by author, via email, 25 August 2010.
2. Harsha Walia, personal interview by author, 6 February 2010.
3. Tom Mertes, *A Movement of Movements: Is Another World Really Possible?* (London: Verso, 2004).
4. International Olympic Committee, *Olympic Charter*, 93.

5. Michael Hardt and Antonio Negri, *Empire* (London: Harvard University Press, 2000), 124, 45.
6. Reg Johanson, *Escraches* (Vancouver, BC, Coast Salish Territory: Left Hand Press, 2010), n.p. Used with permission.
7. Barbara Yaffe, "PM's Strategy of Controlling Message Fails to Silence Opponents," *Vancouver Sun,* 12 February 2010, B2.
8. Tarrow, *The New Transnational Activism,* 170–172.
9. Lance W. Bennett, "Social Movements beyond Borders: Understanding Two Eras of Transnational Activism," in *Transnational Protest and Global Activism,* ed. Donatella della Porta and Sidney Tarrow (New York: Rowman & Littlefield, 2005), 213.
10. Lenskyj, *Olympic Industry Resistance,* 65.
11. David Eby, personal interview by author, 5 February 2010.
12. Gord Hill, personal interview by author, 18 August 2010.
13. Christine O'Bonsawin, "'There Will Be No Law That Will Come against Us': An Important Episode of Indigenous Resistance and Activism in Olympic History," in *The Palgrave Handbook of Olympic Studies,* ed. Helen Jefferson Lenskyj and Stephen Wagg Basingstoke (New York: Palgrave Macmillan, 2012), 475.
14. Nancy J. Parezo, "A 'Special Olympics': Testing Racial Strength and Endurance at the 1904 Louisiana Purchase Exhibition" in *The 1904 Anthropology Days and Olympic Games: Sport, Race, and American Imperialism,* ed. Susan Brownell, 59–126 (Lincoln: University of Nebraska Press, 2008); Mark Dyreson, "The 'Physical Value' of Races and Nations: Anthropology and Athletics at the Louisiana Purchase Exhibition," in *The 1904 Anthropology Days and Olympic Games: Sport, Race, and American Imperialism,* ed. Susan Brownell, 127–155 (Lincoln: University of Nebraska Press, 2008).
15. Parezo, "A 'Special Olympics.'"
16. O'Bonsawin, "'There Will Be No Law That Will Come against Us,'" 475.
17. James E. Sullivan, "Anthropology Days at the Stadium," in *Spalding's Official Athletic Almanac for 1905,* ed. James E. Sullivan (New York: American Sports Publishing, 1905), 251.
18. Parezo, "A 'Special Olympics,'" 92. This was all lost on Sullivan. Anyone who broke a rule was summarily disqualified, but then organizers realized they wouldn't have enough participants for the finals.
19. Parezo, "A 'Special Olympics,'" 89, 96.
20. Sullivan, "Anthropology Days at the Stadium," 257.
21. Sullivan, "Anthropology Days at the Stadium," 253.
22. Quoted in Parezo, "A 'Special Olympics,'" 112. Parezo sums up Sullivan's political corollary—because he believed "Native peoples were intellectually, socially, cognitively, and morally inferior by nature," they "were not as good prospects for assimilation as European immigrants" (97).
23. de Coubertin, *Olympism,* 695, 407, 409, 742.
24. de Coubertin, *Olympism,* 695.
25. Montréal 1976, Games of the XXI Olympiad, "Official Report," Volume 1 (Ottawa: COJO, 1978), 306.
26. Forsyth, "Teepees and Tomahawks," 72.
27. Hans Tammemagi, "Olympic Games a Showcase for Native Culture," *Indian Country Today,* 24 March 2010.

28. International Olympic Committee, *Olympic Charter*, 11.
29. Kim Pemberton, "Aboriginal Groups Divided on Whether to Support Olympics," *Vancouver Sun*, 6 February 2010.
30. See Hamar Foster and Alan Grove, "'Trespassers on the Soil': *United States v. Tom* and a New Perspective on the Short History of Treaty Making in Nineteenth-Century British Columbia" *B.C. Studies* 138/139 (2003): 51–84; Cole Harris, *Making Native Space: Colonialism, Resistance, and Reserves in British Columbia* (Vancouver: UBC Press, 2002). There are currently sixty First Nations in British Columbia participating in various stages of the treaty process: www.bctreaty.net.
31. Taiaiake Alfred, "Deconstructing the British Columbia Treaty Process," *Balayi: Culture, Law and Colonialism* 3 (2001): 42.
32. Some suggested the slogan may have alienated potential supporters thereby limiting the numbers that came out to the streets in support. See Charlie Smith, "Did the Anti-Olympic Movement Miss the Mark by Focusing on Stolen Aboriginal Land?" *Georgia Strait*, 21 February 2010, http://www.straight.com/article-292384/vancouver/did-antiolympic-movement-miss-mark-focusing-stolen-aboriginal-land.
33. O'Bonsawin, "'No Olympics on Stolen Native Land'" 152.
34. Economist Intelligence Unit, "Global Liveability Report," January 2010, http://www.eiu.com/site_info.asp?info_name=The_Global_Liveability_Report&page=noads&rf=0#.
35. Frontier Centre for Public Policy, "The 6th Annual Demographia International Housing Affordability Survey: 2010 Ratings for Metropolitan Markets," 39, http://www.fcpp.org/publication.php/3153.
36. Andy Merrifield, *Henri Lefebvre: A Critical Introduction* (New York: Routledge, 2006), 69–70, emphasis in original.
37. Am Johal, personal interview by author, 5 February 2010.
38. Richard B. Perelman, *Olympic Retrospective: The Games of Los Angeles* (Los Angeles: Los Angeles Olympic Organizing Committee, 1985), 119.
39. Boykoff, *Celebration Capitalism and the Olympic Games.*
40. Holger Preuss, *The Economics of Staging the Olympics: A Comparison of the Games, 1972–2008* (Cheltenham, UK: Edward Elgar, 2004), 290.
41. Daphne Bramham, "Olympics Bill Tops $6 billion—So Far," *Vancouver Sun*, 23 January 2009; Damian Inwood, "City Spent $550 Million on Olympics," *Vancouver Province*, 16 April 2010. Taxpayers spent $1 billion on a convention center built right beside Vancouver's extant convention center. Housing advocates noted between clenched teeth that such money could solve street homelessness in British Columbia.
42. Peter Birnie and Tiffany Crawford, "'Discouraged' Chairwoman Quits Over Lack of Provincial Support," *Vancouver Sun*, 19 August 2010; "School Board Riled Over Budget Review," *CBC*, 14 April 2010; Rod Mickleburgh, "BC Arts Groups Blast Funding Cuts," *Globe and Mail*, 12 July 2010.
43. Micheal Vonn, personal interview by author, 18 August 2010.
44. Gord Hill interview, 18 August 2010.
45. Gary Mason, "The Real Threat to the Olympics Could Be a Bloody Protest," *Globe & Mail*, 11 February 2010, A21.
46. Office of the Privacy Commissioner of Canada, "Privacy and Security at the Vancouver 2010 Winter Games," August 2009, http://www.priv.gc.ca/fs-fi/02_05_d_42_ol_e.cfm#004.

47. Micheal Vonn interview, 18 August 2010. In addition, David Eby noted, "There are some cameras that are still in public space now that are the 'legacy' of the Olympic period." The BCCLA is concerned that the "legacy cameras'" might eventually end up in public schools. David Eby interview, 6 August 2010.

48. Darah Hansen, "Victoria Cop Infiltrated Anti-Games Group, Jamie Graham Says," *Vancouver Sun,* 2 December 2009.

49. Christopher Shaw, personal interview by author, 17 August 2010.

50. International Olympic Committee, "Brand Protection: Olympic Marketing Ambush Protection and Clean Venue Guidelines," (Lausanne, Switzerland: Olympic Committee, 2005).

51. Michael Barnholden, personal interview by author, 19 August 2010.

52. David Eby interview, 6 August 2010.

53. Neil Smith and Deborah Cowen, "'Martial Law in the Streets of Toronto': G20 Security and State Violence," *Human Geography* 3, no. 3 (2010): 38, emphasis in original.

54. Edward W. Soja, *Seeking Spatial Justice* (Minneapolis: University of Minnesota Press, 2010), 89.

55. Henri Lefebvre, *The Production of Space,* trans. Donald Nicholson-Smith (Oxford: Blackwell, 1991) 365, emphasis in original.

56. "Olympic Cauldron Fence Thwarts Visitors," *CBC,* 16 February 2010. VANOC eventually moved the fence closer to the cauldron and added a rooftop viewing area to accommodate disenchanted Olympics-goers who were unable to secure an unobstructed glimpse of the torch.

57. Mustafa Dikeç, "Justice and the Spatial Imagination," *Environment and Planning A* 33 (2001): 1792, emphasis in original.

58. Reg Johanson, personal interview by author, 16 August 2010.

59. Harsha Walia, personal interview by author, 18 August 2010.

60. Cecily Nicholson, personal interview by author, 6 August 2010.

61. Hardt and Negri, *Empire,* 61, 208, 44, emphasis in original.

62. Aaron Vidaver, personal interview by author, 11 August 2010. In 2002 Vidaver participated in the Woodwards squat, a crucial precedent to the Olympics space seizures.

63. Nathan Crompton, personal interview by author, 19 August 2010.

64. Dave Diewert and Harsha Walia, personal interviews by author, 17 August 2010, 18 August 2010.

65. Mertes, "Grass-Roots Globalism," 110.

66. Harsha Walia interview, 18 August 2010.

67. Although more than one hundred organizations signed on in support of the action, numerous activists noted the conspicuous absence of the labor movement from anti-Olympics organizing.

68. Henri Lefebvre, *Writings on Cities,* trans. Eleonore Kofman and Elizabeth Lebas (Oxford: Blackwell, 1996), 112.

69. Aaron Vidaver interview.

70. Mustafa Dikeç, "Police, Politics, and the Right to the City," *GeoJournal* 58 (2003): 93.

71. Dave Diewert, personal interview by author, 17 August 2010; Harsha Walia interview, 18 August 2010.

72. Am Johal, personal interviews, 5 February 2010 and 17 August 2010. The tents were ethically sourced in China. For more information, see www.redtents.org.

73. Lefebvre, *The Production of Space,* 383.

74. Cecily Nicholson interview, 6 August 2010. For the audio archive of Evening News events, see http://radiomultiple.org/.

75. See http://shortrangepoeticdevice.blogspot.com/.

76. Earl and Kimport, *Digitally Enabled Social Change,* 124–125.

77. Nicholas Perrin, personal interview by author, 18 August 2010.

78. Herbert H. Haines, *Black Radicals and the Civil Rights Mainstream, 1954–1970,* (Knoxville: The University of Tennessee Press, 1988), 3.

79. Foster and Grove, "'Trespassers on the Soil,'" 53.

80. Robert Matas, "Olympics Protest's Vandalism Denounced," *Globe and Mail,* 15 February 2010.

81. David Eby interview, 6 August 2010.

82. Michael Hardt, "Today's Bandung?" *New Left Review* 14 (2001): 115–116.

83. Walter J. Nicholls, "The Urban Question Revisited: The Importance of Cities for Social Movements," *International Journal of Urban and Regional Research* 32, no. 4 (2008): 842.

84. "Olympic Village Social Housing Units Still Empty," *CBC,* 13 August 2010.

85. David Eby interview, 6 August 2010.

86. Jeff Derksen, "Art and Cities during Mega-Events: On the Intersection of Culture, Everyday Life, and the Olympics in Vancouver and Beyond. Part IV," *Camera Austria* 111 (2010): 60–61.

87. Dave Diewert and Franklin López, personal interviews by author, 17 August 2010.

88. Neil Smith, "Scale Bending and the Fate of the National," in *Scale and Geographic Inquiry: Nature, Society, and Method,* ed. Eric Sheppard and Robert B. McMaster (Oxford: Blackwell, 2004), 193.

89. Harsha Walia interview, 18 August 2010.

90. Miloon Kothari, "Report of the Special Rapporteur on Adequate Housing as a Component of the Right to an Adequate Standard of Living, and on the Right to Non-Discrimination in this Context." United Nations Human Rights Council, 17 February 2009, http://www2.ohchr.org/english/bodies/hrcouncil/docs/10session/A.HRC.10.7.Add.3.pdf, 24; Raquel Rolnik, "Report of the Special Rapporteur on Adequate Housing as a Component of the Right to an Adequate Standard of Living, and on the Right to Non-Discrimination in this Context." United Nations Human Rights Council, 2009, https://www.un.org/wcm/webdav/site/sport/shared/sport/pdfs/Resolutions/A-HRC-13-20/A-HRC-13-20_EN.pdf, 8, 10.

91. Paul Routledge, "'Our Resistance Will Be as Transnational as Capital': Convergence Space and Strategy in Globalising Resistance," *GeoJournal* 52 (2000): 27.

92. International Olympic Committee, "IOC Marketing Media Guide: Vancouver 2010," 35. *Vancouver Sun* reporter Jeff Lee served double duty for the Olympics, writing for both the *Sun* and freelancing for the IOC's magazine *The Olympic Review,* penning a piece called "Feeling the Buzz." It should be noted that Lee sometimes asked hard questions about the Olympics for the *Sun,* but neither he nor his newspaper was forthcoming about his conflict of interest. See Andrew MacLeod, "Sun's Olympics Reporter Was Paid to Write for IOC's Magazine," *The Tyee,* 22 May 2009.

93. Jules Boykoff, "Surveillance, Spatial Compression, and Scale: The FBI and Martin Luther King, Jr." *Antipode* 39, no. 4 (2007): 729–756.

94. Micheal Vonn interview, 18 August 2010; British Columbia Civil Liberties Association, "Provincial Government Shuts BCCLA out of International Media Centre" 10 February 2010, http://www.bccla.org/news.htm.

95. Gord Hill interview, 18 August 2010.

96. Carty, *Wired and Mobilizing,* 91; Boykoff, *The Suppression of Dissent,* 290.

97. Mark Andrejevic, *iSpy: Surveillance and Power in the Interactive Era* (Lawrence: University Press of Kansas, 2007), 2.

98. Franklin López, personal interview by author, 17 August 2010.

99. Jodi Dean, *Democracy and Other Neoliberal Fantasies: Communicative Capitalism and Left Politics* (Durham: Duke University Press, 2009), 49, 24, emphasis in original.

100. Bennett, "Social Movements Beyond Borders."

101. Dawn Paley, personal interview by author, 17 August 2010.

102. Smith and Cowen, "'Martial Law in the Streets of Toronto.'"

103. Government of Canada, G8-G20 Integrated Security Unit, "FAQs," http://www.g8-g20isu.ca/g20/faq-eng.htm.

104. Harsha Walia interview, 18 August 2010.

105. David Harvey, "The Right to the City," *New Left Review* 53 (2008): 32.

106. Lefebvre, *Writings on Cities,* 158; For more on the US Right to the City Movement, see http://www.righttothecity.org/.

107. Soja, *Seeking Spatial Justice,* 59.

108. Franklin López interview, 17 August 2010.

109. Reg Johanson and Mercedes Eng, personal interviews by author, 16 August 2010.

Chapter 3   London Calling

1. To access the documents, see http://wikileaks.org/the-gifiles.html.

2. WikiLeaks, "Public Policy Question for Coca-Cola," 2 June 2009, EMAIL-ID 5413843, http://wikileaks.org/gifiles/docs/5413843_public-policy-question-for-coca-cola-.html.

3. WikiLeaks, "Bhopal update—03-07-11," 7 March 2011, EMAIL-ID 389943, http://wikileaks.org/gifiles/docs/389943_bhopal-update-03-07-11-.html.

4. WikiLeaks, "DOW CONFIDENTIAL: Bhopal Monitoring Report Friday, November 18, 2011" 19 November 2011, EMAIL-ID 407784, http://wikileaks.org/gifiles/docs/407784_dow-confidential-bhopal-monitoring-report-friday-november-18.html.

5. Colin Toogood, personal interview by author, 22 August 2012.

6. Julian Cheyne, personal interview by author, 2 May 2012.

7. Julian Cheyne interview, 10 August 2012.

8. Julian Cheyne interview, 2 May 2012.

9. Meredith Alexander, personal interview by author, 11 July 2012.

10. Julian Cheyne interview, 17 October 2011.

11. Boris Johnson, "Put a Sock in It, We're on to a Winner," *The Sun,* 20 July 2012, http://www.thesun.co.uk/sol/homepage/features/4439396/Boris-Put-a-sock-in-it-were-on-to-a-winner.html.

12. Kerry-anne Mendoza, personal interview by author, 2 August 2012.

13. Isaac Marrero-Guillamón, personal interview by author, 19 June 2012.

14. Jess Worth, personal interview by author, 10 May 2012.

15. Emily Coats, personal interview by author, 20 May 2012.

16. Agent Monstris, personal interview by author, 5 August 2012.

17. David Renton, personal interview by author, 20 July 2012.

18. Preuss, *The Economics of Staging the Olympics,* 290.
19. London 2012, "Candidate File, Vol. 1," 25.
20. National Audit Office, "The Budget for the London 2012 Olympic and Paralympic Games," London, 2007, 6. London's candidature file employed a £1 to $1.60 conversion rate.
21. National Audit Office, "The Budget," 4.
22. Mike Wells, personal interview by author, 11 July 2012.
23. House of Commons, Culture, Media, and Sport Committee (hereafter CMSC), "London 2012 Olympic Games, Games and Paralympic Games: Funding and Legacy, Second Report of Session 2006–07," 1: 5.
24. Ibid., 48.
25. Ibid., 3, emphasis added.
26. CMSC, "London 2012 Olympic Games," 2: 69.
27. CMSC, "London 2012 Olympic Games," 1: 4.
28. Preuss, *The Economics of Staging the Olympics.*
29. Gareth A. Davies, "Mayor Tricked Govt. into 2012 Olympic Bid, *Telegraph*, 25 April 2008.
30. Julian Cheyne, "The Aftermath 2012," *Games Monitor*, 11 July 2011, http://www.gamesmonitor.org.uk/node/1305.
31. Amy Oliver, "Cost of Olympics to spiral to £24bn," *Daily Mail,* 27 January 2012, http://www.dailymail.co.uk/news/article-2092077/London-2012-Olympics-cost-spiral-24bn—10-TIMES-higher-2005-estimate.html.
32. "The Greatest Sideshow on Earth," *The Economist*, 22 July 2010, http://www.economist.com/node/16647677.
33. Julian Cheyne and Martin Slavin, personal interviews by author, 25 July 2011.
34. CMSC, "London 2012 Olympic Games," 1: 10, emphasis added.
35. London 2012, "London 2012 'Public Transport Games' Plan Launched," 28 February 2007, http://www.london2012.com/press/media-releases/2007/02/london-2012-public-transport-games-plan-launched.php.
36. John Horne and Garry Whannel, *Understanding the Olympics* (London and New York: Routledge, 2012), 101.
37. Hélène Mulholland, "David Cameron Claims London 2012 Will Bring £13bn 'Gold for Britain,'" *Guardian*, 5 July 2012, http://www.guardian.co.uk/politics/2012/jul/05/david-cameron-london-2012-gold-britain.
38. Simon Jenkins, "The Olympics Were a Celebration Worthy of Nero—and as Extravagant," *Guardian*, 27 December 2012, http://www.guardian.co.uk/commentisfree/2012/dec/27/olympics-nero-orgasmic-hangover.
39. Martyn Herman, "Olympics-London 2012 Under Budget Despite High Running Costs," *Reuters*, 23 October 2012, http://www.reuters.com/article/2012/10/23/olympics-budget-idUSL3E8LN4KF20121023.
40. "UK Economy Returns to Growth with Help from Olympics," *BBC*, 25 October 2012, http://www.bbc.co.uk/news/business-20078231.
41. "Louise Cooper on UK AAA-Rating and Triple-Dip Recession," *BBC*, 7 January 2013, http://www.bbc.co.uk/news/uk-politics-20935599.
42. See http://www.youthfightforjobs.com/wordpress/wordpress/?p=519.
43. Suzanne Beishon, personal interview by author, 28 July 2012.
44. Martin Hickman, "Britain Flooded with 'Brand Police' to Protect Sponsors," *Independent*, 16 July 2012, http://www.independent.co.uk/news/uk/home-news/

britain-flooded-with-brand-police-to-protect-sponsors-7945436.html#; Simon Goodley, Josephine Moulds, and Simon Rogers, "London 2012: Olympic Sponsors Waive Tax Break," *Guardian*, 18 July 2012, http://www.guardian.co.uk/sport/2012/jul/18/london-2012-visa-olympic-tax.

45. Simon Rogers, "London 2012 Olympic Sponsors List: Who Are They and What Have They Paid?" *Guardian*, 19 July 2012, http://www.guardian.co.uk/sport/datablog/2012/jul/19/london-2012-olympic-sponsors-list.

46. The IOC also contributed funds to help stage the Games.

47. Tom Gardner, "London 2012 Organisers Switched Traffic Lights Green to Ease Gridlock for Olympic VIPs During Bid to Host the Games," *Daily Mail*, 13 May 2012, http://www.dailymail.co.uk/news/article-2143943/London-2012-organisers-admit-switching-traffic-lights-green-Olympic-VIPs-win-bid.html; Michael Joseph Gross, "Jumping through Hoops," *Vanity Fair*, June 2012, http://www.vanityfair.com/culture/2012/06/international-olympic-committee-london-summer-olympics.

48. James Ball, "Torchbearers Picked by Sponsors Keep Flame of Commerce Alive," *Guardian*, 6 June 2012, http://www.guardian.co.uk/sport/2012/jun/06/torchbearers-nominated-olympics-sponsors.

49. Sponsors received 8 percent of tickets, while 12 percent went to National Olympic Committees and another 5 percent to other members of the Olympic movement, including accredited journalists. Mark Easton, "Empty Seats and the Privilege of the Games," *BBC*, 3 August 2012, http://www.bbc.co.uk/news/uk-19109997.

50. Rajeev Syal, "Cherie Blair: London's Secret Lobbying Weapon," *Guardian*, 22 July 2012, http://www.guardian.co.uk/sport/2012/jul/22/cherie-blair-london-olympics-2012.

51. Moody's Investors Service, "Olympics Will Give Only Short-Term Boost to Corporates," 1 May 2012, http://www.moodys.com/research/Moodys-Olympics-will-give-only-short-term-boost-to-corporates—PR_244640. The firm also commented, "the benefits are likely to be largely short-lived, providing only a temporary fillip to corporate earnings."

52. "Adidas Sales Top 14.5b Euros," *AFP*, 27 December 2012.

53. HM Revenue & Customs, "Accredited Individuals and 2012 Partner Workers: Business Profits Exemption," n.d., http://www.hmrc.gov.uk/2012games/tax-exemptions/bus-profits-exemption.htm; Tim Hunt, "The Great Olympic Tax Swindle, *Ethical Consumer*, 5 July 2012, http://www.ethicalconsumer.org/commentanalysis/corporatewatch/thegreatolympictaxswindle.aspx.

54. Hunt, "The Great Olympic Tax Swindle."

55. Simon Goodley, Josephine Moulds, and Simon Rogers, "London 2012: Olympic Sponsors Waive Tax Break," *Guardian*, 18 July 2012, http://www.guardian.co.uk/sport/2012/jul/18/london-2012-visa-olympic-tax; 38 Degrees, "Hurray! Now What Next?" 26 July 2012, http://blog.38degrees.org.uk/2012/07/26/hurray-now-what-next/; Anna Lezard, "Coca Cola Decides to Pay their Olympic Taxes," *New Statesman*, 18 July 2012, http://www.newstatesman.com/blogs/business/2012/07/coca-cola-decides-pay-their-olympic-taxes.

56. Earl and Kimport, *Digitally Enabled Social Change*, 5–8.

57. Will Dooling, "Corporate 'Sin Washing'—Embracing the Olympic Brand Pays Off for Sponsors," *Truthout*, 11 August 2012, http://truth-out.org/news/item/10830-corporate-sin-washing-embracing-the-olympic-brand-pays-off-for-sponsors.

58. Heather Rogers, *Green Gone Wrong: How Our Economy Is Undermining the Environmental Revolution* (New York: Scribner, 2010), 4.

59. London 2012, "London 2012," preface.

60. London 2012, "Candidate File, Vol. 1," 75.

61. London 2012, "Candidate File, Vol. 1," 24–25.

62. LOCOG, "London 2012 Sustainability Report: A Blueprint for Change" http://www.london2012.com/mm%5CDocument%5CPublications%5CSustainabilit y%5C01%5C24%5C09%5C14%5Clondon-2012-sustainability-report-a-blueprint -for-change.pdf, 87.

63. Commission for a Sustainable London 2012 (hereafter CSL), "Sustainable Sourced?: A Snapshot Review of the Sustainability of London 2012 Merchandise" London: The Commission, 2011. http://www.cslondon.org/wp-content/ uploads/downloads/2011/10/Sustainably-Sourced-2011.pdf, 2.

64. Meredith Alexander interview, 11 July 2012.

65. CSL, "Breaking the Tape: Pre-Games Review," London: The Commission, 2012. http://www.cslondon.org/wp-content/uploads/downloads/2012/06/CSL _Annual_Review_20111.pdf, 3.

66. Meredith Alexander interview, 11 July 2012.

67. To see the videos, go to www.greenwashgold.org.

68. Rupert Neate, "Olympic Medal Pollution Protesters Disrupt Rio Tinto Meeting," Guardian, 19 April 2012, http://www.guardian.co.uk/business/2012/apr/19/ olympic-medal-pollution-protesters-rio-tinto.

69. Meredith Alexander interview, 11 July 2012.

70. Danny Chivers, personal interview by author, 9 August 2012.

71. Mark Brown, "Galleries Renew £10m BP Deal Despite Environmental Protests," Guardian, 19 December 2011, http://www.guardian.co.uk/culture/2011/dec/19/ galleries-renew-bp-deal-protests.

72. Danny Chivers, "BP or Not BP, That Is the Question," London Late, 7 August 2012, 16.

73. Text of soliloquy reprinted with permission of Richard Howlett. To see a video of the performance, see "BP or Not BP? The Debut Performance of the Reclaim Shakespeare Company," http://www.youtube.com/watch?v =oMAImPJHqHk&feature=player_embedded.

74. Richard Howlett, personal interview by author, 6 August 2012.

75. Danny Chivers interview, 9 August 2012.

76. Emily Dickinson, The Complete Poems of Emily Dickinson (New York: Little Brown and Company, 1961), 506.

77. Richard Howlett interview, 6 August 2012.

78. Danny Chivers interview, 9 August 2012.

79. Richard Howlett interview, 6 August 2012.

80. See http://bp-or-not-bp.org/.

81. Gerbaudo, Tweets and the Streets, 161–162.

82. "Oiling the wheels of the Shakespeare festival," Guardian, 22 April 2012, http:// www.guardian.co.uk/stage/2012/apr/22/oiling-wheels-shakespeare-festival.

83. Jess Worth interview, 6 August 2012.

84. See http://bp-or-not-bp.org/news/museum/.

85. Richard Howlett interview, 6 August 2012.

86. Emily Jupp, "The Great Shakespearean Flashmob Strikes Again," Independent, 14 November 2012, http://www.independent.co.uk/arts-entertainment/theatre -dance/news/the-great-shakespearean-flashmob-strikes-again-8316440.html.

87. Colin Toogood interview, 22 August 2012.

88. Bridget Botelho, personal interview by author, 2 August 2012.
89. Colin Toogood interview, 22 August 2012.
90. Ibid.
91. Paul Sonne, "Dow's Olympic Goals," *Wall Street Journal*, 9 August 2012, B3.
92. Lefebvre, *The Production of Space*, 365.
93. Oliver Pickup, "IOC President Jacques Rogge Insists He Is 'Working Class' Despite VIP Treatment," *Telegraph*, 23 July 2012, http://www.telegraph.co.uk/sport/olympics/9419914/London-2012-Olympics-IOC-President-Jacques-Rogge-insists-he-is-working-class-despite-VIP-treatment.html.
94. Games Monitor, "Taxi," 9 October 2011, http://gamesmonitor.org.uk/blog/1365.
95. David Millward, "Cab Drivers Create Gridlock in Games Lane Protest," *Telegraph*, 17 July 2012, http://www.telegraph.co.uk/sport/olympics/news/9406127/Cab-drivers-create-gridlock-in-Games-Lane-protest.html; Alan Jones, "Taxi Drivers Bring Forth Olympic Traffic Lanes Protest," *Independent*, 27 July 2012, http://www.independent.co.uk/news/uk/home-news/london-2012-taxi-drivers-bring-forward-olympic-traffic-lanes-protest-7982113.html.
96. Center on Housing Rights and Evictions (hereafter COHRE), "Fair Play for Housing Rights: Mega-events, Olympic Games and Housing Rights," (Geneva, 2007).
97. COHRE, "One World, Whose Dream?: Housing Rights Violations and the Beijing Olympic Games." (Geneva, 2008), 8.
98. Julian Cheyne interview, 25 July 2011.
99. Julian Cheyne interview, 2 May 2012.
100. Charles Williams, "Olympic Hurdle," *Building Design*, 5 December 2003, http://www.bdonline.co.uk/olympic-hurdle/3030828.article.
101. Julian Cheyne interview, 25 July 2011.
102. Mary Smith, "When the Games Come to Town: Host Cities and the Local Impacts of the Olympics" (London East Research Institute Working Papers, December 2008), 54.
103. Interviews with Clays Lane residents: Julian Cheyne, 2 May 2012 and Mike Wells, 11 July 2012.
104. London 2012, "London 2012," 34.
105. Estelle du Boulay, personal interview by author, 3 August 2012.
106. Martin Slavin, personal interview by author, 25 July 2011.
107. Dave Hill, "The Battle Begins on a Newham Estate," *Guardian*, 13 June 2012, http://www.guardian.co.uk/sport/2012/jun/13/london-2012-legacy-battle-newham.
108. Olympic Delivery Authority, "Planning Information for the Temporary Basketball Facility at Leyton Marsh," London, January 2012, http://www.london2012.com/documents/oda-planning/planning-update-for-the-temporary-basketball-training-facility-at-leyton-mar.pdf.
109. Fizle Sagar, personal interview by author, 4 August 2012.
110. Katherine Underwood, "Campaigners Lose Battle to Keep Paralympics Basketball Courts Off Hackney Marsh," *Hackney Citizen*, 13 February 2012, http://hackneycitizen.co.uk/2012/02/13/campaigners-lose-basketball-courts-battle-paralympic-games-leyton-marsh/.
111. Charlie Charman, personal interview by author, 4 August 2012.
112. Vicky Sholund, personal interview by author, 4 August 2012.
113. Charlie Charman interview, 4 August 2012.

114. Melanie Strickland, personal interview by author, 7 August 2012.
115. Peter Walker, "Police Arrest Six at East London Olympics Facility Protest Camp," *Guardian*, 10 April 2012, http://www.guardian.co.uk/uk/2012/apr/10/police -arrest-london-olympics-occupy-protest.
116. Vicky Sholund interview, 4 August 2012.
117. Ibid.
118. Fizle Sagar interview, 4 August 2012.
119. For NOGOE's web site, see http://www.nogoe2012.com/
120. NOGOE Newsletter, September 2009, 5, http://www.nogoe2012.com/downloads/ 2009-september-newsletter-nogoe.pdf and NOGOE, "Greenwich Park, Application Nos 09/2598 and 09/2599: Annex D," 27 January 2010, http://www.nogoe2012 .com/appendices/2010-01-27-NOGOE-objection-annex-D-ecology.pdf.
121. NOGOE Newsletter, January 2010, 2, http://www.nogoe2012.com/downloads/ 2010-january-newsletter-nogoe.pdf.
122. NOGOE Newsletter, November 2009, 2, http://www.nogoe2012.com/ downloads/2009-november-newsletter-nogoe.pdf.
123. Owen Gibson, "London 2012 Test Event Draws Polite Protest," *Guardian*, 4 July 2011, http://www.guardian.co.uk/sport/2011/jul/04/london-olympics-test-event -greenwich-park?INTCMP=SRCH.
124. Rachel Mawhood, personal interview via e-mail by author, 9 January 2013.
125. Julian Cheyne interview, 25 July 2011.
126. David Renton interview, 20 July 2012.
127. Graeme Hayes and John Horne, "Sustainable Development, Shock and Awe?: London 2012 and Civil Society," *Sociology* 45, no. 5 (2011): 759.
128. David Featherstone, *Resistance, Space and Political Identities: The Making of Counter-Global Networks* (Oxford: Wiley-Blackwell, 2008), 7.
129. Philip Boyle and Kevin P. Haggerty "Spectacular Security: Mega-Events and the Security Complex," *International Political Sociology* 3 (2009): 259, 264, emphasis in original.
130. London 2012, "Candidate File, Vol. 3," 27.
131. Alan Cowell, "Subway and Bus Blasts in London Kill at Least 37," *New York Times*, 7 July 2005, A6.
132. London Assembly, "Policing Costs," 2–3.
133. Owen Gibson, "Police 'Have Learned Lessons of Riots,'" *Guardian*, 8 March 2012, http://www.guardian.co.uk/sport/2012/mar/09/london-2012-olympics-police-riots.
134. Mark Townsend, "Police Plan Preemptive Arrests to Stop Disruption," *Observer*, 2 June 2012, http://www.guardian.co.uk/uk/2012/jun/02/olympic-games-2012 -police-arrests?newsfeed=true.
135. Nick Hopkins, Robert Booth, and Owen Gibson, "MoD to Set Up Temporary Base for Troops," *Guardian*, 13 July 2012, http://www.guardian.co.uk/2012/ jul/13/olympic-security-temporary-base-troops.
136. Martin Robinson, "Welcome to London! Royal Navy's Largest Warship Sails Down the Thames as Armed Forces Put on Show of Strength for Olympics," *Daily Mail*, 13 July 2012, http://www.dailymail.co.uk/news/article-2173122/ Royal-Navys-largest-warship-sails-Thames-armed-forces-strength-Olympics .html#ixzz25cw7IozD.
137. Sandra Laville, "Metropolitan Police Plastic Bullets Stockpile up to 10,000 after UK Riots," *Guardian*, 3 May 2012, http://www.guardian.co.uk/uk/2012/may/03/

metropolitan-police-plastic-bullets-stockpile-riots; Ben Quinn, "Fast-track Court System Planned for London Olympics," *Guardian*, 25 June 2012, http://www .guardian.co.uk/law/2012/jun/26/fast-track-court-london-olympics.

138. Gavin Thomas, "Sonic Device Deployed in London During Olympics," *BBC*, 12 May 2012, http://www.bbc.co.uk/news/uk-england-london-18042528.

139. Robert Booth and Nick Hopkins, "Olympic Security Chaos: Depth of G4S Security Crisis Revealed," *Guardian*, 12 July 2012, http://www.guardian.co.uk/sport/2012/jul/12/london-2012-g4s-security-crisis.

140. Jules Boykoff and Pete Fussey, "London's Shadow Legacies: Security and Activism at the 2012 Olympics," *Contemporary Social Science* (forthcoming).

141. Sandra Laville, "Olympics Welcome Does Not Extend to All in London as Police Flex Muscles," *Guardian*, 4 May 2012, http://www.guardian.co.uk/uk/2012/may/04/olympics-welcome-london-police.

142. Estelle du Boulay interview, 3 August 2012.

143. Metropolitan Police Commissioner Bernard Hogan-Howe, "Total Policing," October 2011, http://www.feraa.org.uk/assets/content/documents/Commissioners_letter_to_Londoners.pdf.

144. Estelle du Boulay interview, 3 August 2012.

145. Space Hijackers, "Second Manifesto of the Space Hijackers," n.d., http://www .spacehijackers.org/html/manifesto.html.

146. For an academic treatment of Space Hijackers, see Paul Gilchrist and Neil Ravenscroft, "Space Hijacking and the Anarchopolitics of Leisure," *Leisure Studies* (2012): 1–20.

147. Agent Maxwell, personal interview by author, 20 July 2012.

148. Agent Monstris interview, 5 August 2012.

149. Agent Square Mile, personal interview by author, 5 August 2012.

150. Ian Steadman, "Olympic Protesters Suspended from Twitter over Trademark Violation," *Wired*, 23 May 2012, http://www.wired.co.uk/news/archive/2012-05/23/space-hijackers-suspended-over-olympic-protest; Shiv Malik, "Twitter Suspends Account for Using London 2012 Olympics Logo," *Guardian*, 23 May 2012, http://www.guardian.co.uk/sport/2012/may/23/twitter-london-2012-olympic-logo.

151. http://www.protestlondon2012.com/news.html.

152. Andrejevic, *iSpy*.

153. http://www.protestlondon2012.com/sitevisit.html.

154. Agent Maxwell interview, 20 July 2012.

155. The activist shared the bail conditions with me.

156. On "leaderless" resistance, see Carne Ross, *The Leaderless Revolution: How Ordinary People Will Take Power and Change Politics in the 21st Century*. (New York: Plume, 2011). For a convincing refutation of such leaderless activism and alternative "choreographic leadership," see Gerbaudo, *Tweets and the Streets*, 134–157.

157. Public Order Act 1986, Part II, Section 12, http://www.legislation.gov.uk/ukpga/1986/64/section/12.

158. "Critical Mass Police Ban Blocked by Law Lords," *Guardian*, 26 November 2008, http://www.guardian.co.uk/uk/2008/nov/26/critical-mass-london-police.

159. Fabian Flues, personal interview by author, 28 July 2012.

160. Agent Rachmetoff, personal interview by author, 5 August 2012.

161. For example, see http://i.imgur.com/3NcgA.jpg.

162. Kerry-anne Mendoza interview, 2 August 2012.

163. Tom Richards, "How the Met Police Criminalised the Critical Mass Bike Ride," *Guardian*, 18 March 2013, http://www.guardian.co.uk/environment/bike-blog/2013/mar/18/police-activism.

164. Alexander Cockburn, "The Tenth Crusade," *The Nation*, 5 September 2002, http://www.thenation.com/article/tenth-crusade.

165. Harjeet Kaur, personal interview via e-mail by author, 9 August 2012.

166. Kevin Blowe, personal interview by author, 11 July 2012.

167. Randeep Ramesh, "Atos Holds £3bn of Government Gontracts," *Guardian*, 28 August 2012, http://www.guardian.co.uk/society/2012/aug/28/atos-3bn-government-contracts-paralympics; Nick Sommerlad, "32 Die a Week after Failing Test for New Incapacity Benefit," *Mirror*, 4 April, 2012, http://blogs.mirror.co.uk/investigations/2012/04/32-die-a-week-after-failing-in.html.

168. "Hundreds March in Olympics Protest in East London," *BBC*, 28 July 2012, http://www.bbc.co.uk/news/uk-england-london-19028574.

169. Julian Cheyne interview, 2 May 2012.

170. David Renton, Public talk, Houseman's Bookshop, London, 8 August 2012.

171. Kerry-Anne Mendoza interview, 2 August 2012.

172. Gerbaudo, *Tweets and the Streets*, 161, 42, emphasis in original.

173. Agent Maxwell interview, 20 July 2012.

174. Kerry-Anne Mendoza interview, 2 August 2012.

175. Boykoff, *The Suppression of Dissent*, 290.

176. Agent Maxwell interview, 20 July 2012.

177. Boykoff, *The Suppression of Dissent*, 290.

Chapter 4   Media and the Olympics

1. "How Does Media Cover the Games?" *Olympic Review* (1996): 60; LOCOG, "Olympic Park Flythrough 2011," 31 March 2011, http://www.london2012.com/news/articles/2011/3/olympic-park-flythrough-2011.html.

2. Owen Gibson, "BBC Olympic Staff to Outnumber Team GB Athletes," *Guardian,* 25 April 2012, http://www.guardian.co.uk/sport/2012/apr/25/bbc-olympics-staff-coverage-london-2012.

3. Lenskyj, *Olympic Industry Resistance,* 4.

4. Nicolien Van Luijk and Wendy Frisby, "(Re)Framing of Protest at the 2010 Winter Olympic Games," *International Journal of Sport Policy and Politics* 4, no. 3 (2012): 350.

5. John Horne and Garry Whannel, "The 'Caged Torch Procession': Celebrities, Protesters and the 2008 Olympic Torch Relay in London, Paris and San Francisco," *Sport in Society* 13, no. 5 (2010): 766.

6. Christopher A. Shaw, *Five Ring Circus: Myths and Realities of the Olympic Games* (Gabriola Island: New Society Publishers, 2008), 16–17.

7. Greg Bishop, "In the Shadow of the Olympics," *New York Times,* 5 February 2010, B10.

8. Christine Brennan, "Despite Difficult First Days, Games Aren't Beyond Repair," *USA Today,* 15 February 2010, 3D.

9. "Worried about His Safety, Weir Stays with Other Athletes: Figure Skater Has Received Threats from Anti-fur Activists," *Washington Post,* 14 February 2010, D6.

10. Rod Mickleburgh, "Harnessing Games Spirit to Tackle Homelessness," *Globe and Mail,* 5 February 2010, S3.

11. Lena Sin, "Anti-Olympics Activists Provide Border 'Guide' for Visiting Protesters," *Vancouver Province,* 7 February 2010, A13.

12. Ian Bailey and Justine Hunter, "Harper Targeted by Insite Supporters," *Globe and Mail,* 11 February 2010, S1.

13. Harsha Walia, "Stop Civil Obedience: Fight the Games," *Vancouver Sun,* 8 February 2010, A13.

14. Robert Matas, "As Canada Watches the Games . . . Activist Fears He's Being Watched Too," *Globe and Mail,* 9 February 2010, S1.

15. Gary Mason, "The Real Threat to the Olympics Could be a Bloody Protest," *Globe and Mail,* 11 February 2012, A21.

16. Neil Boyd, "It's Time to Stop Fighting the Games and Join the Party," *Vancouver Sun,* 22 February 2010, A15.

17. Michael Smyth, "Hate Explains Downtown Clash with Police: Morons, Hoping to Get Arrested, Create a Dangerous Scene," *Vancouver Province,* 14 February 2010, A4.

18. Robert Matas, "Protest Group Refuses to Apologize for Vandalism During Vancouver March," *Globe and Mail,* 14 February 2010, A6.

19. Jon Ferry, "Violent Protesters Sully My Olympic Paradise: Window-Smashing Punks Trigger Costly Security Overload," *Vancouver Province,* 22 February 2010, A13.

20. Dean Pilling, "Death of the Protest," *Vancouver Province,* 16 February 2010, A19.

21. Stephen Hume, "There's No Need to Hide If You Believe What You Say: True Civil Disobedience Means Taking Responsibility for Your Actions, Not Wearing a Mask and Slinking Away," *Vancouver Sun,* 17 February 2010, A17.

22. Matas, "Protest Group Refuses to Apologize."

23. Doug Ward, "Black Bloc Taints Anti-Olympic Movement," *Vancouver Sun,* 27 February, A17.

24. Sarah Boesveld, "Lead Protester in Window-Smashing Rampage Arrested, Police Say," *Globe and Mail,* 17 February 2010, A2.

25. Michael Smyth, "How to Avoid Olympic Hangover: Smoothly Operating Transport, Security Essential for Games to Work," *Vancouver Province,* 10 February 2010, B8.

26. Pete McMartin, "Why I Loathe the Olympics and Why I Hope They Succeed," *Vancouver Sun,* 6 February 2010, A4.

27. Barbara Yaffe, "PM's Strategy of Controlling Message Fails to Silence Opponents," *Vancouver Sun,* 12 February 2010, B2.

28. Stephen Hume, "Stop Whining: Just Enjoy the Games," *Vancouver Sun,* 10 February 2010, A23.

29. Rod Mickleburgh, "Harnessing Games Spirit to Tackle Homelessness," *Globe and Mail,* 5 February 2010, S3.

30. Ian Bailey, Wendy Stueck, and Robert Matas, "The Woes That Weren't," *Globe and Mail,* 1 March 2010, S3.

31. Mason, "The Real Threat to the Olympics."

32. Doug Ward, "'Activist' Councillor Feels Little Solidarity with Protesters," *Vancouver Sun,* 15 February 2010, A13.

33. Bailey, Stueck, and Matas, "The Woes that Weren't."

34. Ward, "Black Bloc Taints Anti-Olympic Movement."

35. Boesveld, "Lead Protester in Window-Smashing Rampage Arrested, Police Say."

36. Robert Matas, "Security's New Look: A Long Reach and a Gentle Touch," *Globe and Mail,* 20 February 2010, S1.

37. Hume, "There's No Need to Hide If You Believe What You Say."

38. Ethan Baron, "Protester Thanks Cops for Kindness: Officer Guards Her Civil Right," *Vancouver Province*, 22 February 2010, A6.

39. Stephen Hume, "Scoffs and Sneers Can't Break Our Cheers: Games Win Gold," *Vancouver Sun*, 1 March 2010, D2.

40. Mark Hume, "Aboriginal Experience at the Games: The Happy Side," *Globe and Mail*, 27 February 2010, S1.

41. Earl and Kimport, *Digitally Enabled Activism*, 198.

42. Robert W. Entman, *Projections of Power: Framing News, Public Opinion, and U.S. Foreign Policy* (Chicago: University of Chicago Press, 2004), 5.

43. Maxwell T. Boykoff and Jules M. Boykoff, "Climate Change and Journalistic Norms: A Case Study of U.S. Mass-Media Coverage," *Geoforum* 38, no. 6 (2007): 1190–1204

44. Shantar Iyengar and Jennifer A. McGrady, *Media Politics: A Citizen's Guide* (New York: W.W. Norton & Company, 2007).

45. Danny Hayes and Matt Guardino, "Whose Views Made the News?: Media Coverage and the March to War in Iraq," *Political Communication* 27, no. 1 (2010): 59–87; Jonathan Mermin, *Debating War and Peace* (Princeton, NJ: Princeton University Press, 1999).

46. Ryan J. Barilleaux, "The President, 'Intermestic' Issues, and the Risks of Policy Leadership," *Presidential Studies Quarterly* 15, no. 4 (1985): 754–767.

47. W. Lance Bennett, Regina G. Lawrence, and Steven Livingston, "None Dare Call It Torture: Indexing and the Limits of Press Independence in the Abu Ghraib Scandal," *Journal of Communication* 56 (2006): 468.

48. See http://www.mediauk.com/article/32696/the-most-popular-newspapers-in-the-uk.

49. Audit Bureau of Circulations, http://accessabc.wordpress.com/2012/05/01/the-top-u-s-newspapers-for-march-2012/.

50. Reg Gratton, "The Media," in *Staging the Olympics: The Event and Its Impact*, ed. Richard Cashman and Anthony Hughes, 121–131 (Sydney: University of New South Wales Press, 1999).

51. Whannel, "The Rings and the Box"; Don Morrow and Janice Waters, "Method in Sport History: A Content Analysis Approach," *Canadian Journal of History of Sport* 13, no. 2 (1982): 30–37.

52. Due to quirks in the collection of articles from the *Daily Mail* and the *Independent*, we performed Boolean searches using the terms "Olympics," "politics," "protest," and "economics."

53. Gratton, "The Media," 130–131.

54. More precisely, after identifying the predominant themes, I randomly selected a forty-two-article minisample that evenly represented the time frame of the universe of articles (see Barney G. Glaser, *Theoretical Sensitivity: Advances in the Methodology of Grounded Theory* (Mill Valley, CA: The Sociology Press, 1978), 56–61). In order to measure the validity of the coding structure, a research assistant and I ran an inter-coder reliability test; we independently coded the minisample for the ten themes and carried out a statistical comparison to make sure our coding for each theme reached statistically significant agreement. This reliability test attained 91.8 percent coder agreement, which sits comfortably within the acceptable range of reliability coefficients. Every theme had acceptable coder agreement in terms of their reliability coefficients: Olympics economics

(80 percent); corporate sponsor politics (83.3 percent); policing and security (90.9 percent); feminism, sexism, and gender equality (100 percent); infrastructure readiness (100 percent); the politics of tickets to events (100 percent); geopolitical relations (100 percent); media issues (85.7 percent); (9) Olympic legacy (100 percent); (10) activism and protest (85.7 percent). See Kimberly A. Neuendorf, *The Content Analysis Guidebook,* (Thousand Oaks, CA: Sage, 2002), 142–143; Daniel Riffe, Stephen Lacy, and Frederick G. Fico, *Analyzing Media Messages: Using Quantitative Content Analysis in Research* (Mahwah, NJ: Lawrence Erlbaum, 1998), 131.

55. We ran an open-closed coding on the randomly selected thirty-one-article minisample in order to inductively identify predominant frames. To measure the validity of the coding structure, we tested inter-coder reliability by independently closed-coding the sample for the five predominant frames. We then ran a statistical comparison to ensure each frame attained statistically significant agreement. Overall, our reliability test achieved 93.2 percent coder agreement, well within the acceptable range of reliability coefficients. Every frame had acceptable coder agreement. The four predominant frames and their reliability coefficients were: Principled Resistance Frame (95 percent); Disruption Frame (89 percent); Criminality Frame (83 percent); and Freak Frame (100 percent). See Neuendorf, *The Content Analysis Guidebook,* 142–143; Riffe, Lacy, and Fico, *Analyzing Media Messages,* 131.

56. Individual news stories can contain multiple frames, and were thus coded as such.

57. Boykoff and Laschever, "The Tea Party Movement, Framing, and the US Media"; Jules Boykoff, "Framing Dissent: Mass Media Coverage of the Global Justice Movement," *New Political Science* 28 (June 2006): 201–228.

58. Christopher Martin, *Framed!: Labor and the Corporate Media* (Ithaca: Cornell University Press, 2004); Melvin Small, *Covering Dissent: The Media and the Vietnam War Movement* (New Brunswick, NJ: Rutgers University Press, 1994); Boykoff, "Framing Dissent."

59. Martin, *Framed!,* 7, 4, 54, 50.

60. Ibid., 8–11.

61. Alan Jones, "Bus Drivers Accept Games Cash Offers," *Independent,* 18 July 2012; David Millward, "London Bus Workers Win Olympic Bonus," *Telegraph,* 18 July 2012.

62. IOC, *Olympic Charter,* 77.

63. London Organising Committee of the Olympic Games and Paralympic Games (LOCOG), "Rule 40 Guidelines," July 2011, 6, http://www.london2012.com/mm/Document/Publications/General/01/25/29/32/rule-40-guidelines_Neutral.pdf.

64. Adam Shergold, "Athletes Launch 'Gag' Protest against the Olympic Rule That Bans Them from Promoting Their Own Sponsors," *Daily Mail,* 31 July 2012.

65. Ken Belson, "Olympians Take to Twitter to Protest Endorsement Rule," *New York Times,* 31 July 2012, B11.

66. Andrejevic, *iSpy,* 5.

67. IOC, "IOC Social Media, Blogging and Internet Guidelines for Participants and Other Accredited Persons at the London 2012 Olympic Games," Lausanne: 31 August, 2011. http://www.olympic.org/Documents/Games_London_2012/IOC_Social_Media_Blogging_and_Internet_Guidelines-London.pdf, 1.

68. IOC, *Olympic Charter,* 93.

69. Mark Staniforth, "Australian Damien Hooper Escapes Punishment after Wearing Tee-shirt Displaying Aboriginal Flag," *Independent,* 30 July 2012.

70. Jerome Taylor, "UK Tamil Community Set for Mass Protests," *Independent,* 25 July 2012.

71. Kenfrey Kiberenge, "Ivory Coast President Heckled by Protesters Ahead of Olympic Opening Ceremony Visit," *Independent,* 27 July 2012.

72. Jill Reilly, "Argentine Athletes Plan to Use Olympics to Stage Black Power-Style Protest over Falklands," *Daily Mail,* 24 June 2012; "Argentina May Use Olympics for Falklands Protest, Warns Foreign Office," *Telegraph,* 24 June 2012.

73. Scott Johnson, "The Not So Funny Fiasco of the London Games, So Far," *New York Times,* 20 July 2012.

74. See Alan Jones, "Hopes Raise for Moves to Avert London Bus Strike," *Independent,* 20 June 2012.

75. "London Braced for Fresh Travel Chaos as Tube Workers Vote for Strike," *Telegraph,* 12 June 2012; Alan Jones, "London Bus Strike Causes Travel Chaos," *Independent,* 22 June 2012.

76. Ainsley Thomson, "U.K. Border Officials Threaten to Strike Day Before Olympics," *Wall Street Journal,* 20 July 2012, A12.

77. David Millward, "Border Force Staff to Walk Out ahead of Olympics," *Telegraph,* 19 July 2012.

78. Emma Clark, "Bus Drivers Bring London to a Halt as They Strike Over Demands for £500 Olympics Bonus," *Daily Mail,* 22 June 2012.

79. "Olympic Saboteurs Shame the Nation," *Daily Mail,* 24 July 2012.

80. John Stevens, "Captain Crow's Cruise: On the Deck of a Riverboat, Beer in Hand, the Union Hardliner Plotting Strikes That Could Hit the Olympics," *Daily Mail,* 27 June 2012.

81. "The Olympic Strike Will Bring Shame on Britain," *Telegraph,* 19 July 2012.

82. "An Olympic Security Mess: Better Government Contracts Could Shield Taxpayers from Contractor Failure—Before the Fact," *Wall Street Journal,* 19 July 2012.

83. See, for example: Jules Boykoff and Martha Gies, "'We're Going to Defend Ourselves': The Portland Chapter of the Black Panther Party and the Local Media Response," *Oregon Historical Quarterly* 111 (Fall 2010): 278–311.

84. Sandra Laville, "Police Arrested Actors for Spilling Custard, Say Olympic Protesters," *Guardian,* 20 July 2012. See also Tom Peck, "Father of Olympic Branding: My Rules Are Being Abused," *Independent,* 21 July 2012, http://www.independent.co.uk/sport/olympics/news/father-of-olympic-branding-my-rules-are-being-abused-7962593.html.

85. "Protesters Clash with Police Close to Olympic Stadium," *Telegraph,* 27 July 2012.

86. Alice Speri, "Cycle Activists Arrested at Olympic Protest," *Wall Street Journal,* 28 July 2012.

87. Jeffrey Walker, "The Body of Persuasion: A Theory of the Enthymeme," *College English* 56, no. 1 (1994): 46–65.

88. Townsend, "Police Plan Preemptive Arrests to Stop Disruption."

89. Cahal Milmo, "Scotland Yard Defends Arrests of Critical Mass Cyclists," *Independent,* 29 July 2012.

90. Kevin Johnson, "Demonstrations Drowned Out; National Pride, Athletic Success Mute Planned Protests," *USA Today,* 13 August 2012, 4D.

91. Rob Preece, "Ukrainian Feminists Stage Topless Protest near Tower Bridge Over Olympic Body's Support for Bloody Islamist Regimes," *Daily Mail,* 2 August 2012.

92. If a source was quoted multiple times in the same article, I only tallied them once.

93. In terms of raw numbers, union activists were sourced eighty-four times, grass-roots activists fifty-six times, and athlete activists eighteen times.

94. Peck, "Father of Olympic Branding."

95. Stephen Castle, "Britain Adds Troops for Olympics and Tries to Avert Strike at Airport," *New York Times*, 25 July 2012, 9.

96. Christopher Hope, "BBC's Garry Richardson Accused of Bias by Unions Over Border Strike," *Telegraph*, 22 June 2012.

97. The remaining 1 percent was a residual category of "other," which included two anonymous sources.

98. Daniel Hallin, "The Media, the War in Vietnam, and Political Support: A Critique of the Thesis of an Oppositional Media," *Journal of Politics* 46, no. 1 (1984): 14.

99. For example, see David Baker, "'Don't Play Games with Our Lives': Londoners Protest against Plans for Olympic Defence Systems on Top of Flats," *Daily Mail*, 30 June 2012; Jerome Taylor, "Adidas Faces Protests Over 'Sweatshop' Goods," *Independent*, 14 July 2012; Ben Glaze, "Jeremy Hunt Urges Border Staff to Work On," *Independent*, 25 July 2012.

100. E. E. Schattschneider, *The Semisovereign People: A Realist's View of Democracy in America* (New York: Holt, Rinehart and Winston, 1960), 68, emphasis in original.

101. Horne and Whannel, "The 'Caged Torch Procession,'" 766. Also see Wing-Shing Tang, "The 2008 Olympic Torch Relay in Hong Kong: A Clash of Governmentalities," *Human Geography* 1, no. 1 (2008): 106–110.

102. See http://stoptheolympicmissiles.org/.

103. Donna Bowater, "Olympics Sponsor Adidas to Be Targeted by Sweatshop Protesters," *Telegraph*, 7 June 2012.

104. Koopmans and Statham, "Ethnic and Civic Conceptions of Nationhood," 228.

105. Christine Brennan, "Chaos of London a Welcome Sight after Sterile Beijing," *USA Today*, 25 July 2012, 7C; Peter Walker and Greg Jones, "Anish Kapoor's House in London Occupied by Protesters," *Guardian*, 22 June 2012.

106. Boykoff, *Beyond Bullets*, 28.

107. Miah, García, and Zhihui, "'We Are the Media,'" 339, 343.

108. Whannel, "The Television Spectacular," 30.

Chapter 5   Looking Ahead through the Rearview Mirror

1. Kurt Anderson, "The Protester," *Time*, 14 December 2011.

2. Michel Foucault, *Fearless Speech* (Los Angeles: Semiotext(e), 2001), 13–14. Plato used the term *parrhesia* pejoratively, meaning the aimless—and often off-target—chattering of the masses. But more commonly parrhesia enjoys positive connotations in classical Greek texts.

3. Ibid., 15, emphasis in original.

4. Ibid., 22.

5. Ibid., 73, emphasis in original. The public sphere was only one arena for the *parrhesiastes*, the others being small groups of people in the community and personal relationships. See 107–142.

6. Michel Foucault, *Power/Knowledge: Selected Interviews and Other Writings, 1972–1977* (New York: Pantheon Books, 1980), 93.

7. John Carlos and Dave Zirin in conversation, University of Brighton, Chelsea School of Sport, 15 May 2012.

8. Jules Boykoff, "With Heads and Hands Held High: An Interview with John Carlos," *Street Roots*, 23 November 2012, 1.

9. ESPN Films and Maggie Vision Productions, "Return to Mexico City," 2009.

10. See, for example, the range of heroes celebrated in Gerald M. Pomper, *On Ordinary Heroes and American Democracy* (Boulder: Paradigm Publishers, 2007).

11. Bent Flyvbjerg, Nils Bruzelius, and Werner Rothengatter, *Megaprojects and Risk: An Anatomy of Ambition* (Cambridge: Cambridge University Press, 2003), 5.

12. Iain Lindsay, "Olympicisation: Growing for Gold," *Urbanities* 1, no. 1 (2011): 29.

13. IOC, *Olympic Charter*, 93.

14. London Olympic Games and Paralympic Games Act 2006, 47–48, http://www.legislation.gov.uk/ukpga/2006/12/pdfs/ukpga_20060012_en.pdf.

15. Peck, "Father of Olympic Branding."

16. Keith Bradsher, "China Finds American Allies for Security," *New York Times*, 28 December 2007.

17. WikiLeaks, "Brazil: Blackout—Causes and Implications," 1 December 2009, http://wikileaks.ch/cable/2009/12/09BRASILIA1383.html.

18. Alfred E. Senn, *Power, Politics, and the Olympic Games* (Champaign, IL: Human Kinetics, 1999), 276.

19. Number of National Olympic Committees: http://www.olympic.org/national-olympic-committees. UN member states: http://www.un.org/en/members/growth.shtml.

20. Pew Research Center, "Olympics Bridge Gender Divide In Sports Interest," 1 February 2010, http://pewresearch.org/pubs/1481/interest-men-women-winter-olympics-super-bowl-world-cup.

21. Amy Chozick, "NBC Unpacks Trove of Data From Olympics," *New York Times*, 26 September 2012, B3.

22. John Plunkett, "BBC Olympics Coverage Watched by 90% of UK Population," *The Guardian*, 13 August 2012.

23. Featherstone, *Resistance, Space and Political Identities*, 53.

24. Gillham and Noakes, "'More than a March in a Circle,'" 343.

25. Duncombe, *Dream*, 126.

26. Benjamin Shepard, *Play, Creativity, and Social Movements: If I Can't Dance, It's Not My Revolution* (London: Routledge, 2011), 23.

27. Gerbaudo, *Tweets and the Streets*, 134–157. To be sure, Gerbaudo also spotlights the importance of street organizing. The crux of his book is how social media can constitute a springboard to such activism.

28. Mikhail Bakhtin, *Rabelais and His World*, trans. Helene Iswolsky (Cambridge: The M.I.T. Press, 1968), 7, 8.

29. Mikhail Bakhtin, *Problems of Dostoevsky's Poetics*, trans. Caryl Emerson (Minneapolis: University of Minnesota Press, 1984), 122.

30. Ibid., 123.

31. Haugerud, *No Billionaire Left Behind*, 53.

32. Shepard, *Play, Creativity, and Social Movements*, 260.

33. Ibid., 269–270.

34. Debord, *The Society of the Spectacle*, 12.

35. Terry Eagleton, "Wittgenstein's Friends," *New Left Review* I/135 (1982): 90.

36. Graham St. John, "Protestival: Global Days of Action and Carnivalized Politics in the Present," *Social Movement Studies* 7, no. 2 (2008): 167–190

37. Dean, *Democracy and Other Neoliberal Fantasies*, 24.

38. Ibid., 30.

39. Ibid., 31.

40. Ibid., 33.

41. Ibid., 36.

42. Ibid., 47.

43. Isaac Marrero Guillamón personal interview by author, 19 June 2012.

44. Zirin, *Welcome to the Terrordome*, 133.

45. "State Bank to Cover Loss-Making Olympics Projects," *RIA Novosti*, 14 June 2013, http://en.rian.ru/russia/20130614/181670051/State-Bank-to-Cover-Loss -Making-Olympic-Projects.html; Corey Flintoff, "Despite Critics, Russia Promises a Grand Olympic Spectacle," *National Public Radio*, 11 June 2013, http://www .npr.org/blogs/parallels/2013/06/11/190722902/despite-critics-russia-promises-a -grand-olympic-spectacle.

46. Fred Weir, "Putin Warns of Growing Terror Risks as Kremlin Arrests Opposition Leader," *Christian Science Monitor*, 17 October 2012, http://www.csmonitor .com/World/Europe/2012/1017/Putin-warns-of-growing-terror-risks-as-Kremlin -arrests-opposition-leader.

47. Fred Weir, "Russian NGOs in Panic Mode over Proposed 'High Treason' Law," *Christian Science Monitor*, 26 September 2012, http://www.csmonitor.com/ World/Europe/2012/0926/Russian-NGOs-in-panic-mode-over-proposed-high -treason-law; Fred Weir, "Many Russian NGOs Face 'Foreign Agent' Label," *Christian Science Monitor*, 5 July 2012, http://www.csmonitor.com/World/ Europe/2012/0705/Many-Russian-NGOs-face-foreign-agent-label; Fred Weir, "Russian Activists Sound Alarm at Soaring Fines for Civil 'Disorder,'" *Christian Science Monitor*, 5 June 2012, http://www.csmonitor.com/World/Europe/2012/ 0605/Russian-activists-sound-alarm-at-soaring-fines-for-civil-disorder; David M. Herszenhorn and Andrew E. Kramer, "Russian Protesters Challenge Permit Law," *Boston Globe*, 16 December 2012, http://bostonglobe.com/news/world/2012/ 12/16/couple-thousand-demonstrators-march-moscow-unsanctioned-protest/ ANwYEoofs5wsfiakq67E7H/story.html; Fred Weir, "Putin Warns of Growing Terror Risks as Kremlin Arrests Opposition Leader," *Christian Science Monitor*, 17 October 2012, http://www.csmonitor.com/World/Europe/2012/1017/Putin -warns-of-growing-terror-risks-as-Kremlin-arrests-opposition-leader; Miriam Elder, "Censorship Row over Russian Internet Blacklist," *Guardian*, 12 November 2012, http://www.guardian.co.uk/world/2012/nov/12/censorship-row-russian -internet-blacklist.

48. Jeré Longman, "Outrage over Antigay Law Does Not Spread to Olympic Officials," *New York Times*, 7 August 2013, B10; "Sochi, Sport and Security: Russia Bans Protests during Winter Olympics, Limits Access," *Russia Today*, 24 August 2013, http://rt.com/news/sochi-protest-ban-olympics-931/.

49. Dana Wojokh, personal interview by author, 29 July 2012.

50. W. Alejandro Sánchez Nieto, "The Olympic Challenge: Russia's Strategy for the Establishment of Security in the North Caucasus before 2014," *Journal of Slavic Military Studies* 24 (2011): 582–604

51. Tamara Barsik, personal interview by author, 29 July 2012.

52. Bryan C. Clift and David L. Andrews, "Living Lula's Passion? The Politics of Rio 2016," in *The Palgrave Handbook of Olympic Studies*, ed. by Helen Jefferson Lenskyj and Stephen Wagg Basingstoke (New York: Palgrave Macmillan, 2012), 219.

53. Payne, *Olympic Turn Around*, 169.

54. Brazilian Olympic Committee, "Candidature File for Rio de Janeiro to Host the 2016 Olympic and Paralympic Games, Volume 1." 2009. http://rio2016.com/sites/default/files/parceiros/candidature_file_v1.pdf; Theresa Williamson, "It's Just the Beginning; Change Will Come," *New York Times*, 19 June 2013, http://www.nytimes.com/roomfordebate/2013/06/19/will-the-protests-in-brazil-lead-to-change/its-just-the-beginning-change-will-come-to-brazil.

55. Samantha R. McRoskey, "Security and the Olympic Games: Making Rio an Example," *Yale Journal of International Affairs* (2010): 102.

56. Theresa Williamson and Maurício Hora, "In the Name of the Future, Rio Is Destroying Its Past," *New York Times*, 13 August 2012, A17.

57. Taylor Barnes, "Rio's Olympic Land Grab," *Christian Science Monitor*, 8 March 2012, http://www.csmonitor.com/World/Americas/Latin-America-Monitor/2012/0308/Rio-s-Olympic-land-grab.

58. Jonathan Watts, "Brazilian Politicians Struggle with How to Respond to Another Night of Protests," *Guardian*, 19 June 2013, http://www.guardian.co.uk/world/2013/jun/19/brazil-protests-continue-authorities-scramble; Dave Zirin, "As Brazil's Protests Continue, the Ghosts of Mexico City Must Be Heard," *The Nation*, 20 June 2013, http://www.thenation.com/blog/174909/brazils-world-cupolympic-protests-continue-ghosts-mexico-city-must-be-heard.

59. Jonathan Watts, "Brazil Erupts in Protest: More than a Million on the Streets," *Guardian*, 21 June 2013, http://www.guardian.co.uk/world/2013/jun/21/brazil-police-crowds-rio-protest.

60. Simon Romero, "Brazil's Leftist Ruling Party, Born of Protests, Is Perplexed by Revolt," *New York Times*, 19 June 2013, http://www.nytimes.com/2013/06/20/world/americas/brazil-protests.html.

61. "Rio 2016 Model Venue Exercise," *Around the Rings*, 21 June 2013, http://www.aroundtherings.com/articles/view.aspx?pv=xqv&id=43624; "Despite Protests, IOC Says 2016 Olympics Will 'Bring Significant Benefits' to Rio and Brazil," *Associated Press*, http://www.washingtonpost.com/sports/olympics/despite-protests-ioc-says-2016-olympics-will-bring-significant-benefits-to-rio-and-brazil/2013/06/20/87762f78-d9b0-11e2-b418-9dfa095e125d_story.html.

62. Christopher Gaffney, "Mega-Events and Socio-Spatial Dynamics in Rio de Janeiro, 1919–2016," *Journal of Latin American Geography* 9 no, 1 (2010): 23.

63. Orwell, *Shooting an Elephant and Other Essays*, 152.

64. Marc Perelman, *Barbaric Sport: A Global Plague*. (London: Verso, 2012), 39–40.

65. Karl Marx, "Contribution to the Critique of Hegel's Philosophy of Law, Introduction," in *Karl Marx, Frederick Engels Collected Work* (London: Lawrence & Wishart, 1974 [1844]), 3:174, emphasis in original. Marx went on to write, "To abolish religion as the *illusory* happiness of the people is to demand their real happiness. The demand to give up illusions about the existing state of affairs is the *demand to give up a state of affairs which needs illusions*. The criticism of religion is therefore *in embryo the criticism of the vale of tears*, the *halo* of which is religion" (175, emphasis in original).

Bibliography

Alfred, Taiaiake. "Deconstructing the British Columbia Treaty Process." *Balayi: Culture, Law and Colonialism* 3 (2001): 37–65.

Andrejevic, Mark. *iSpy: Surveillance and Power in the Interactive Era*. Lawrence: University Press of Kansas, 2007.

Andrews, David L., and Stephen Wagg. Introduction to *East Plays West: Sport and the Cold War*, edited by Stephen Wagg and David L. Andrews, 1–10. London: Routledge, 2007.

Bairner, Alan. *Sport, Nationalism, and Globalization: European and North American Perspectives*. Albany: State University of New York Press, 2001.

Bakhtin, Mikhail. *Problems of Dostoevsky's Poetics*. Translated by Caryl Emerson. Minneapolis: University of Minnesota Press, 1984.

———. *Rabelais and His World*. Translated by Helene Iswolsky. Cambridge, MA: The M.I.T. Press, 1968.

Barilleaux, Ryan J. "The President, 'Intermestic' Issues, and the Risks of Policy Leadership." *Presidential Studies Quarterly* 15, no. 4 (1985): 754–767.

Barney, Robert K. "The Olympic Games in Modern Times." In *Onward to the Olympics: Historical Perspectives on the Olympic Games*, edited by Gerald P. Schaus and Stephen R. Wenn, 221–241. Waterloo, ON: Wilfrid Laurier University Press, 2007.

Barney, Robert K., Stephen R. Wenn, and Scott G. Martyn. *Selling the Five Rings: The International Olympic Committee and the Rise of Olympic Commercialism*. Salt Lake City: The University of Utah Press, 2004.

Benford, Robert D., and David A. Snow. "Framing Processes and Social Movements: An Overview and Assessment." *Annual Review of Sociology* 26 (2000): 611–639.

Bennett, W. Lance. "Social Movements Beyond Borders: Understanding Two Eras of Transnational Activism." In *Transnational Protest and Global Activism*, edited by Donatella della Porta and Sidney Tarrow, 203–226. New York: Rowman & Littlefield, 2005.

Bennett, W. Lance, Regina G. Lawrence, and Steven Livingston. "None Dare Call It Torture: Indexing and the Limits of Press Independence in the Abu Ghraib Scandal." *Journal of Communication* 56 (2006): 467–485.

Bennett, W. Lance, and Alexandra Segerberg. "The Logic of Connective Action: Digital Media and the Personalization of Contentious Politics." *Information, Communication & Society* 15, no. 5 (2012): 739–768.

Booth, Douglas. *The Race Game: Sport and Politics in South Africa*. London: Frank Cass Publishers, 1998.

Bourdieu, Pierre. "Program for a Sociology of Sport." *Sociology of Sport Journal* 8 (1988): 153–161.

Boykoff, Jules. "The Anti-Olympics: Fun at the Games." *New Left Review* 67 (January–February 2011): 41–59.

———. *Beyond Bullets: The Suppression of Dissent in the United States*. Oakland: AK Press, 2007.

———. *Celebration Capitalism and the Olympic Games*. New York: Routledge, 2013.

———. "Framing Dissent: Mass Media Coverage of the Global Justice Movement." *New Political Science* 28 (June 2006): 201–228.

———. "Limiting Dissent: The Mechanisms of State Repression in the United States." *Social Movement Studies* 6 (December 2007): 281–310.

———. *The Suppression of Dissent: How the State and Mass Media Squelch USAmerican Social Movements*. New York: Routledge, 2006.

———. "Surveillance, Spatial Compression, and Scale: The FBI and Martin Luther King, Jr." *Antipode* 39, no. 4 (2007): 729–756.

Boykoff, Jules, and Pete Fussey. "London's Shadow Legacies: Security and Activism at the 2012 Olympics." *Contemporary Social Science* (forthcoming).

Boykoff, Jules, and Martha Gies. "'We're Going to Defend Ourselves': The Portland Chapter of the Black Panther Party and the Local Media Response." *Oregon Historical Quarterly* 111, no. 3 (Fall 2010): 278–311.

Boykoff, Jules, and Eulalie Laschever. "The Tea Party Movement, Framing, and the US Media." *Social Movement Studies* 10, no. 4 (2011): 341–366.

Boykoff, Maxwell T., and Jules M. Boykoff. "Climate Change and Journalistic Norms: A Case Study of U.S. Mass-Media Coverage." *Geoforum* 38. no. 6 (2007): 1190–1204.

Boyle, Philip, and Kevin P. Haggerty. "Spectacular Security: Mega-Events and the Security Complex." *International Political Sociology* 3 (2009): 257–274.

Brazilian Olympic Committee, "Candidature File for Rio de Janeiro to Host the 2016 Olympic and Paralympic Games, Volume 1." 2009. http://rio2016.com/sites/default/files/parceiros/candidature_file_v1.pdf.

Burdsey, Daniel. *British Asians and Football: Culture, Identity, Exclusion*. London: Routledge, 2007.

———. "That Joke Isn't Funny Anymore: Racial Microaggressions, Color-Blind Ideology and the Mitigation of Racism in English Men's First-Class Cricket." *Sociology of Sport Journal* 28 (2011): 261–283.

Burns, Jimmy. *Barça: A People's Passion*. London: Bloomsbury, 1999.

Carrington, Ben. "Cricket, Culture and Identity: An Exploration of the Role of Sport in the Construction of Black Masculinities." In *Practising Identities: Power and Resistance*, edited by Sasha Roseneil and Julie Seymour, 11–32. Basingstoke, UK: Palgrave, 1999.

———. *Race, Sport, and Politics: The Sporting Black Diaspora*. London: Sage, 2010.

———. "'What's the Footballer Doing Here?': Racialized Performativity, Reflexivity, and Identity." *Cultural Studies <=> Critical Methodologies* 8 (2008): 423–452.

Carter, Thomas F. "The Olympics as Sovereign Subject Maker." In *Watching the Olympics: Politics, Power, and Representation*, edited by John Sugden and Alan Tomlinson, 55–68. London: Routledge, 2012.

Carty, Victoria. *Wired and Mobilizing: Social Movements, New Technology, and Electoral Politics.* New York: Routledge, 2011.

Centre on Housing Rights and Evictions (COHRE). "Fair Play for Housing Rights: Mega-events, Olympic Games and Housing Rights." Geneva, 2007.

———. "One World, Whose Dream?: Housing Rights Violations and the Beijing Olympic Games." Geneva, 2008.

Clift, Bryan C., and David L. Andrews. "Living Lula's Passion? The Politics of Rio 2016." In *The Palgrave Handbook of Olympic Studies,* edited by Helen Jefferson Lenskyj and Stephen Wagg, 210–229. Basingstoke, UK: Palgrave Macmillan, 2012.

Commission for a Sustainable London 2012. "Breaking the Tape: Pre-Games Review." London: The Commission, 2012. http://www.cslondon.org/wp-content/uploads/downloads/2012/06/CSL_Annual_Review_20111.pdf.

———. "Sustainable Sourced?: A Snapshot Review of the Sustainability of London 2012 Merchandise." London: The Commission, 2011. http://www.cslondon.org/wp-content/uploads/downloads/2011/10/Sustainably-Sourced-2011.pdf.

Cottrell, M. Patrick, and Travis Nelson. "Not Just the Games? Power, Protest and Politics at the Olympics." *European Journal of International Relations* 17, no. 4 (2011): 729–753.

Dean, Jodi. *Democracy and Other Neoliberal Fantasies: Communicative Capitalism and Left Politics.* Durham: Duke University Press, 2009.

Debord, Guy. *The Society of the Spectacle.* Translated by Donald Nicholson-Smith. New York: Zone Books, 1995.

de Coubertin, Pierre. *Olympism: Selected Writings.* Edited by Norbert Müller. Lausanne: International Olympic Committee, 2000.

DeNora, Tia. *Beethoven and the Construction of Genius: Musical Politics in Vienna, 1792–1803.* Berkeley: University of California Press, 1997.

———. "Musical Patronage and Social Change in Beethoven's Vienna." *American Journal of Sociology* 97 (1991): 310–346.

Derksen, Jeff. "Art and Cities during Mega-Events. On the Intersection of Culture, Everyday Live, and the Olympics in Vancouver and Beyond. Part IV." *Camera Austria* 111 (2010): 60–61.

Diani, Mario. "The Concept of Social Movement." *The Sociological Review* 40, no. 1 (1992): 1–25.

Dickinson, Emily. *The Complete Poems of Emily Dickinson.* New York: Little Brown and Company, 1961.

Dikeç, Mustafa. "Justice and the Spatial Imagination." *Environment and Planning A* 33 (2001): 1785–1805.

———. "Police, Politics, and the Right to the City." *GeoJournal* 58 (2003): 91–98.

Duncombe, Stephen. *Dream: Re-Imagining Progressive Politics in an Age of Fantasy.* New York: The New Press, 2007.

Dyreson, Mark. "The 'Physical Value' of Races and Nations: Anthropology and Athletics at the Louisiana Purchase Exhibition." In *The 1904 Anthropology Days and Olympic Games: Sport, Race, and American Imperialism,* edited by Susan Brownell, 127–155. Lincoln: University of Nebraska Press, 2008.

Eagleton, Terry. "Wittgenstein's Friends." *New Left Review* I/135 (1982): 64–90.

Earl, Jennifer. "Political Repression: Iron Fists, Velvet Gloves, and Diffuse Control." *Annual Review of Sociology* 37 (2011): 13.1–13.24.

———. "Tanks, Tear Gas, and Taxes: Toward a Theory of Movement Repression." *Sociological Theory* 21 (2003): 44–68.

Earl, Jennifer, and Katrina Kimport. *Digitally Enabled Social Change: Activism in the Internet Age*. Cambridge, MA: The MIT Press, 2011.

Earl, Jennifer, Katrina Kimport, Greg Prieto, Carly Rush, and Kimberly Reynoso. "Changing the World One Webpage at a Time: Conceptualizing and Explaining Internet Activism." *Mobilization: An International Journal* 15, no. 4 (2010): 425–466.

Edwards, Harry. *The Revolt of the Black Athlete*. New York: The Free Press, 1969.

England, Kim V. L. "Getting Personal: Reflexivity, Positionality, and Feminist Research." *The Professional Geographer* 46, no. 1 (1994): 80–89.

Entman, Robert W. "Framing: Toward Clarification of a Fractured Paradigm." *Journal of Communication* 43 (1993): 51–58.

———. *Projections of Power: Framing News, Public Opinion, and U.S. Foreign Policy*. Chicago: University of Chicago Press, 2004.

Espagnac, Sylvie. "The IOC in Session in Salt Lake City." *Olympic Review* 27 (2002): 9–12.

Featherstone, David. *Resistance, Space and Political Identities: The Making of Counter-Global Networks*. Oxford: Wiley-Blackwell, 2008.

Fernandez, Luis A. *Policing Dissent: Social Control and the Anti-Globalization Movement*. New Brunswick, NJ: Rutgers University Press, 2008.

Flowers, Julianne F., Audrey A. Haynes, and Michael H. Crespin. "The Media, the Campaign, and the Message." *The American Journal of Political Science* 47 (2003): 259–273.

Flyvbjerg, Bent, Nils Bruzelius, and Werner Rothengatter. *Megaprojects and Risk: An Anatomy of Ambition*. Cambridge: Cambridge University Press, 2003.

Forsyth, Janice. "Teepees and Tomahawks: Aboriginal Cultural Representation at the 1976 Olympic Games." In *The Global Nexus Engaged: Past, Present, Future Interdisciplinary Olympic Studies: Sixth International Symposium for Olympic Research*, edited by Kevin Wamsley, Robert K. Barney, and Scott G. Martyn, 71–75. London, ON: International Centre for Olympic Studies, 2002.

Foster, Hamar, and Alan Grove. "'Trespassers on the Soil': United States v. Tom and a New Perspective on the Short History of Treaty Making in Nineteenth-Century British Columbia." *B.C. Studies* 138/139 (2003): 51–84.

Foucault, Michel. *Fearless Speech*. Los Angeles: Semiotext(e), 2001.

———. *Power/Knowledge: Selected Interviews and Other Writings, 1972–1977*. New York: Pantheon Books, 1980.

Gaffney, Christopher. "Mega-Events and Socio-Spatial Dynamics in Rio de Janeiro, 1919–2016." *Journal of Latin American Geography* 9, no. 1 (2010): 7–29.

Gamson, William. "Bystanders, Public Opinion, and the Media." In *The Blackwell Companion to Social Movements*, edited by David A. Snow, Sarah A. Soule, and Hanspeter Kriesi, 242–261. London: Blackwell Publishing, 2004.

Gerbaudo, Paolo. *Tweets and the Streets: Social Media and Contemporary Activism*. London: Pluto Press, 2012.

Gerlach, Larry. "An Uneasy Discourse: Salt Lake 2002 and Olympic Protest." In *Pathways: Critiques and Discourse in Olympic Research,* edited by Robert K. Barney, 141–150. London, ON: International Centre for Olympic Studies, 2008.

Gilchrist, Paul, and Neil Ravenscroft. "Space Hijacking and the Anarchopolitics of Leisure." *Leisure Studies* (2012): 1–20.

Gillham, Patrick F., Bob Edwards, and John A. Noakes. "Strategic Incapacitation and the Policing of Occupy Wall Street Protests in New York City, 2011." *Policing & Society* (2012): 1–22.

Gillham, Patrick F., and John A. Noakes. "'More than a March in a Circle': Transgressive Protests and the Limits of Negotiated Management." *Mobilization: An International Quarterly* 12, no. 4 (2007): 341–357.

Gillan, Kevin, and Jenny Pickerill. "The Difficult and Hopeful Ethics of Research on, and with Social Movements." *Social Movement Studies* 11, no. 2 (2012): 133–143.

Giulianotti, Richard. "Participant Observation and Research into Football Hooliganism: Reflections on the Problem of Entrée and Everyday Risks." *Sociology of Sport Journal* 12, no. 1 (1995): 1–20.

Glaser, Barney G. *Theoretical Sensitivity: Advances in the Methodology of Grounded Theory.* Mill Valley, CA: The Sociology Press, 1978.

Goldstone, Jack A. "More Social Movements or Fewer?: Beyond Political Opportunity Structures to Relational Fields." *Theory and Society* 33 (2004): 333–365.

Goodwin, Jeff, and James M. Jasper. "Caught in a Winding, Snarling Vine: The Structuralist Bias of Political Process Theory." *Sociological Forum* 14, no. 1 (1999): 27–54.

Granovetter, Mark S. "The Strength of Weak Ties." *American Journal of Sociology* 78, no. 6 (1973): 1360–1380.

Gratton, Chris, and Ian P. Henry, eds. *Sport in the City: The Role of Sport in Economic and Social Regeneration.* London: Routledge, 2001.

Gratton, Chris, and Ian Jones. *Research Methods for Sport Studies.* Abingdon, UK: Routledge, 2004.

Gratton, Reg. "The Media." In *Staging the Olympics: The Event and Its Impact*, edited by Richard Cashman and Anthony Hughes, 121–131. Sydney: University of New South Wales Press, 1999.

Gruneau, Richard. *Class, Sports, and Social Development.* Amherst: The University of Massachusetts Press, 1983.

Haines, Herbert H. *Black Radicals and the Civil Rights Mainstream, 1954–1970.* Knoxville: The University of Tennessee Press, 1988.

Hallin, Daniel. "The Media, the War in Vietnam, and Political Support: A Critique of the Thesis of an Oppositional Media." *Journal of Politics* 46, no. 1 (1984): 2–24.

Hardt, Michael. "Today's Bandung?" *New Left Review* 14 (2001): 112–118.

Hardt, Michael, and Antonio Negri. *Empire.* London: Harvard University Press, 2000.

Hargreaves, Jennifer. *Sporting Females: Critical Issues in the History and Sociology of Women's Sports.* London: Routledge, 1994.

Harlow, Summer. "Social Media and Social Movements: Facebook and an Online Guatemalan Justice Movement that Moved Offline." *New Media & Society* 14, no. 2 (2012): 225–243.

Harris, Cole. *Making Native Space: Colonialism, Resistance, and Reserves in British Columbia.* Vancouver: UBC Press, 2002.

Hartmann, Douglas. *Race, Culture, and the Revolt of the Black Athlete: The 1968 Olympic Protests and Their Aftermath.* Chicago: University of Chicago Press, 2003.

Harvey, David. "The Right to the City." *New Left Review* 53 (2008): 23–40.

Harvey, Jean, John Horne, and Parissa Safai. "Alterglobalization, Global Social Movements, and the Possibility of Political Transformation through Sport." *Sociology of Sport Journal* 26 (2009): 383–403.

Haugerud, Angelique. *No Billionaire Left Behind: Satirical Activism in America.* Stanford, CA: Stanford University Press, 2013.

Hayes, Danny, and Matt Guardino. "Whose Views Made the News?: Media Coverage and the March to War in Iraq." *Political Communication* 27, no. 1 (2010): 59–87.

Hayes, Graeme, and John Horne. "Sustainable Development, Shock and Awe?: London 2012 and Civil Society." *Sociology* 45, no. 5 (2011): 749–764.

Hindman, Matthew. *The Myth of Digital Democracy*. Princeton, NJ: Princeton University Press, 2009.

Hoofd, Ingrid H. *Ambiguities of Activism: Alter-Globalism and the Imperatives of Speed*. New York: Routledge, 2012.

Horne, John. *Sport in Consumer Culture*. New York: Palgrave Macmillan, 2006.

Horne, John, and Garry Whannel. "The 'Caged Torch Procession': Celebrities, Protesters and the 2008 Olympic Torch Relay in London, Paris and San Francisco." *Sport in Society* 13, no. 5 (2010): 760–770.

———. *Understanding the Olympics*. London: Routledge, 2012.

House of Commons, Culture, Media, and Sport Committee. "London 2012 Olympic Games and Paralympic Games: Funding and Legacy, Second Report of Session 2006–07, Vol. 1." London: the House of Commons, 2007.

———. "London 2012 Olympic Games and Paralympic Games: Funding and Legacy, Second Report of Session 2006–07, Vol. 2." London: the House of Commons, 2007.

"How Does Media Cover the Games?" *Olympic Review* (1996): 60–61.

Hutchins, Brett, and Janine Mikosza. "The Web 2.0 Olympics: Athlete Blogging, Social Networking and Policy Contradictions at the 2008 Beijing Games." *Convergence: The International Journal of Research into New Media Technologies* 16, no. 3 (2010): 279–297.

International Olympic Committee. "Brand Protection: Olympic Marketing Ambush Protection and Clean Venue Guidelines." Lausanne, Switzerland: 2005.

———. "IOC Marketing Media Guide: Vancouver 2010." Lausanne: 2010. http://www.olympic.org/Documents/Reports/EN/IOC-MEDIAGUIDE-2010-EN.pdf.

———. "IOC Social Media, Blogging and Internet Guidelines for Participants and Other Accredited Persons at the London 2012 Olympic Games." Lausanne: 31 August 2011. http://www.olympic.org/Documents/Games_London_2012/IOC_Social_Media _Blogging_and_Internet_Guidelines-London.pdf.

———. "IOC Social Media, Blogging and Internet Guidelines for Participants and Other Accredited Persons at the Sochi 2014 Olympic Winter Games." Lausanne: 15 June 2013. http://www.olympic.org/Documents/social_media/IOC_Social_Media_Blogging_and _Internet_Guidelines-English.pdf.

———. *Olympic Charter*. Lausanne, Switzerland: 9 September 2013. http://www.olympic .org/Documents/olympic_charter_en.pdf.

———. "The Olympic Movement in Society." Copenhagen: 5 October 2009. http:// www.olympic.org/Documents/Conferences_Forums_and_Events/2009_Olympic _Congress/Olympic_Congress_Recommendations.pdf.

Iyengar, Shanto, and Jennifer A. McGrady. *Media Politics: A Citizen's Guide*. New York: W.W. Norton & Company, 2007.

Jennings, Andrew. "The Love That Dare Not Speak Its Name: Corruption and the Olympics." In *The Palgrave Handbook of Olympic Studies*, edited by Helen Jefferson Lenskyj and Stephen Wagg, 461–473. Basingstoke, UK: Palgrave Macmillan, 2012.

———. *The New Lords of the Rings*. London: Pocket Books, 1996.

Johanson, Reg. *Escraches*. Vancouver, BC, Coast Salish Territory: Left Hand Press, 2010.

Johnson, James H. "Beethoven and the Birth of Romantic Musical Experience in France." *19th-Century Music* 15 (1991): 23–35.

Juris, Jeffrey S. "Reflections on #Occupy Everywhere: Social Media, Public Space, and Emerging Logics of Aggregation." *American Ethnologist* 39, no. 2 (2012): 259–279.

Karamichas, John. "The Olympics and the Environment." In *The Palgrave Handbook of Olympic Studies*, edited by Helen Jefferson Lenskyj and Stephen Wagg, 381–393. Basingstoke, UK: Palgrave Macmillan, 2012.

Kaufman, Peter, and Eli A. Wolff. "Playing and Protesting: Sport as a Vehicle for Social Change." *Journal of Sport and Social Issues* 34, no. 2 (2010): 154–175.

Keck, Margaret, and Kathryn Sikkink. *Activists beyond Borders: Advocacy Networks in International Politics*. Ithaca: Cornell University Press, 1998.

Kellner, Douglas. *Media Spectacle*. London: Routledge, 2003.

Kennelly, Jacqueline. *Citizen Youth: Culture, Activism, and Agency in a Neoliberal Era*. New York: Palgrave Macmillan, 2011.

Killanin, Lord. *My Olympic Years*. New York: William Morrow and Company, 1983.

Klosterman, Chuck. *IV: A Decade of Curious People and Dangerous Ideas*. New York: Scribner, 2006.

Koopmans, Ruud, and Paul Statham. "Ethnic and Civic Conceptions of Nationhood and the Differential Success of the Extreme Right in Germany and Italy." In *How Social Movements Matter*, edited by Mario Giugni, Doug McAdam, and Charles Tilly, 225–251. Minneapolis: University of Minnesota Press, 1999.

Kothari, Miloon. "Report of the Special Rapporteur on Adequate Housing as a Component of the Right to an Adequate Standard of Living, and on the Right to Non-Discrimination in this Context." United Nations Human Rights Council, 17 February 2009. http://www2.ohchr.org/english/bodies/hrcouncil/docs/10session/A.HRC.10.7.Add.3.pdf.

Kraska, Peter B. "Militarization and Policing—Its Relevance to 21st Century Police." *Policing: A Journal of Policy and Practice* 1, no. 4 (2007): 501–513.

Lefebvre, Henri. *The Production of Space*. Translated by Donald Nicholson-Smith. Oxford: Blackwell, 1991.

———. *Writings on Cities*. Translated by Eleonore Kofman and Elizabeth Lebas. Oxford: Blackwell, 1996.

Lenskyj, Helen Jefferson. *The Best Olympics Ever?: Social Impacts of Sydney 2000*. Albany: State University of New York Press, 2002.

———. *Inside the Olympic Industry: Power, Politics, and Activism*. Albany: State University of New York Press, 2000.

———. *Olympic Industry Resistance: Challenging Olympic Power and Propaganda*. Albany: State University of New York Press, 2008.

Leong, Sze Tsung. "Control Space." In *Mutations*, edited by Rem Koolhaas, Stefano Boeri, Sanford Kwinter, Nadia Tazi, and Hans Ulrich Obrist, 185–195. Barcelona: Actar, 2001.

Lindsay, Iain. "Olympicisation: Growing for Gold." *Urbanities* 1, no. 1 (2011): 21–31.

LOCOG. "London 2012 Sustainability Report: A Blueprint for Change." 2011. http://www.london2012.com/mm%5CDocument%5CPublications%5CSustainability%5C01%5C24%5C09%5C14%5Clondon-2012-sustainability-report-a-blueprint-for-change.pdf.

London 2012. "Candidate File, Vol. 1." London 2004 http://webarchive.nationalarchives.gov.uk/20070305103412/http://www.london2012.com/news/publications/candidate-file.php.

———. "Candidate File, Vol. 2." London 2004 http://webarchive.nationalarchives.gov.uk/20070305103412/http://www.london2012.com/news/publications/candidate-file.php.

———. "London 2012: A Vision for the Olympic and Paralympic Games." London, 2004.

London Assembly, Budget and Performance Committee. "Policing Costs for the London 2012 Olympic and Paralympic Games." 2011. http://www.london.gov.uk/moderngov/mgConvert2PDF.aspx?ID=6547.

Maguire, Joseph. *Power and Global Sport: Zones of Prestige, Emulation, and Resistance*. Abingdon, UK: Routledge, 2005.

Mandell, Richard D. *The Nazi Olympics.* Urbana: University of Illinois Press, 1987.

Markovits, Andrei, and Lars Rensmann. *Gaming the World: How Sports Are Reshaping Global Politics and Culture.* Princeton, NJ: Princeton University Press, 2010.

Martin, Christopher. *Framed! Labor and the Corporate Media.* Ithaca: Cornell University Press, 2004.

Marx, Karl. *Capital: A Critique of Political Economy, Vol. 1: A Critical Analysis of Capitalist Production.* Translated by Ben Fowkes. New York: Penguin Books, 1976.

———. "Contribution to the Critique of Hegel's Philosophy of Law, Introduction." In *Karl Marx, Frederick Engels Collected Work, Volume 3*, 175–187. London: Lawrence & Wishart, 1974 [1844].

McAdam, Doug. "Conceptual Origins, Current Problems, Future Directions." In *Comparative Perspectives on Social Movements: Political Opportunities, Mobilizing Structures, and Cultural Framings*, edited by Doug McAdam, John D. McCarthy, and Mayer N. Zald, 23–40. New York: Cambridge University Press, 1996.

———. "Recruitment to High-Risk Activism: The Case of Freedom Summer." *American Journal of Sociology* 92, no. 1 (1986): 64–90.

McAdam, Doug, John D. McCarthy, and Mayer N. Zald. "Introduction: Opportunities, Mobilizing Structures, and Framing Processes—Toward a Synthetic, Comparative Perspective on Social Movements." In *Comparative Perspectives on Social Movements: Political Opportunities, Mobilizing Structures, and Cultural Framings*, edited by Doug McAdam, John D. McCarthy, and Mayer N. Zald, 1–20. New York: Cambridge University Press, 1996.

McAdam, Doug, Sidney Tarrow, and Charles Tilly. *Dynamics of Contention.* Cambridge: Cambridge University Press, 2001.

McCammon, Holly J., Courtney Sanders Muse, Harmony D. Newman, and Teresa M. Terrell. "Movement Framing and Discursive Opportunity Structures: The Political Successes of the U.S. Women's Jury Movements." *American Sociological Review* 72 (2007): 725–749.

McChesney, Robert W. *Digital Disconnect: How Capitalism Is Turning the Internet Against Democracy.* New York: The New Press, 2013.

McRoskey, Samantha R. "Security and the Olympic Games: Making Rio an Example." *Yale Journal of International Affairs* (2010): 91–105.

Mermin, Jonathan. *Debating War and Peace.* Princeton, NJ: Princeton University Press, 1999.

Merrifield, Andy. *Henri Lefebvre: A Critical Introduction.* New York: Routledge, 2006.

Mertes, Tom. "Grass-Roots Globalism." *New Left Review* 17 (2001): 101–110.

———. *A Movement of Movements: Is Another World Really Possible?* London: Verso, 2004.

Messner, Michael A. *Out of Play: Critical Essays on Gender and Sport.* Albany: State University of New York Press, 2007.

———. *Taking the Field: Women, Men, and Sports.* Minneapolis: University of Minnesota Press, 2002.

Meyer, David S. "Political Opportunity and Nested Institutions." *Social Movement Studies* 2 (2003): 17–35.

Miah, Andy, Beatriz García, and Tian Zhihui. "'We Are the Media': Nonaccredited Media and Citizen Journalists at the Olympic Games." In *Owning the Olympics: Narratives of the New China*, edited by Monroe E. Price and Daniel Dayan, 320–345. Ann Arbor: The University of Michigan Press, 2008.

Morozov, Evgeny. *The Net Delusion: The Dark Side of Internet Freedom.* New York: Public Affairs, 2011.

Morrow, Don, and Janice Waters. "Method in Sport History: A Content Analysis Approach." *Canadian Journal of History of Sport* 13, no. 2 (1982): 30–37.

National Audit Office. "The Budget for the London 2012 Olympic and Paralympic Games." London, 2007.

Neuendorf, Kimberly A. *The Content Analysis Guidebook.* Thousand Oaks, CA: Sage, 2002.

Newman, Joshua I. "A Detour Through 'NASCAR Nation': Ethnographic Articulations of Neoliberal Sporting Spectacle." *International Review for the Sociology of Sport* 42, no. 3 (2007): 289–308.

Newman, Joshua I., and Michael D. Giardina. *Sport, Spectacle, and NASCAR Nation: Consumption and the Cultural Politics of Neoliberalism.* New York: Palgrave Macmillan, 2011.

Nicholls, Walter J. "The Urban Question Revisited: The Importance of Cities for Social Movements." *International Journal of Urban and Regional Research* 32, no. 4 (2008): 841–859.

Nixon, Rob. "Apartheid on the Run: The South African Sports Boycott." *Transitions* 58 (1992): 68–88.

O'Bonsawin, Christine M. "'No Olympics on Stolen Native Land': Contesting Olympic Narratives and Asserting Indigenous Rights within the Discourse of the 2010 Vancouver Games." *Sport in Society* 13, no. 1 (2010): 143–156.

———. "'There Will Be No Law That Will Come against Us': An Important Episode of Indigenous Resistance and Activism in Olympic History." In *The Palgrave Handbook of Olympic Studies*, edited by Helen Jefferson Lenskyj and Stephen Wagg, 474–486. Basingstoke, UK: Palgrave Macmillan, 2012.

Orwell, George. *A Collection of Essays.* New York: Harcourt Brace Jovanovich Publishers, 1946.

———. "The Sporting Spirit." *Shooting an Elephant and Other Essays*, 151–155. New York: Harcourt, Brace & World, 1950.

Parezo, Nancy J. "A 'Special Olympics': Testing Racial Strength and Endurance at the 1904 Louisiana Purchase Exhibition." In *The 1904 Anthropology Days and Olympic Games: Sport, Race, and American Imperialism*, edited by Susan Brownell, 59–126. Lincoln: University of Nebraska Press, 2008.

Payne, Michael. *Olympic Turn Around: How the Games Stepped Back from the Brink of Extinction to Become the World's Best Known Brand—And a Multi-Billion Dollar Global Franchise.* London: London Business Press, 2005.

Perelman, Marc. *Barbaric Sport: A Global Plague.* London: Verso, 2012.

Perelman, Richard B. *Olympic Retrospective: The Games of Los Angeles.* Los Angeles: Los Angeles Olympic Organizing Committee, 1985.

Pomper, Gerald M. *On Ordinary Heroes and American Democracy.* Boulder: Paradigm Publishers, 2007.

Pound, Richard W. *Inside the Olympics: A Behind-the-Scenes Look at the Politics, the Scandals, and the Glory of the Games.* Canada: Wiley, 2004.

Preuss, Holger. *The Economics of Staging the Olympics: A Comparison of the Games, 1972–2008.* Cheltenham, UK: Edward Elgar, 2004.

Price, Monroe E. "On Seizing the Olympic Platform." In *Owning the Olympics: Narratives of the New China*, edited by Monroe E. Price and Daniel Dayan, 86–114. Ann Arbor: The University of Michigan Press, 2008.

Rider, Toby C., and Kevin B. Wamsley. "Myth Heritage and the Olympic Enterprise." In *The Palgrave Handbook of Olympic Studies*, edited by Helen Jefferson Lenskyj and Stephen Wagg, 289–303. Basingstoke, UK: Palgrave Macmillan, 2012.

Riffe, Daniel, Stephen Lacy, and Frederick G. Fico. *Analyzing Media Messages: Using Quantitative Content Analysis in Research.* Mahwah, NJ: Lawrence Erlbaum, 1998.

Rogers, Heather. *Green Gone Wrong: How Our Economy Is Undermining the Environmental Revolution.* New York: Scribner, 2010.

Rolnik, Raquel. "Report of the Special Rapporteur on Adequate Housing as a Component of the Right to an Adequate Standard of Living, and on the Right to Non-Discrimination in this Context." United Nations Human Rights Council, 2009. https://www.un.org/wcm/webdav/site/sport/shared/sport/pdfs/Resolutions/A-HRC-13-20/A-HRC-13-20_EN.pdf.

Ross, Carne. *The Leaderless Revolution: How Ordinary People Will Take Power and Change Politics in the 21st Century*. New York: Plume, 2011.

Routledge, Paul. "'Our Resistance Will Be as Transnational as Capital': Convergence Space and Strategy in Globalising Resistance." *GeoJournal* 52 (2000): 25–33.

Sánchez Estellés, Isis. 2010. "The Political-Opportunity Structure of the Spanish Anti-War Movement (2002–2004) and its Impact." *The Sociological Review* 58, no. 2 (2010): 246–269.

Sánchez Nieto, W. Alejandro. "The Olympic Challenge: Russia's Strategy for the Establishment of Security in the North Caucasus before 2014." *Journal of Slavic Military Studies* 24 (2011): 582–604.

Sands, Robert R. *Sport Ethnography*. Champaign, IL: Human Kinetics, 2002.

Schattschneider, E. E. *The Semisovereign People: A Realist's View of Democracy in America*. New York: Holt, Rinehart and Winston, 1960.

Senn, Alfred E. *Power, Politics, and the Olympic Games*. Champaign, IL: Human Kinetics, 1999.

Shaw, Christopher A. *Five Ring Circus: Myths and Realities of the Olympic Games*. Gabriola Island: New Society Publishers, 2008.

Shepard, Benjamin. *Play, Creativity, and Social Movements: If I Can't Dance, It's Not My Revolution*. London: Routledge, 2011.

Shirky, Clay. *Here Comes Everybody: The Power of Organizing without Organizations*. New York: Penguin Books, 2008.

Silk, Michael L. "Sporting Ethnography: Philosophy, Methodology, and Reflection." In *Qualitative Methods in Sports Studies*, edited by David L. Andrews, Daniel S. Mason, and Michael L. Silk, 65–103. Oxford: Berg, 2005.

Silk, Michael L., and David L. Andrews. "Sport and the Neoliberal Conjuncture: Complicating the Consensus." In *Sport and Neoliberalism: Politics, Consumption, and Culture*, edited by David L. Andrews and Michael L. Silk, 1–19. Philadelphia: Temple University Press, 2012.

Silk, Michael L., David L. Andrews, and Daniel S. Mason. "Encountering the Field: Sports Studies and Qualitative Research." In *Qualitative Methods in Sports Studies*, edited by David L. Andrews, Daniel S. Mason, and Michael L. Silk, 1–20. Oxford: Berg, 2005.

Small, Melvin. *Covering Dissent: The Media and the Vietnam War Movement*. New Brunswick, NJ: Rutgers University Press, 1994.

Smith, Mary. "When the Games Come to Town: Host Cities and the Local Impacts of the Olympics." London East Research Institute Working Papers, December 2008.

Smith, Neil. "Scale Bending and the Fate of the National." In *Scale and Geographic Inquiry: Nature, Society, and Method*, edited by Eric Sheppard and Robert B. McMaster, 192–212. Oxford: Blackwell, 2004.

Smith, Neil, and Deborah Cowen. "'Martial Law in the Streets of Toronto': G20 Security and State Violence." *Human Geography* 3, no. 3 (2010): 29–46.

Soja, Edward W. *Seeking Spatial Justice*. Minneapolis: University of Minnesota Press, 2010.

Space Hijackers. "Second Manifesto of the Space Hijackers," n.d. http://www.spacehijackers.org/html/manifesto.html.

Stalker, Glenn J., and Lesley J. Wood. "Reaching Beyond the Net: Political Circuits and Participation in Toronto's G20 Protests." *Social Movement Studies* 12, no. 2 (2013): 178–198.

St. John, Graham. "Protestival: Global Days of Action and Carnivalized Politics in the Present." *Social Movement Studies* 7, no. 2 (2008): 167–190.

Sugden, John, and Alan Tomlinson. "Afterword: 'No Other Anything . . .': The Olympic Games Yesterday and Today." In *Watching the Olympics: Politics, Power, and Representation*, edited by John Sugden and Alan Tomlinson, 242–251. London: Routledge, 2012.

———. "Digging the Dirt and Staying Clean: Retrieving the Investigative Tradition for a Critical Sociology of Sport." *International Review for the Sociology of Sport* 34, no. 4 (1999): 385–397.

Sullivan, James E. "Anthropology Days at the Stadium." In *Spalding's Official Athletic Almanac for 1905*, edited by James E. Sullivan, 249–264. New York: American Sports Publishing, 1905.

Sustar, Lee, and Aisha Karim, eds. *Poetry & Protest: A Dennis Brutus Reader*. Chicago: Haymarket Books, 2006.

Tang, Wing Shing. "The 2008 Olympic Torch Relay in Hong Kong: A Clash of Governmentalities." *Human Geography* 1, no. 1 (2008): 106–110.

Tarrow, Sidney. *The New Transnational Activism*. New York: Cambridge University Press, 2005.

———. *Power in Movement: Social Movements and Contentious Politics*, 2nd ed. Cambridge: Cambridge University Press, 1998.

Timms, Jill. "The Olympics as a Platform for Protest: A Case Study of the London 2012 'Ethical' Games and the Play Fair Campaign for Workers' Rights." *Leisure Studies* 31, no. 3 (2012): 355–372.

Tomlinson, Alan. "Carrying the Torch for Whom?: Symbolic Power and Olympic Ceremony." In *The Olympics at the Millennium: Power, Politics, and the Games*, edited by Kay Schaffer and Sidonie Smith, 167–181. New Brunswick, NJ: Rutgers University Press 2000.

———. "The Disneyfication of the Olympics?: Theme Parks and Freak Shows of the Body." In *Post-Olympism?: Questioning Sport in the Twenty-first Century*, edited by John Bale and Mette Krogh Christensen, 147–163. Oxford: Berg, 2004.

———. "The Making—and Unmaking?—of the Olympic Corporate Class." In *The Palgrave Handbook of Olympic Studies*, edited by Helen Jefferson Lenskyj and Stephen Wagg, 233–247. Basingstoke, UK: Palgrave Macmillan, 2012.

Tufekci, Zeynep, and Christopher Wilson. "Social Media and the Decision to Participate in Political Protest: Observations from Tahrir Square." *Journal of Communication* 62 (2012): 363–379.

Van Luijk, Nicolien, and Wendy Frisby. "(Re)Framing of Protest at the 2010 Winter Olympic Games." *International Journal of Sport Policy and Politics* 4, no. 3 (2012): 343–359.

Vásquez Montalbán, Manuel. *An Olympic Death*. Translated by Ed Emery. London: Serpent's Tail, 1992.

Walker, Jeffrey. "The Body of Persuasion: A Theory of the Enthymeme." *College English* 56, no. 1 (1994): 46–65.

Wamsley, Kevin. "The Global Sport Monopoly: A Synopsis of 20th Century Olympic Politics." *International Journal* 57, no. 3 (2002): 395–410.

———. "Laying Olympism to Rest." In *Post-Olympism?: Questioning Sport in the Twenty-first Century*, edited by John Bale and Mette Krogh Christensen, 231–242. Oxford and New York: Berg, 2004.

Wamsley, Kevin B., and Guy Schultz. "Rogues and Bedfellows: The IOC and the Incorporation of the FSFI," 113–118. *Fifth International Symposium for Olympic Research*. Western Ontario University, 2000.

Watt, Paul. "'It's Not for Us': Regeneration, the 2012 Olympics and the Gentrification of East London." *City* 17, no. 1 (2013): 99–118.

Whannel, Garry. "The Rings and the Box: Television Spectacle and the Olympics." In *The Palgrave Handbook of Olympic Studies*, edited by Helen Jefferson Lenskyj and Stephen Wagg, 261–273. Basingstoke, UK: Palgrave Macmillan, 2012.

———. "The Television Spectacular." In *Five-Ring Circus: Money, Power, and Politics at the Olympic Games*, edited by Alan Tomlinson and Garry Whannel, 30–43. Sydney: Pluto Press, 1984.

Wheaton, Belinda. "'Just Do It': Consumption, Commitment, and Identity in the Windsurfing Subculture." *Sociology of Sport Journal* 17, no. 3 (2000): 254–274.

Wheeler, Robert F. "Organized Sport and Organized Labour: The Workers' Sport Movement." *Journal of Contemporary History* 13 (1978): 191–210.

Wilson, Brian. "Ethnography, the Internet, and Youth Culture: Strategies for Examining Social Resistance and 'Online-Offline' Relationships." *Canadian Journal of Education* 29, no. 1 (2006): 307–328.

Worden, Minky, ed. *China's Great Leap: The Beijing Games and Olympian Human Rights Challenges.* New York: Seven Stories Press, 2008.

Zervas, Konstantinos. "Anti-Olympic Campaigns." In *The Palgrave Handbook of Olympic Studies*, edited by Helen Jefferson Lenskyj and Stephen Wagg, 533–548. Basingstoke, UK: Palgrave Macmillan, 2012.

Zirin, Dave. *Welcome to the Terrordome: The Pain, Politics, and Promise of Sports.* Chicago: Haymarket Books, 2007.

Index

About the Author

JULES BOYKOFF is the author of *Celebration Capitalism and the Olympic Games* (2013). His writing on the Olympics has appeared in academic outlets like *Contemporary Social Science, Human Geography*, and *Olympika: The International Journal of Olympic Studies*, as well as publications like the *Guardian, New Left Review*, and the *New York Times*. He teaches political science at Pacific University in Oregon.

CPSIA information can be obtained at www.ICGtesting.com
Printed in the USA
BVOW04s0207190614

356560BV00005B/1/P